Buried Alive

Buried Alive

A History of Premature Burials and Accidental Interments

A.J. Griffiths-Jones

PEN & SWORD
HISTORY

First published in Great Britain in 2024 by
Pen & Sword History
An imprint of Pen & Sword Books Limited
Yorkshire – Philadelphia

Copyright © A.J. Griffiths-Jones 2024

ISBN 978 1 03611 170 0

The right of A.J. Griffiths-Jones to be identified as
Author of this Work has been asserted by him in accordance
with the Copyright, Designs and Patents Act 1988.

A CIP catalogue record for this book is
available from the British Library

Typeset by Mac Style
Printed in the UK by CPI Group (UK) Ltd, Croydon, CR0 4YY.

FSC
MIX
Paper | Supporting
responsible forestry
FSC® C013604

Pen & Sword Books Limited incorporates the imprints of After
the Battle, Atlas, Archaeology, Aviation, Discovery, Family History,
Fiction, History, Maritime, Military, Military Classics, Politics,
Select, Transport, True Crime, Air World, Frontline Publishing, Leo
Cooper, Remember When, Seaforth Publishing, The Praetorian Press,
Wharncliffe Local History, Wharncliffe Transport, Wharncliffe True
Crime and White Owl.

For a complete list of Pen & Sword titles please contact

PEN & SWORD BOOKS LIMITED
47 Church Street, Barnsley, South Yorkshire, S70 2AS, England
E-mail: enquiries@pen-and-sword.co.uk
Website: www.pen-and-sword.co.uk
or
PEN AND SWORD BOOKS
1950 Lawrence Rd, Havertown, PA 19083, USA
E-mail: uspen-and-sword@casematepublishers.com
Website: www.penandswordbooks.com

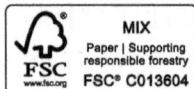

For My Dad, Raymond Griffiths
(1940–2020)

With Special Thanks to Doctor Zahi Hawass

Contents

Foreword

Premature interment, overhasty burial, untimely entombment, call it what you will but there is something undoubtedly chilling when one conjures up the imagery of being buried alive. Perhaps it is the lingering asphyxiation, possible hypothermia, gradual dehydration and inevitable starvation that would follow such an event, the realisation that there is no escape from the underground grave, all mourners dispersed and unable to hear the muffled cries, nothing more than darkness and the inability to claw your way free.

The phrase 'saved by the bell' is reputed to have originated in the early eighteenth century, when physicians had limited means to ascertain whether a person was truly dead or were affected by a condition such as being in a coma or trance. Occasionally, relatives of the deceased would bury their loved ones with bell ropes, so that if they woke up, the bell could be rung, and they could be saved from suffocating inside the coffin. In fact, it became common practice to lay out the recently departed in German 'dead-houses', each corpse attached to strings or wires in order to detect the slightest movement, long before their European counterparts had recognised the need for longer periods before burial. Sadly, years ago, cases of persons being buried alive were not uncommon. However, the saying itself is actually derived from boxing slang, and has no connection to those poor mites whose premature burial literally cost them their lives. Taphophobia, the fear of being buried and waking up alive within your own grave was, and still is for some, a genuine concern, with several prominent people expressing their anxiety when close to death themselves. Lord Chesterfield, in 1769, was quoted as saying "All I desire for my own burial is not to be buried alive."

George Washington made a similar plea on his deathbed, requesting, "Have me decently buried, but do not let my body be put into a vault in less than two days after I am dead." The most fearful of all was surely Frederic Chopin, whose last words were, "Swear to make them cut me open, so that I won't be buried alive." He requested that his heart be cut out to ensure death. Hans Christian Anderson, the Danish fairy tale writer, also had an immense fear of being buried alive. Each night before he slept, Anderson laid a note on his bedside table reading: 'I only *seem* to be dead.' Both Anderson and Alfred Nobel, the acclaimed Swedish chemist, asked to have their arteries cut open.

English novelist and playwright Wilkie Collins left a missive among his papers directing that when he died a thorough examination of his body was to be made by a skilled surgeon. Lady Burton, wife of Captain Sir Richard Burton, ordered that her body should be pierced with a needle in the region of the heart. Mr Edmund Yates, of the *World*, Miss Ada Cavendish, actress, Miss Harriet Martineau, the authoress, may all be mentioned as instances of men and women who have left instructions that they should not be interred until everything possible had been done to make sure that they were lifeless. In some cases, it was severance of a vein, in others even decapitation that was resolved upon. Others, with a similar end in view, adopted different means.

The signalling invention of Edgar Allan Poe – who wrote this subject up in his characteristically weird fashion, is familiar to most readers. Poe seemed to have a dark obsession with the subject matter related to taphophobia and his horror story *The Premature Burial* is a typical example of his exploration into the fear. Other works by the author, including *The Fall of the House of Usher*, *The Cask of Amontillado*, and *The Black Cat*, explore a similar theme.

Then there is the apparatus of a Russian inventor, which consisted of a mechanism placed in the throat of the corpse. If consciousness returned, and an effort were made to breathe, the effort set in motion certain wires, which resulted in a bell ringing in the cemetery-keeper's lodge. In 1897, Sir Henry Littlejohn told his students at Edinburgh University of a fancy new coffin, fitted with patent springs so constructed that on the slightest indication of returning life they would immediately open the coffin lid and thus save the victim.

However, we must endeavour to separate myth and nightmare from truth, to unravel the fireside stores of spine-tingling tales created to frighten and shock, from the real-life cases throughout history that have been documented and testified to by medical men and clergy alike. As we look back through the centuries to fathom the likelihood of such a fate in modern times, considering medical advancement and the riddance of toxic disease, we must ask ourselves, is it really possible, with medical progress and modern technology, that one could be buried alive?

Of course, there are also cases of intended premature burial, through acts of torture, murder, ritual, and belief, which are none the less horrifying but deserve their own explanation, which we will look at in detail. There are also the fakirs, entertainers and eccentrics who commit themselves to the grave in order to astound crowds and gain public notoriety, all at the risk of losing their life.

The revival of supposed corpses, triggered by sudden jolts of the coffin, over-eager embalmers and natural consciousness after a coma, have stunned and confounded those attending the funerals of their supposed dead loved ones and sometimes the ramifications of a corpse's 'sudden awakening' has had a profound effect on their nearest and dearest.

People's fear of being buried alive lessened with the option of cremation but, as an inquest in Westminster in December 1908 on sixty-six-year-old registered medical practitioner John Laird of Pimlico in London showed, even those in the medical profession at the turn of the twentieth century held fears of being confined to their coffin whilst still breathing. Mr Robert Cornwall, the deceased's solicitor, stated that sixteen years before, Mr Laird made a Will in which he gave express directions for his cremation. He subsequently called at Mr Cornwall's office and emphasised his wish for cremation saying he was afraid of being buried alive. Medical evidence at the inquest of John Laird showed that the cause of death was oedema of the brain. Answering the coroner, Mr Cornwall said he was satisfied that the deceased's death was a natural one. The coroner replied that great care had to be taken where directions for cremation were given. A verdict in accordance with the medical evidence was returned.

Another victim of taphophobia, Miss Frances Power Cobbe, who died suddenly at her home in Mengwrt, North Wales, in April 1904, had a great dread of being buried alive and took elaborate precautions against such a thing happening. She always kept upon her study desk a telegram addressed to Dr Walter Hadwen, of Gloucester, reading as follows: 'Pray come immediately, Miss Cobbe seriously ill – Housekeeper' and left directions for it to be sent directly to the medic should any alarming symptoms appear. After the death of Frances Cobbe, instructions were found in her Will to the effect that her medical adviser, Dr Hadwen, was to sever the arteries in her neck and windpipe, so as to render revival impossible. The Will also stipulated that if this operation was not performed and witnessed by one of the executors, all Miss Cobbe's bequests would become null and void. Among the other provisions of the will were the following instructions: 'That the body should be driven to the grave in Miss Cobbe's own carriage and be interred in a coffin merely sufficient to carry the body decently to its place of burial.'

Thankfully, there are many recorded instances where the intervention or quick thinking of others has prevented premature burial, such as the case of the late Sir Hugh Ackland, of Devonshire, who apparently died of a fever and was laid out as dead. The nurse, with two of the footmen, sat up with the corpse, and the weather being extremely cold at the time, Lady Ackland sent them a bottle of brandy to drink during the night. One of the servants told the other how their master had dearly loved a brandy when he was alive, and he was resolved that he should take one glass now that he was dead. The fellow accordingly poured out a bumper and forced it down His Lordship's throat. A gurgling immediately ensued, followed by a violent motion of the neck and upper part of the breast.

The other footman and the nurse were so terrified that they ran downstairs, and the brandy genius, hastening away with rather too much speed, tumbled down headfirst. The noise of the fall and the ensuing cries alarmed a young gentleman who was staying in the house. He got up and immediately went to the room where the supposed corpse lay and found, to his astonishment, Sir Hugh sitting upright. He called the servants to put the old man into a warm bed and sent for a physician and apothecary. Within a few weeks, Sir Hugh was restored to good health and lived for several years afterwards. The Baronet often told the story, and, when he actually died, left the 'brandy' footman a handsome annuity.

Across the globe the formation of societies and associations comprised of medical men and clergy have endeavoured to reduce statistics of premature burial and to create guidelines, in order for the general physician to ascertain whether a person is truly dead. So too have inventors created mechanisms and gadgets to save those who have awoken in their silent tombs. In several parts of Europe mortuaries made their own provision for preventing premature interment by setting up elaborate contraptions for the detection of motion in a supposed corpse. We will also explore the ritual killings by burial alive of tribes and religions, some of which still occur in remote regions, and what triggers the beliefs of those who succumb willingly to death in this manner.

In the following chapters, you will discover true stories of the poor souls who were subjected to such a horrific fate, those who survived to tell their story and the measures taken by various humane societies to prevent persons from being buried alive. Each case was documented in newspapers and, through thorough investigative research, sources have been catalogued with details remaining unchanged.

Chapter One

Early Cases

One of the very first recorded cases of persons being buried alive was during Emperor Qin Shi Huang's reign between 213 and 206 BC. The first ruler of a unified China, he was known for his fascination with immortality. During his lifetime, Emperor Qin (see top right image on page 1 of the plate section) ordered thousands of books to be burned following the advice of chief adviser Li Si, in order to avoid scholars comparing Qin's reign with those of past rulers. The only books allowed to escape the burning pyres were those on astrology, agriculture, medicine, divination, and the history of the Qin state. However, according to the Records of the Grand Historian, Emperor Qin, in his search for prolonged life, was deceived by two alchemists, and ordered more than 460 Confucian scholars of alchemy to be buried alive, believing them to be plotting against him. An account by Wei Hong in the second century, however, puts the figure at over 1,000.

Emperor Qin's huge funerary compound contains some 8,000 life-sized terracotta soldiers at Xian. However, whilst unearthing the statues, archaeologists found something else, the human remains of thousands who were most likely buried alive within the tomb of the deceased ruler. These poor souls died as part of a belief that that the emperor needed the living to take care of him in the afterlife. Further *Records of the Grand Historian* by Han dynasty scholar Sima Qian (206 BCE–220 CE) state that after Qin Shi Huang died, his son and successor Hu Hai ordered his soldiers to 'execute and bury all his father's concubines who had never given birth' because, he claimed, 'it was inappropriate to let them leave the palace.' Sima didn't specify exactly how many died on Hu Hai's orders, it was simply recorded as 'a large number.' By 2021, of the 99 small tombs that archaeologists had discovered inside the mausoleum, 10 have been excavated and all of them contain the bones of numerous young women.

Thousands of construction workers also became victims after the mausoleum was finished. Having become privy to the inner-workings of the vault, which included booby traps to protect it and the treasures inside from grave robbers, seemingly palace officials were concerned that some of the more unscrupulous labourers might share the secrets with others. The solution was to lock the gates after the funeral, trapping all of the workers inside. Historical records show that the number of those incarcerated alive could be as high as 720,000!

Similarly, the fourteenth century traveller, Ibn Batuta, wrote the following after watching the burial of a great khan:

> The Khan who had been killed, with about a hundred of his relatives, was then brought, and a large sepulchre was dug for him under the earth in which a most beautiful couch was spread, and the Khan was with his weapons laid upon it. With him they placed all the gold and silver vessels he had in his house, together with four female slaves, and six of his favourite mamluks, or slave soldiers, with a few vessels of drink. They were then all closed up, and the earth heaped upon them to the height of a large hill.

Leading Egyptologist Dr Zahi Hawass has confirmed that ancient Egyptians neither buried servants alive with their masters nor used immurement as a form of capital punishment. However, in May 1914, Dr. George A. Reisner, Professor of Egyptology at Harvard who was conducting explorations and excavations in Egypt, sent word to the *New York Tribune* that he had discovered evidence of a people and a civilisation that existed in Egypt 3,700 years ago, and of which no record or evidence had previously existed. He made the discovery at a point marking one of the outposts to the south of an ancient Egyptian civilisation near Kerma, not far from the Nile. According to Dr. Reisner the inhabitants were neither Egyptians nor negroes, and he claimed that their pottery was the finest and most beautiful ever made in the Nile Valley. Many of the treasures in ivory, stone and pottery which Dr Reisner sent to the Boston Museum of Fine Arts were taken from the graves of chiefs. Apparently six or seven subjects were buried alive with the body of each chief.

In September 1915, Professor Charles G. Seligman, in his presidential address to the Anthropological sector, referred to burials alive and other remarkable customs. He outlined the early history of the Anglo-Egyptian Sudan from the standpoint of the ethnologist and, referring to the discoveries at Kerma, said that the remains of the Hyksos period were especially interesting. Professor Reisner had described a people who razed the buildings of their predecessors and buried their dead in the debris, and whose funerary customs were entirely 'un-Egyptian.' Each burial pit contained a number of graves, in every one of which several bodies had been interred. The chief personage lay on a carved bed, around which lay a varying number of bodies, both male and female. Several had their fingers twisted into their hair or had covered their faces with their hands. One woman had struggled over on to her back and was clutching her throat, but most of them lay composed as if resigned to die quietly according to the custom of their fathers. Professor Reisner could not observe any marks of violence but judging from the contorted positions of some of the bodies he thought that they had been buried alive. Among other ancient burial customs mentioned were that of Uganda, where the body of a dead King was opened, the internal organs removed, emptied, and then washed in beer before being replaced. Describing the ancient tombs of Egypt, Professor Seligman mentioned one type in which a shaft was left open for the soul to pass in and out of the burial pit.

The ancients were far more scrupulous in safeguarding interment while life existed than their European counterparts. The Egyptians kept the bodies of the dead under careful supervision by the priests until satisfied that life was extinct, previous to embalming them by means of antiseptic balsams. The Greeks were also aware of the dangers of premature burial and would often cut off a corpse's fingers before cremation upon a pyre to see whether death had truly occurred.

The celebrated Greek philosopher, Democritus, was of the opinion that the signs of death were not sufficiently certain. He believed that in apoplexies, syncope and suffocations, such as those persons who had been hanged, strangled, drowned, shut up in confined places or suddenly cut off from breathing, such as hysterical or hypochondriac patients, signs of death could be deceiving. However, as J.J. Bruhier d'Ablaincourt pointed out in his 1746 publication, this misfortune was less owing to the imperfection of medicine, than to the ignorance or negligence of physicians, and the carelessness, poverty, or even sometimes the wicked disposition of those who have the care and management of the sick.

Occasionally a case of premature burial sends a thrill of horror through the community, but the lesson which it taught in ancient times was that less haste should be manifested in committing dead bodies to their silent homes, but it was not always heeded and in some instances the body was hardly cold before the undertaker was called to perform his sad office. However, the ancient Greeks and Romans took warning and prohibited the early burial of the dead.

An early recorded instance of recovery of life of an individual about to be buried was that of a woman in Agrigentum, in ancient Greece, whose funeral was stopped by Empedocles, a man of great medical skill, and she was restored to life. After this a law was passed forbidding interment of deceased persons until three full days had elapsed. Custom extended this period to the sixth or seventh day, during which precautions were taken to restore animation, if it was simply suspended, and often with effect.

The Romans also had their attention turned to this matter in the time of Pompeii, by a physician, who detected signs of life in a person supposed to be dead and was on a funeral pyre which had already been lighted. The flames were extinguished, and the individual was resuscitated. Aviola, another Roman, was less fortunate. Having fallen into a lethargic fit, he was taken for dead, the funeral pyre erected, flames lighted, and the corpse placed upon it. The heat caused Aviola to quickly recover his senses and he attempted to rise from the pyre. Spectators rushed to save him, but they were too late and Aviola was burned alive. The praetor Lamia had a similar fate, and the life of Tubero was saved by signs of life being discovered just as he was about to be laid on the funeral pyre.

In consequence of these examples, the Romans increased the interval between death and burial, and more closely scrutinised the signs of death. Custom as well as law required that after death the nearest relative should close the eyes of the deceased. The body was then bathed in warm water, with the twofold purpose of rendering it ready to be anointed with oil, or to cause consciousness should the person only be in a comatose state. After a variety of ceremonies, which were continued for seven or eight days, the corpse was then carried to the funeral pyre and burned in the presence of relatives and friends.

Legend tells us that the fifth century Roman Emperor Flavius Zeno, whose reign was plagued by domestic revolts and religious dissention, was buried alive in Constantinopole after becoming insensible from drinking. According to eleventh and twelfth century Greek historians Joannes Zonaras and George Kedrenos, cries of 'Have pity on me!' could be heard from within the sarcophagus for three days after his apparent death on 9 April 491 AD, as it lay within the Church of the Holy Apostles, but due to the hatred felt towards Zeno's wife and subjects, Empress Ariadne refused to have the tomb opened. If these claims are indeed true, Emperor Zeno would have died a gradual death caused by dehydration and asphyxiation.

For Muslims, it was customary to bury their dead no more than twenty-four hours after death. Speedy burials stem from ancient times when heat and hygiene conditions were far from ideal. In effect, they were protecting the living from sanitary issues. In the case of assassinated Libyan revolutionary Muammar Gaddafi, for example, there was a delay, as his body was put on display, in order to convince people that he really was dead. Unfortunately, we must presume that this haste in preparing the corpse has led to premature interments throughout history, although unless there was reason to disinter a body from its grave, in all likelihood the majority of cases would go unrecorded. Islam does not allow cremation as the religion places an emphasis on the preservation of the body in both life and death. In some cases, if there is a need to do so, embalming is permitted.

Burial alive has been used as a form of capital punishment for centuries and in many nations. In ancient Rome, Vestal Virgins were constituted as a class of priestess whose principal duty it was to maintain the sacred fire dedicated to Vesta, the goddess of home and family. They lived under a strict vow of chastity and those who broke their celibacy vows were immured in small caves, and the rapists of virgins suffered the same fate. However, the Order of the Vestal

Virgins existed for almost 1,000 years, with only ten recorded immurements. Their fate of one such woman was chronicled as follows:

> When condemned by the college of pontifices, she was stripped of her vittae and other badges of office, was scourged, attired like a corpse, placed in a closed litter, borne through the forum attended by her weeping kindred with all the ceremonies of a real funeral to a rising ground called the *Campus Sceleratus*. This was located just within the city walls, close to the Colline Gate. A small vault underground had been previously prepared, containing a couch, a lamp, and a table with a little food. The *Pontifex Maximus*, having lifted up his hands to heaven and uttered a secret prayer, opened the litter, led forth the culprit, and placed her on the steps of the ladder which gave access to the subterranean cell. He delivered her over to the common executioner and his assistants, who led her down, drew up the ladder, and having filled the pit with earth until the surface was level with the surrounding ground, left her to perish deprived of all the tributes of respect usually paid to the spirits of the departed.

Similarly, Flavius Basiliscus, emperor in the Eastern Roman Empire from AD 475–476, was deposed and sent to Cappadocia with his family. They were imprisoned deep in a dry cistern and died from cold and hunger.

In 1149, Otto III of Olomouc of the Moravian Premyslid dynasty immured Abbott Deocar and 20 monks in the Rhadisch monastery refectory, where they eventually starved to death. Otto III's ire had been stirred when one of the monks had fondled his wife, Durana, during her stay there. However, the great leader had happened to confiscate all of the monastery's wealth prior to the immurement, which seems a much more likely motive.

In Germany during the Middle Ages, live burial was the penalty for infanticide, while in Italy murderers were pushed into the ground head-first with only their feet sticking out to mark the spot. In the Netherlands in the sixteenth century, during a time when Protestant churches were being ousted by the Catholic authorities, women found guilty of heresy were punished with live burial. The last to be executed in this way was Anna Utenhoven, who was considered an anabaptist as she neither attended Mass or confession. She was placed in a pit at Vilvoorde in 1597. In the late 1580s, Utenhoven was employed as a servant for the Rampart sisters in Brussels. As Anna declined to recant her religious beliefs, which were cited as heresy, an illegal act under Catholic Habsburg rule, the priest ordered her arrest on 21 December 1594. An ecclesiastical court found her guilty and condemned her to death by burial alive, a punishment used for female heretics that had not been used in over twenty years. Anna Utenhoven was held in the Council of Brabant's prison, Treurenberch.

In 1596, the newly appointed Archbishop Mathias Hovius visited Anna in her cell and tried to convince her to recant. Hovius worried that the woman was spreading heretical influence within the prison and claimed that her stay must be terminated by either converting to Catholicism or ending in her death. In March 1597, Albert VII, governor of the Spanish Netherlands, wrote to the Council of Brabant urging Utenhoven's execution. A few months later she was visited by Jesuit priests, pleading with her to convert in order to save herself. Anna refused and also declined their generous offer of allowing her a further six months to consider the offer. On 17 July 1597, Anna Utenhoven was taken to Vilvoorde. She was given a chance to recant her faith whilst her head was still above ground, but she refused and was suffocated by the earth being piled on top of her (see bottom image on page 1 of the plate section). Dutch citizens protested and urged the Habsburg authorities to stop this cruel form of punishment. As a result, heresy was afterwards punished by deportation or hefty fines. Anna Utenhoven became the subject of Jacobus Viverius' poem *De Uytspraecke van Anna vyt den Hove*, which the poet used to argue against Spanish rule within the Netherlands.

Throughout history one may also find instances of sacrificial burial alive, for the prosperity of a site or building, for example, whilst in other cases the immurement of persons within walls and foundations came as a form of punishment. Many claim that the carved white marble tomb located on the grounds of Lahore's Punjab Civil Secretariat complex in India is the most beautiful one in the world. Made of exquisitely carved stone, it certainly is striking. Further enhancing its beauty is the poignant story behind it.

At the end of the sixteenth century, Akbar was Emperor of Hindustan. In his harem there was a stunning girl called Anar Kali, 'Pomegranate Blossom.' Akbar's son, Prince Salim, and Anar Kali fell in love. When Akbar learned of this, he threatened to disinherit Salim for his relationship with Anar Kali and decreed that the girl must be buried alive within the walls of his palace, which she was. Prince Salim, who later ascended to the throne as King Jahangir, ordered a tomb to be built in Anar Kali's honour as a token of his love. Just before the final blocks were inserted, he said to those grouped around it: "Do not look upon this as a tomb, but rather a temple of love." The earliest Western account mentioning the relationship between the Prince and Anar Kali was written by British traveller William Finch, who reached Lahore in February 1611, eleven years after the supposed death of Anar Kali. An excerpt of his olde English account says:

King Akbar caused her to be inclosed quicke within a wall in his moholl, where she died, and the King (Jahangir), in token of his love commands a sumptuous tomb to be built of stone in the midst of four square garden richly walled, with a gate and divers rooms over it.

Wives who murdered their spouses in feudal Russia were buried alive in a sacred site simply called 'The Pit,' but this was replaced in 1689 with the far more humane punishment of beheading. There were also reported cases of live burials during the Cossack-Polish War, between 1648 and 1657, particularly of Jews, who were seen as their immediate oppressors by the peasants. Under the law of Queen Margaret I of Denmark, adulterous Scandinavian women were punished with premature burial whilst men would be beheaded. However, in the Ribe City Statute in 1269, a female thief was also recorded as being buried alive.

Completed around the year 1290, during the reign of Edward I, *Fleta* was the treatise on the common law of England. Written in Latin, its author is unknown, and only one complete manuscript of the book now survives, being housed in the British Library. Although there is no documented evidence to support the penalty of being buried alive as ever inflicted in Britain during medieval times, the following is stated in *Fleta xxxviii.3:*

Those who have dealings with Jews or Jewesses, those who commit bestiality, and sodomists, are to be buried alive after legal proof that they were taken in the act, and public conviction.

However, Tacitus, the Roman historian and politician, referred to it among ancient Germans in Germania. Men convicted of being sodomites, rapists and those practising bestiality were all subjected to live interment from the mid-thirteenth to sixteenth century. In later centuries, women convicted of murder were also punished in this way. It was a particularly brutal way to die, with thorn branches and nettles lining a deep pit into which the criminal was laid. More thorns and nettles would be piled over the person and finally earth thrown on top to suffocate them. It was a long and painful death which was later replaced with drowning in a sewn-up sack, executioners preferring this method as the death struggles were unable to be seen or heard under the water.

The punishment for men found guilty of paederasty, homosexual intercourse with young boys, varied according to class and status. In 1409 and 1532 in Augsburg, Germany, two men were burned alive for their offences. However, four clerics found guilty of the same crime in 1409 were locked in a wooden casket and hung up in the Perlachturm, a bell tower in front of the church of St. Peter am Perlach, until they starved to death.

One of the first documented cases of a person accidentally being buried alive was in the fourteenth century. John Duns Scotus, a renowned philosopher, was reportedly found outside of his coffin with bloodied hands. Born around 1265, Duns Scotus was a Scottish Catholic priest and theologian, having been educated at a university behind St. Ebbes Church in Oxford. Towards the end of 1302, Duns Scotus was lecturing at the prestigious University of Paris but was expelled later that year for supporting Pope Boniface VIII in his feud with King Philip IV of France over the taxation of church property. The philosopher died suddenly in Cologne in November 1308, but the story concerning his premature burial failed to be supported due to the absence of Duns Scotus' servant, the only man who could verify his master's susceptibility to falling into a coma.

Doctor John James Crafft, physician at Neufchastel, remitted the following account of premature burial:

> Burgundy, and especially the town of Dijon, was in the year 1558 afflicted with a violent plague, which cut off the inhabitants so fast that there was not time to make a separate grave for each dead person, for which reason large pits were made and filled with as many bodies as they could contain. In this deplorable conjuncture Madame Nicole Lentillet shared the common fate, and after labouring under the disorder for some days, fell into a syncope so profound that she was taken for dead and accordingly buried in a pit with other dead bodies. The next morning after her interment she returned to life and made the strongest efforts she could to get out, but her weakness and the weight of the bodies with which she was covered rendered her incapable of executing her design. In this wretched situation she remained for four days, until the gravedigger, coming to inter other bodies, took her up and carried her to her own house, where she recovered a perfect state of health.

Dr Crafft also made mention of a young lady from Auxbourg, who falling into a syncope was buried in a deep vault, without being covered with earth because her friends thought it sufficient to have the vault carefully shut up. Some years after, a member of the same family happened to die and so the vault was opened. The body of the young woman was found on the stairs at the entry, without any fingers on her right hand!

An instance of a human being immured alive which is well authenticated was that of Geronimo of Oran, in the wall of the fort near the gate Bab-el-Oued, of Algiers, in 1568. The fort is composed of blocks of pise, a concrete made of stones, lime, and sand, mixed in certain proportions, trodden down and rammed hard into a mould, and exposed to dry in the sun. When thoroughly baked and solid it is turned out of the mould and is then ready to use. Geronimo was a Christian who had served in a Spanish regiment. He was taken by pirates and given to the Dey (literally meaning '*uncle*' this title was given to the Honorary Rulers of Algiers). When the fort was in construction, the Arabs endeavoured to induce Geronimo to renounce his faith, and after refusing to do so he was bound hand and foot and put into one of the moulds. The concrete was then rammed around him and then the block was put into the walls. Don Diego de Haedo, the contemporary author of the *Topography of Algiers*, said, 'On examining with attention the blocks of pise which form the walls of the fort, a block will be observed in the north wall of which the surface has sunk in, and looks as if it has been disturbed, for the body in decaying left a hollow in the block, which has caused the sinkage.' On December 27 1853, the block was exhumed. The old fort was demolished to make room for the modern '*Fort des vingt-quatre-heures*,' under the direction of Captain Susoni, when a petard, or small bomb, which had been placed beneath two or three courses of pise near the ground, exploded, and exposed a cavity containing a human skeleton, the whole of which was visible, from the neck to the knees, in a perfect state of preservation. The remains, the cast of the head, and the broken block of pise, are now in the former Cathedral Saint Philip, now the Ketchaoua Mosque, in Algiers.

Immurement as a form of punishment includes cases of people being confined in extremely tight spaces and being left to die by dehydration or starvation. Occasionally, it was used as a form of life imprisonment and those enclosed were regularly given food and water. There are records showing that some people survived months and years in this way. According to Latvian legend, three people were immured in tunnels underneath Grobina Castle when the daughter of a knight refused the hand of a suitor chosen by her father.

Some immurements took place at the request of those being entombed alive, such as that of fourth century nun Alexandra, who immured herself in a vault for ten years with a tiny vent allowing her to receive very small food rations. Saint Jerome also mentioned one follower who spent his life inside a cistern and consumed only five fresh figs a day. In the case of Jeanne, a nun from Lespenasse, who had committed acts of heresy in 1246, she was confined to a small cell inside her own convent with a gap for food to be pushed through.

The term 'double jeopardy' is a procedural defence that prevents an accused person from being tried twice on the same charges. One lucky criminal narrowly escaped due to this loophole in the law, but only after suffering a horrific ordeal and with terrible consequences. On 27 March 1634 John Bartondale was condemned to death in York, hanged on the gallows and buried. That afternoon a passer-by heard noises coming from the grave and realised that Bartondale was buried alive. He was rescued, only to be taken back to the assizes. Pleading that he could not be hanged twice for the same offence, and supported by the public, Bartondale was pardoned. Unfortunately, records of Bartondale's crime no longer exist.

A similar instance occurred in the year 1650, when Anne Green was executed at Oxford. After hanging for the usual period of time, her body was taken away. However, signs of life were detected, and methods used to bring her around. Anne lived for many years after and gave a very distinct account of what she had suffered from the moment she was 'turned off.' This made such an outcry at the time that forty of the Prime Wits of the University wrote copies of Latin and English verses about the occasion. A circumstantial account of the whole affair was printed the next year in a quarto pamphlet of three and a half sheets, bearing the title *News from the Dead* in the *Revival of Ann Green*.

Another example of this situation happened in Scotland, where a woman was hanged for the murder of her bastard child which, however, she constantly denied both before and after her execution. By the care of her friends, the woman was revived some hours after she was hanged. She lived for many years in the village of Musselburgh, where people visited and gave her money to hear the story of her near-death experience.

In a document entitled *The Most Lamentable and Deplorable Accident* we learn a fearful tale from the seventeenth century:

Friday last June 22. befell Lawrence Cawthorn, a Butcher in St. Nicholas Shambles in Newgate Market, who being suspected to be Dead, by the two hasty covetousness and cruelty of his Land-lady Mrs. Cook in Pincock-lane, was suddenly and inhumanely buryed. Together With the report of his moving of the Body as it was carrying by the Bearers to his Grave, and the treating of his Winding sheet with his own hands, and the Lamentable Shrieks and Groans he made on the Saturday and Sunday following.

As also the Examination and Commitment of his Land-Lord and Land-Lady by the Lord Mayor to the Prison of Newgate; And opening the Grave, the body exposed to publick view on the Munday following. And the Virdict and Sentence which the Jury passed upon the sight of the Body, & the Examination of several witnesses following. For the further satisfaction of the people who have bin so extremely mis-informed in the particulars of this sad Accident, that the very name of the person is most falsely represented.

LONDON, Printed for W. Gilbertsan, 1661

So, what were the circumstances surrounding the case of Lawrence Cawthorn? For the year, 1661, it was particularly well documented, and some witnesses testified that Cawthorn was subject to having strange fits, and that sometimes he would lie in a trance like a dead man for many hours. However, on the morning in question, everyone who looked at the body agreed that Lawrence was truly dead. It was concluded that the man had died of 'Quinsey', a disease which caused swelling of the throat and stopped a person from breathing. The landlady, Mrs Cook, insisted upon an immediate interment, her motive being to take possession of Cawthorn's meagre belongings and free up the room for another tenant. The landlady would also have been recorded as Cawthorn's next of kin, as he had no relatives. Cook went along with her husband to the local victualler where Lawrence was known to drink, knowing that he would contribute towards the burial costs. However, on arrival the victualler claimed that Lawrence owed him a debt of twenty shillings, which he was able to prove. Nevertheless, he was willing to give the man a Christian burial and asked the landlady to hand over her tenant's clothes. This she refused to do, changing accounts but mainly telling all who would listen that Lawrence had actually owed *her* far more than that. It was agreed upon by neighbours that Cawthorn was an honest man, paying but eight-pence a week for his lodging, and could not be so much in her debt. The landlady meanwhile made use of her dead lodger's clothes for her own advantage and prepared for the burial.

Presently the bearers arrived to carry their burden to the grave, with one of them perceiving the corpse to stir in the coffin, but none of them could believe that any person could be so inhumane as to prepare a living man for burial. The body was duly carried to the Christchurch Churchyard and buried. On Saturday and Sunday several people reported hearing great groaning and shrieking from the burial site, and all were equally frightened.

On Monday morning, 24 June 1661, the dead body was dug up and exposed to the public for viewing. Some said that the shroud was torn to pieces, others that Cawthorn's eyes were swollen, the brains beaten out of his head, blood seen at his mouth, and the breast all black and blue. The coroner was sent for, and a verdict of premature burial was recorded by a jury at the inquest. The Lord Mayor had already committed Mr and Mrs Cook to Newgate Gaol for their part in the tragedy of knowingly allowing Cawthorn to go to the grave alive.

According to local legend the walls of Rozafa Castle in Scutari, now called Shkoder, in Albania, are said to contain the body of a woman. Three brothers, all with very beautiful wives, were working hard to build a castle to protect the town but each night, after the men had retired, the walls would fall down. They consulted a wise old man who told the men that the only way to ensure the walls stayed up was to bury a human sacrifice inside the castle brickwork. He suggested that the first wife to arrive the next day with lunch for her husband should be the one to be sacrificed. The brothers agreed and promised not to tell their respective spouses. However, the two older brothers spilled the beans, but the youngest said nothing. Naturally, the following day only the wife of the younger brother showed up with a basket of goodies. Her name was Rozafa.

When her husband explained that she had been chosen as the sacrifice, Rozafa accepted her fate but on one condition, that the brothers leave three holes in the brick around her. The first was for her right breast in order to suckle her newborn son, a second for her right hand to caress him and a third for her right foot to rock his cradle. This was duly done, and the castle walls never collapsed.

Folklore in the Balkans often included tales of peoples being buried alive and both the Romanian folk ditty 'The Arges Monastery' and the Serbian poem 'The Building of Skadar' are examples of this. The last part of the latter is translated to English here:

> With the white bosom outward, He did her whole behest,
> That Yovo might be suckled when he came unto her breast.
> And again she called on Rado, the builder, in this wise:
> 'I prithee, brother Rado, leave a window for mine eyes,
> That I may look to the white house, and easily may see
> When they bring Yovo hither, or bear him back from me.'
> Rado, the master builder, was well pleased with her prayer;
> That she might look to the milk-white house, he left a window there,
> And see the child when they brought him or bore him back again.
> At last they walled her in the wall and stablished the hold amain.
> They brought the babe in the cradle, she suckled him from the stone;
> For seven days she suckled him; thereafter her voice was gone.
> A year she gave the young child suck, and sweet did the white milk flow.
> As it was then in Skadar, so sweet it runneth now.
> Yea, even to-day the white milk flows, for a miracle most high,
> And a healing draught for women whereof the breasts are dry!

Immurement was practised in Mongolia for hundreds of years, and cases were still being reported as late as the early twentieth century. In a report from 1914, it is written: '... the prisons and dungeons of the Far Eastern country contain a number of refined Chinese shut up for life in heavy iron-bound coffins, which do not permit them to sit upright or lie down. These prisoners see daylight for only a few minutes daily when the food is thrown into their coffins through a small hole.'

Maximilian Mission (1650 -1722), the celebrated French writer and traveller, in his *Voyage Through Italy*, Tome I, Letter 5, tells us:

That the number of persons who have been interred as dead, when they were really alive, is very great in comparison of those who have been happily rescued from their graves; for in the town of Cologne, Archbishop Geron, according to Albertus Krantzius, was interred alive and died for want of a reasonable releasement.

As stated in J.J. Bruhier d'Ablaincourt's *The Uncertainty of the Signs of Death* published in 1746, it is not unreasonable to suspect that during times of violent epidemics, such as the plague, or Black Death, vast numbers of people may have been prematurely interred and exposed to a violent death, when a little less haste may have prevented such a dreadful scene. The same may have been said of battles and sieges, where men only unconscious or still struggling with their last breath were thrown into ditches and left for dead.

Earlier, in seventeenth century England, a woman named Alice Blunden of Basingstoke was pronounced dead and buried on 15 July 1674. The account is in *Baigent and Millard's History of Basingstoke*, from which part of this text is taken:

William Blunden was a maltster and his wife was 'a fat, gross woman', who 'had accustomed herself many times to drink brandy'. One evening she imbibed a large quantity of poppy-water and fell into a deep sleep from which she could not be wakened. An apothecary was consulted and it was concluded that Alice had died. William had urgent business in London and left instructions that her funeral should be deferred until his return. However, Alice's relations considered that 'the season of the year being hot, and the corpse fat, it would be impossible to keep her' and she was buried with all due haste. Some days later, boys playing nearby the grave reported haring a voice. Initially they were not believed but upon investigation a little later, it was heard by others and the coffin was pulled from the grave. The body was found to be 'most lamentably beaten' which was thought to have been caused by Alice herself during her incarceration in the coffin. However, those present were unable to find any signs of life and proposed to call the coroner the following morning and meanwhile lowered the body back into the grave overnight. Next day, they found that Alice had torn off a large part of her burial shroud and was scratched all over with a bloody mouth. At that point she was most definitely dead. The coroner recorded a case of premature burial and bound over several people to appear at the Lent Assizes of 1675. Despite the charges, no individuals were convicted but had a 'considerable fine' set upon them for neglect.

In October 1835, navvies working in a Jutland peat bog near Vejle, Denmark, unearthed the remains of a naked woman with two hoops firmly fixed around her waist and chest. Known only as the 'Haraldskaer Woman', after the bog in which she was discovered, her arms and legs were fastened to the bog with wooden hooks, her leather cape and woollen clothing folded on top of the abdomen, leaving no doubt that she had been buried alive. The macabre find caused an immediate stir, with the body being thought to be over a thousand years old, during a dark period in history when burying women alive was punishment for adultery.

Religion has played its part in the immurement of persons alive, both as a form of punishment to those who break their vows and to heretics who refuse to conform, but an altogether different meaning was given to the phrase 'buried alive' after revelations in the late nineteenth century. In November 1890, the *San Francisco Chronicle* received a special dispatch from Naples, Italy, containing the following shocking narrative:

A remarkable case of religious fanaticism has just been brought to light here. In a secluded quarter stands a conventual establishment, known as the 'Nunnery of the Buried Alive', that certainly has been closed to all public knowledge and investigation for generations. Report adds that the religious authorities have prescribed the same secrecy for the past four hundred years regarding what has happened within its walls and the character of its inmates.

The veil, however, is at last removed, and citizens are lost in amazement that such scenes could for years have been enacted in a civilised land with no note of warning sounded. The present revelation is due to the fact that a young girl, crossed in love, was incarcerated within its walls. Her parents, while at first consenting to her banishment, finally became alarmed at their inability to communicate with her, and appealed to the police.

The civil authorities raided the place on Saturday under an order issued by the minister of justice. The door-keeper stoutly resisted, but was overpowered by the gendarmes, who soon found their way into the cells, where sixteen nuns were found in a condition bordering on insanity. They were scantily covered with rags, and their surroundings were filthy in the extreme. Many of the poor creatures had forgotten how to talk and were hardly human in their demeanour. Those who could be induced to speak protested that they were perfectly satisfied with their fate. The young girl for whom the quest was made was found reduced to a mere skeleton. Her parents are nearly crazed with grief at the result of their conduct, though they acted for what they honestly considered the girl's best interests.

The establishment has, of course, been closed, and the victims removed to one of the public institutions, where they will be well cared for. The governor of Naples has ordered the fullest investigation, with a view to punishing those who shall be found to be responsible.

It is an acknowledged fact that the ancient custom of burying monks and nuns alive was practised in many countries of Europe, the medieval survivals of the custom taking the form of what may be described as immuration, or the building up of a wall around the victim. A loaf of bread and jug of water were generally placed in the niche, and writer and explorer Rider Haggard described several ancient monasteries and convents, notably one in Mexico and one at Waltham, England, where skeletons and pitchers built into walls were found by workmen engaged in either tearing down or repairing the building.

The immuring of monks and nuns on breaches of their chastity vows has a long and interesting history. Francesca Medioli wrote the following in her essay 'Dimensions of the Cloister':

At Lodi in 1662 Sister Antonia Margherita Limera stood trial for having introduced a man into her cell and entertained him for a few days; she was sentenced to be walled in alive on a diet of bread and water. In the same year, the trial for breach of enclosure and sexual intercourse against the cleric Domenico Cagianella and Sister Vincenza Intanti of the convent of San Salvatore in Ariano had an identical outcome.

Groups and sects adhered to their own codes of conduct and beliefs, one of those being that of Romany gipsies, who are nowadays somewhat misunderstood and maligned due to social conditions not favouring nomads. Many people will be surprised to hear that British gipsies have rigid laws of cleanliness and morality. One man, for instance, would not take drinking water from a stream because some of his family had washed in it six years before. Chastity is highly valued, with an unchaste girl being driven from the family home, but the traditional ancient punishment within her community was burial alive. Unfaithfulness was also punished, by death, expulsion, or cutting off the nose and ears. As recently as 1875, an old Suffolk gipsy described a certain spot where, as a boy, he saw a girl undergo the punishment of being buried alive for losing her virginity before wedlock.

One might presume that with the increasing use of embalming, the chances of a person being buried alive would be greatly reduced, but in actual fact the art and science of preserving human remains was not universally employed until the early twentieth century. Although earlier methods of practice were fairly widespread in the fifteenth century, it wasn't until William Harvey detailed blood circulation in the seventeenth century that solutions were injected into the corpse. Scottish surgeon William Hunter was the first to advertise embalming to the general public in the mid-eighteenth century, although his methods were met with dubious applause.

In earlier times it became necessary to preserve organs and the human skeleton for anatomical research in medical universities and teaching hospitals, the most famous and scandalous example being the procurement of bodies for Dr Knox in Edinburgh by resurrection men Burke and Hare. Embalming gradually became popular as a part of the grieving process, with family and friends requesting to view the deceased before burial. Also a necessity against the emittance of noxious bodily gases, embalming was a must for those who had died far from home and transportation of the body over long periods needed to occur. In 1867, the discovery of formaldehyde by German chemist August Wilhelm von Hofmann laid the foundation of modern embalming methods.

The fact that embalming had become common practice at the turn of the twentieth century was shown at the sinking of the *Titanic*. An illustrated article in the Chicago 'Day Book', dated 23 April 1912 (see top left image on page 2 of the plate section), reads:

> The cable repair ship *Mackay Bennett*, the 'funeral' ship which put out from Halifax and picked up dead bodies near the scenes of the *Titanic* disaster. The ship carried a large supply of coffins, an undertaker and a staff of embalmers. The Reverend Canon K. Hink was on board to perform funeral service for such bodies as were unrecognizable and too far gone for embalming. The other portrait is of Captain Larnder, the ship's commander.

Chapter Two

Eighteenth & Nineteenth Century Cases

One of the most extraordinary cases of a person being revived after 'supposed death' was related to a hanging. On 26 July 1736, Thomas Reynolds was executed at the Tyburn in London for destroying the turnpikes at Ledbury in Herefordshire. At twenty-eight years of age, Reynolds had honest parents who put him through school and introduced their son to Christian principles. His father decided not to apprentice Thomas into a trade, but instead kept the lad at home to work the family farm. There are few recorded details of Reynolds' crime, but it's his execution that is of most interest. After he was cut down, the wife of James Baylis, who had bought a coffin and shroud with the money that Thomas had given her the previous day, put him into the coffin. A grave was dug not far from the place of execution to which a crowd carried him. As they were lowering the coffin into the grave, one woman requested to see the body and it was duly opened. As soon as air filled the box, Thomas Reynolds moved, breathed, and lifted a hand to his breast.

Those present feared that officers might take Reynolds back to Tyburn and execute him for a second time, so instead carried the coffin along the Oxford Road, every now and again checking to see how the young man was doing. However, despite the chest moving and breath being strongly felt, Reynolds didn't once open his eyes. A surgeon drew blood and saw that it flowed freely and plentifully, causing Thomas to vomit. The mourners then carried the man towards Paddington, but nobody would take him into their house for fear of repercussions. One sympathiser put brandy to Reynolds mouth, and another wrapped his coat around to keep Thomas warm, but it was unfortunately too little help as cold water had been poured into the coffin to try to revive the ailing prisoner. After having carried Reynolds two miles from Tyburn, the crowd turned back towards the town, at which time they realised that the young man had now expired. A second grave was dug there and then, on the Oxford Road, and Thomas Reynolds was finally buried, with no thanks to the mismanagement and application of cold by his friends.

An extract from the Old Bailey records concerning Reynold's death reads:

As his death drew near, he grew more composed, and his conscience did not affright him with those gloomy prospects which generally present themselves to people in his condition; he prepared to meet his fate, if not with constancy, yet with meekness, shewing to the last all the signs that could possibly be expected, both of a general, and particular repentance. As to the accident which happened at his execution, 'twas indeed very singular, but not so unaccountable as some people would make it, since such as have but a very superficial notion of anatomy, may easily conceive how a person very soon cut down ay shew even strong signs of life, and yet be in no condition to recover. If this poor man had fallen into the hands of surgeons instead of the mob, it is very possible that he might have been saved, but amongst such rude attendants as were about him, there is no wonder to be made that he expired, since the pouring liquor down his throat was certainly one of the foolishest things they could do, next to their omitting bleeding and rubbing.

In the year 1742, two cases of premature burial were reported from Europe, one occurred in the city of Florence, Italy, the other in Oviedo, Spain. The first instance was that of a man who was interred in the vault of a church belonging to a nunnery or convent. In the course of the night, the body having been buried the same morning, several of the nuns heard a voice crying, as if in deep distress, coming from the chancel. However, being seized with fear, the women fled from the scene supposing it was some supernatural influence and left the poor wretch to perish. The following morning, some persons who possessed more courage than the nuns, having heard of the shrieks, broke open the tomb. They found the man, then indeed dead, but it was quite evident that his death had been accelerated after being interred, as his hands were greatly lacerated and swollen, and his head much bruised by the endeavours to liberate himself. The second case was not very dissimilar. In Oviedo, a boy, having fallen from a high building, was supposed to have been killed by the impact and was accordingly buried. On the day after his interment, the grave was opened in consequence of some noise being heard by a person who was passing. It was manifest, from the appearance that the boy's body presented, that he had died after being put into the ground. What made the friends of the boy more inexcusable in thus hastening his burial was that his countenance had not undergone any alteration, but looked as blooming and healthy as he did before the accident!

We often hear of people being scared out of their wits by strange occurrences in graveyards, but none can be as frightening as that witnessed by two gentlemen from Cork who felt a sense of curiosity when visiting a vault in 1804. Located in Lower Shandon Churchyard, it belonged to the Grant family and had not been disturbed for almost twenty-two years. To their astonishment they discovered the topmost coffin to be empty, with the lid removed, and the corpse lying prostrate alongside it. From the inscription on the coffin, it appeared that the body was a Mr. Grant, who had been interred in 1782. As many instances of premature burial had occurred in Ireland at the time, it is highly probable that this gentleman was not actually dead and might possibly have recovered but for the culpable haste of his interment.

An article published by Dr Lessing, in the *Edinburgh Journal* of May 1839, related a very painful incident in Sweden. Herr Hildebrand was the proprietor of the Bystandt Ironworks, at which there was a church constructed for the use of the workers employed at the establishment. One evening in 1785 the sexton, in passing this church, heard sounds of groans and piteous cries issuing from the grounds. Unable, from superstitious fear, to reflect calmly on the probable cause of these sounds, he started off in great haste to inform his neighbours. Some of these, gathering a little courage, approached the church, but when they heard a voice distinctly utter exclamations of great distress, they turned and fled. Next morning, when the church was entered, a woman was found stretched lifeless and covered in blood on the cold stone floor. It was a married daughter of Herr Hildebrand, who had recently appeared to die in childbirth, and had been buried the day before with her unborn child in the family vault near the altar. The baby, also dead, was now found in the mother's arms, whose experience during the previous night was too painful to speculate upon.

Burials at sea were all too frequent in the nineteenth century, but occasionally, if a ship was not far from port, a body could be returned for an earthly interment. In March 1794, a young man named Downing, who had entered on board the *Rangecutter* at Falmouth, was found in his hammock apparently dead. He was accordingly taken on shore and interred the same afternoon. It being discovered that Master Downing had been subject to fits, which had held him in a state resembling death for several hours, he was dug up again in the evening. The body was found turned on its side, to have bled from the nose, was still warm, and quite flexible. However, every means for recovery applied proved ineffectual. It was noted in the local newspapers that 'This narrative proves that one of our fellow creatures has waked in his grave, to die the most horrid of deaths, and should appear in every paper in this country as a warning against the indecent haste too frequent in burials.'

Undoubtedly, many a person may have been taken for dead whilst being in a comatose state, with the effects of alcohol being a very familiar cause. Charles Kent, clerk to a brewer in Limerick, Ireland, returned to his father-in-law's house one evening in October 1799, looking rather intoxicated. The next morning, he was found in bed apparently lifeless. A coffin was sent for, and at ten o'clock the same morning he was buried. Some hours later, a woman passing through the churchyard thought she heard a noise issuing from the grave and ran to rouse a neighbouring couple. Several people accompanied the woman back to the burial ground, while others went to fetch the mayor, who had the grave and coffin immediately opened. Sadly, Kent was found turned upon his face, which was greatly mangled by the efforts he had made to break from his terrible confinement and was literally smothered in his own blood.

Notorious cases of premature interment were not confined to those with a disposition to drink, nor were they confined to the working class. Robert E. Lee, the renowned Confederate General who served during the American Civil War (see top right image on page 2 of the plate section), was actually born over a year after his own mother had been buried. Anne Hill Carter Lee was by no means an entirely healthy woman and the physician at Stratford, Virginia, was kept in constant attendance. Mrs Lee suffered from catalepsy and during a prolonged trance she was pronounced dead. The body was prepared for interment and on the morning of the third day after her supposed death the remains were laid in the family vault in the graveyard of the pretty village. Members of the family made frequent visits to pay their last respects and while the sexton was cleaning up and arranging some flowers to be placed on the casket, he heard a faint voice as though someone was calling for assistance. Naturally the old man was somewhat alarmed, but as he had seen many years of service in the 'city of the dead' he did not leave. Listening closely, he again distinctly heard a voice. Satisfied that the noise came from within the casket he immediately set to work to open it, discovering that Mrs Lee was alive inside. Releasing the poor woman from her awful fate, assistance was soon summoned and within a short time she was safe in bed at home. Anne Lee's recovery was slow, but she did eventually regain good health and a little over a year after she was buried alive her youngest son, Robert Edward, was born.

At the turn of the nineteenth century, still more incidents of hasty burial were cropping up in newspaper periodicals. It was reported in Irish circulars that on 22 March 1809, a tragic incident occurred in the vicinity of Camolin, Wexford County. Edward Flinn, a stucco tradesman, left his lodgings early on a Wednesday morning in order to finish a project that he had been working on for a gentleman in the neighbourhood, but he never made it to the site. Flinn was found dead on the side of the road at around eleven o'clock the very same morning, his death a mystery. As was the custom in the early nineteenth century, the body was prepared for burial shortly after discovery and laid to rest the following evening. Word of Flinn's sudden death and hasty interment came to the attention of a local magistrate, who considered the circumstances to be suspicious and the corpse was ordered to be taken up for examination. However, it was soon discovered that the poor man had turned inside the coffin and had bled profusely out of the nose and mouth. It was deemed that not only was Flinn the victim of attempted murder, but he had also been buried alive.

It is naturally a fascinating topic to learn exactly how the victim of syncope might experience the lying in a coffin before their own burial, and many studies have been undertaken to try to understand the level of panic and sheer hopelessness of those trapped within their own unresponsive bodies. This case appears in Dr Crichton's book on Mental Derangement and is taken from a German publication, the *Psychological Magazine*, in 1819. Although the young woman involved was saved from premature burial, it was a close enough shave to merit mention here:

A young lady, an attendant on the Princess of ...., after having been confined to her bed for a length of time with a violent nervous disorder, was at last, to all appearance, deprived of life. Her lips were quite pale, her face resembled the countenance of a dead person, and her body grew cold. She was removed from the room in which she died, was laid in a coffin, and the day of the funeral was fixed on. The day arrived and, according to the custom of the country, funeral songs and hymns were sung before the door. Just as the people were about to nail on the lid of the coffin, a kind of perspiration was observed to appear in the hands and feet of the corpse. A few minutes after, during which time fresh signs of returning life appeared, she at once opened her eyes and uttered a most pitiable shriek; physicians were quickly procured and, in the course of a few days, she was considerably restored and is probably alive at this day.

The description which she herself gave of her situation is extremely remarkable and forms a curious and authentic addition to Psychology. She said, it seemed to her, as if in a dream, that she was really dead; yet she was perfectly conscious of all that happened around her in this dreadful state. The young woman distinctly heard her friends speaking and lamenting her death at the side of her coffin. She felt them pull on the death clothes and lay her in them. This feeling produced a mental anxiety, which was indescribable. She tried to cry, but her soul was without power, and could not act on her body. She had the contradictory feeling, as if she were in her own body, and yet not in it, at one and the same time. It was equally impossible for her to stretch out her arm, or to open her eyes, as to cry, although she continually endeavoured to do so. The internal anguish of her mind was, however, at its utmost height, when the funeral hymns began to be sung, and when the lid of the coffin was about to be nailed on. The thought that she was buried alive was the first one which gave activity to her soul and caused it to operate on her corporeal frame.

Occasionally, the saving of a life due to diligence by loved ones served as a reminder that the medical profession of the nineteenth century had still not found conclusive means to pronounce a person dead without risk of error. At the death of Philip Doddridge, an eminent Virginia lawyer and member of Congress, who died in Washington D.C. in 1832, it was stated as a reason for retaining his body longer than usual that on a former occasion he had narrowly escaped the fate of being buried alive. It was stated that Doddridge had fallen into a cataleptic condition. His respiration had ceased, his pulse no longer throbbed, his limbs were perfectly rigid and his face 'exhibited the sharp outline of death.' The family, physician and friends, with the exception of his wife, all believed Doddridge to be dead. Mrs. Doddridge, however, would not relinquish hope and continued to apply every remedy she could think of to restore vitality, and finally succeeded in administering a small quantity of brandy, which immediately restored her husband to life and allowed him to recover the use of his limbs. Philip Doddridge lived for many years afterwards and was wont to relate, with deep feeling, the painful and horrible sensations he experienced during the period that he was supposed to be dead. He said that though he was completely unable to move his fingers or give the slightest sign of being alive, he could still hear and was conscious of everything going on around him. Doddridge heard the announcement of his death, the lamentations of his family, the directions for the funeral shroud and all the preparations for burial being made. He made desperate efforts to show that he was alive but could not move a muscle. Finally, he heard his wife call for the brandy. It was said that Doddridge was addicted to spirits, and it seems quite ironic that the very stimulant that had most probably induced his state of trance was the very same which restored him to life!

The *Birmingham Journal* stated that a riotous mob assembled in the city in August 1832, and committed great outrages in consequence of a rumour that a cholera victim named John Britton had been buried alive. The mob, consisting chiefly of women and children, gathered in the St. Mary Chapel yard, broke open the coffin, and carried the deceased, on the lid, to the workhouse. Admittance was, however, refused, upon which the mob broke open the workhouse door and deposited the corpse in the mortuary. The excitement caused was so great that it was thought proper to hold an inquest on the body which had been exhumed. One of the claims was that Mr Britton had been poisoned, but this was satisfactorily disproved, and the jury gave a verdict that John Britton was dead when he was buried. One witness, in expressing a belief that the deceased had died of cholera, said he had eaten two large cabbages which were not well boiled. It appeared that the disturbance was caused by a sweetheart of the deceased man, a girl named Anne Price, supposed to be insane, who harangued the mob upon the conduct of the doctors and gave the idea that John had been buried alive. Several people were later examined before the magistrates, charged with participation in the riot. One of the witnesses who gave evidence at the inquest was Rosanna Jaudrell, in whose house Britton died. After leaving the office at its conclusion, a mob threw stones at the poor woman which, together with threats of personal injury, produced such an effect on her that she expired the following Thursday morning.

An extract from a letter dated 8 January 1834 from Frauenfeld, Switzerland, detailed the following case:

On the 6th, a monk of the Convent of Eschingen being dead, his brethren, after the usual ceremonies, conveyed his body into a subterranean vault, used as the common burying place, where deceased members of the community are laid in slight coffins, without any other entombment. Judge, however, of their horror, when on removing the stone that covers the entrance vault, they found at the top of the steps the body of another monk, who had been buried ten days before. It appeared that he was not dead when carried down in his coffin, but only in a state of lethargy, from which he had revived, and contrived to reach the spot where they found him but, being unable to remove the stone or make himself heard, had at length died of exhaustion.

Occasionally, a person requested to be buried alive with good ulterior motive.

In June 1840, John Harris, a prisoner on Blackwell's Island, Jamaica, made his escape by a very novel and ingenious method. Being a good swimmer, Harris felt assured that if he could conceal himself until night outside the prison walls, he could then escape by swimming across the river. He therefore procured the help of fellow convicts to dig a shallow grave, in which he lay down. The inmates covered him lightly with sods of earth and left a small aperture for John to breathe through. The convicts had scarcely finished their funereal labours when the prison guards noticed Harris missing and had the whole island searched in vain. Harris could not be found. The other prisoners were locked up at the usual hour and the wardens retired to rest. As soon as John Harris found that all around him was as silent as the grave in which he lay, he deduced that it was time to leave, and did so, swimming across the river to freedom.

A Madrid newspaper, in Spain, stated that in March 1841 an inhabitant of Granada, being reduced to perfect insensibility by weakness from long illness, was believed to have expired. He was placed in a wooden coffin, carried into the Church of San Mathias and left there prior to the funeral service which was to take place the next day. The sacristan, on opening the church the following morning, found the man quite dead, but prostrate on the altar steps enveloped in his winding sheet. From the state of the coffin, it was evident that during the night the poor soul had recovered his senses and, by violent exertions, had forced open the sides and climbed out, making his way to where he was found before finally dying.

Another ecclesiastical incident was reported when some workmen taking down an old monastic building in Hereford, England, in 1846, came to a prison, in which there was reason to believe that some unfortunate victim was immured alive. A correspondent of the *Hereford Times* gave the following interesting account of the discovery:

In taking down the south-east corner the workmen came to a paving stone which, on being removed, disclosed to view an aperture about eighteen inches by twelve inches in dimensions. On further examination, by removing the walls, it appeared that there was a sort of niche five feet six inches high, it had been plastered on all sides and at the bottom another paving stone. Upon it were a heap of collapsed bones, a glass bottle, an earthen pan, portions of the leather and high heel of shoes, and a piece of wood which, it has been asserted, bears the marks of having been gnawed, as if in the last frenzied effort to sustain a famishing and desperate nature.

In the same year, in *Headley's Letters From Italy*, it was recorded that in the church of San Lorenzo, in the town of San Giovanna, 'is the withered form of a man cased in a side wall. A sort of trapdoor is swung open, when you are shown a human skeleton, perfect in all parts. It stands erect and motionless among naked, jagged stones. This church had been built centuries ago, and remained untouched until when making some repairs, the workmen had occasion to pierce the wall and struck upon the skeleton. The frame indicates a powerful man, and though it is but a skeleton, the whole attitude and aspect give one the impression of a death of agony. The arms are folded across the breast in forced resignation, the head slightly bowed, and the shoulders elevated, as if in the effort to breathe, while the very face, bereft of muscle as it is, seems full of suffering. It is evident it must have been a case of murder, for there are no grave-clothes, no coffin, and no mason work around the body.'

An extraordinary incident in connection with the famine of 1847 was related from Skibbereen, County Cork, Ireland, around which district the pestilence of that black year wrought such terrible havoc. There lived in that town a man named Guerin and his story, related by himself, is that one morning he was lying in the town square when the 'death wagon' came along, picked him up, carted him, with six or seven others who were dead, to one of the pits in the

Abbey Burial Ground. The shallow pit was filled in with a few shovelfuls of earth, and then the gravediggers departed. After a while Guerin recovered his senses and, horror-stricken to find himself surrounded by dead bodies, made feverish efforts to scramble out of the pit. At length he was successful. Guerin lay in the graveyard until some farmers, whose attention was attracted by his moans, found him and carried him to Skibbereen. He was conveyed to the hospital where he quickly recovered.

In 1848 a young woman, the daughter of a baker in New York, had been subjected to chloroform in order to have a tooth extracted and was believed to have died from improper application. She was buried in due course but, doubts having arisen, the grave was opened. It was found that the poor girl had been buried alive, two of her fingers having been broken in an attempt to extricate herself.

It is difficult to imagine the shock of one respectable resident of Montreal, Canada, who had occasion to go to Lachine, nine miles distant, in September 1849. After leaving his family in their usual good health in the morning, he returned in the afternoon. However, when coming within a short distance of his house later that day, he met a funeral procession and inquired who was about to be borne to the grave. Sadly, he was informed that it was his own wife. With deep emotion the man followed the group to the grave and after the funeral service requested that the coffin might be opened so that he could look upon his wife one last time. He gazed on the woman for some time with an agonized heart but, just as the coffin lid was about to be replaced, he thought he saw a slight trembling motion of one of the corpse's arms. He looked again intently, and sure enough the motion was repeated, leaving no doubt that life still remained. Immediately, the woman was lifted from the coffin and taken home where she made a good recovery. It was discovered that the lady had taken so much laudanum that the stupor it produced was mistaken for death!

Many instances of premature interments were reported from the United States in the 1850s and journals published in Canada were continually reporting fresh cases. In October 1849, for example, the *Philadelphia North American* said:

Upon depositing a coffin in the receiving vault of the Light Street Burial Ground, on Sunday, a human hand was found protruding from one of the coffins, which had been there since Friday last. When examined closely the coffin was found bursted open, the body turned entirely round. The hand was firmly clenched, and, from appearances, there can be no doubt that the unfortunate man was buried alive. He had died suddenly and was buried too soon.

The Paris papers related a case of premature interment which occurred in the district of La Mayenne, in 1849. A soldier, who was supposed to have died from indigestion, produced by too copious libations of wine, was about to be buried in the cemetery. The coffin had already been lowered into the grave, when a low groaning was heard just in time. To raise the coffin and tear off the lid took just a few minutes and the man who was about to be buried alive was taken out. It was said that the soldier intended to bring action against his officious friends for premature interment.

A religious custom prevented a person from being buried alive in 1852, but this was actually the second time that the same person escaped a terrible fate. Ten years before, a three-year-old child named Eulalie was attacked by typhus fever. She was the daughter of respectable tradespeople and after a fortnight's illness appeared to expire. Seeking relief to their sorrow, Eulalie's parents left the house, asking two of the girl's aunts to attend to the funeral. As the family belonged to the Reformed Church, it was resolved, in compliance with the usual custom, to wash the body before placing it in a burial shroud. While the water was warming one of the aunts proposed that it should be made quite hot and that the deceased child's foot should be placed in it. This was done and suddenly the two females heard a slight sigh. They then began to apply friction to different parts of the body and succeeded in restoring little Eulalie to life.

The girl continued to enjoy good health until 1852, when she was diagnosed with a condition described as '*brain fever*' and after suffering for some time she appeared to have died. A physician declared Eulalie dead and signed a certificate for her interment. One of the aunts was present and watched over the body in the company of a nurse. In the course of conversation, the aunt happened to mention the strange circumstance that had happened when Eulalie was younger, causing the nurse to recommend that hot water should be applied to the girl's foot again. Eulalie's leg was accordingly plunged into a bucket of hot water. This produced a similar effect to years before and the girl recovered.

An incident occurred in St. George's burial ground, North Circular Road, London, which left some room to suppose that an unfortunate woman had come by her death in consequence of premature burial. Around ten o'clock in the morning on 22 February 1854, Mrs Barker, of 2 Blessington Place, was taken to the burial ground to be interred. The gravediggers had lowered her coffin to its final resting place and had begun to perform their last duties by flinging in the earth, a large portion of which had been deposited in place, when sounds were heard to issue from beneath it. The men, concluding that the noises were coming from the coffin, quickly began to remove the soil and uncover the coffin. A physician was sent for, a Dr Dollan, of Dorset Street, but he was too late to be of any service, for life was found to be extinct. The following day at one o'clock, Henry Davis, county coroner, held an inquest at the gatehouse to inquire into the cause of death of Mrs Barker. A jury having been sworn, the following evidence was given:

Mary Jane Brown, daughter of the caretaker of the burial ground, deposed that the body of Catherine Barker was brought for interment in a mourning coach, accompanied by two women and a man. The grave was dug but was a little short and had to be lengthened. The gravedigger, Mary Brown's father, and Mr Walker, the sexton, let down the body into the grave and the gravedigger, Thomas Cuffe, began to cover it with earth. The grave was about four feet deep. The persons who had come with the body left and when the grave was half full Brown heard a sound and called Cuffe's attention. They then both heard a knocking sound and became alarmed. Brown told Cuffe to take the earth away, but only after being paid a second time. They then broke open the lid and found the deceased to have a very black and swollen face, 'like a bullock's liver'.

The next two witnesses gave very conflicting evidence. James Cuthbertson, surgeon, examined the body of Catherine Barker and stated that from external appearances he saw nothing to account for the noise as stated by Brown and Cuffe. The limbs were not displaced, but a slight displacement of the shoulders had taken place. Both hands and knees were unmoved. The dead woman had a diseased liver and an enlarged heart, 'as if she drank with dropsical effusion.' He did not think that she could have been buried alive.

However, medical student Robert Quale felt the woman's face for about a minute after the coffin was opened. He said that she appeared turned a little on one side and she appeared to him to be not more than an hour dead. When he saw her, it was one o'clock, and she had been interred at ten. The Coroner carefully considered the evidence given but the jury found the verdict that Catherine Barker had died from 'tubercated' state of the liver, diseased heart and general dropsical effusion.

In December 1863 a type of scarlet fever swept away one-eighth of the population of Whitehaven, in England, with the mortality rate being attributed to bad sanitary conditions, poor drainage of the streets and the absence of water closets, or toilets. Mr Bell, a well-respected china and earthenware dealer from the area, was struck with the typhus fever and, despite the most skilful treatment, died. The news of his death was telegraphed to Dublin and Belfast, places where Mr Bell was known in business. Fortunately, Mrs Bell, by the most natural act, placed her hand on the region of her husband's heart and felt it beating. Without delay she applied hot water bottles to her husband's feet and administered hot brandy with the effect that Mr Bell recovered and opened his eyes. However, this escape from premature burial was not without cost, for Bell lost the use of one eye and his hearing was greatly impaired.

A terrible story reported from Agen and attested by both a doctor and the Directeurs des Pompes Funebres, showed that fears of premature burial in France were not unfounded, in consequence of the law commanding interment within twenty-four hours after death. A young lady from Agen died in 1868 and was buried in the cemetery of Sainte Foi. A year later her mother also died, having previously expressed a wish to be laid in the same coffin as her daughter. A large coffin was accordingly constructed to contain the two corpses, and the body of the young lady was exhumed. It was then discovered that the winding-sheet had been torn open, and the right hand, which was disengaged from its folds, was deeply marked with bites. On the lid of the coffin were some marks made with the crucifix which lay on her breast, and the whole circumstances of the case left no doubt that the unfortunate young woman had been a victim to the horrors of premature burial. Intense excitement prevailed in the local neighbourhood and an official inquiry was made on the subject.

Later the same year, the French public were still in uproar on the subject of premature burial, doubtlessly roused by a report in the *Petit Journal*. It claimed that in November 1869, an inhabitant of Lyons lost a daughter aged twelve. Half an hour before the funeral, the disconsolate father wished to see his child once more. The coffin was opened but a doubt came over the man at the sight of his child, whose features were unaltered and still tinged with colour. A doctor was sent for and declared that he shared the father's doubts. The funeral was nevertheless proceeded with, for the mourners were waiting in the church. Having reached the cemetery, the coffin was let down into the vault, but the father immediately sent for Monsieur Delay, the engineer and inventor of an electric alarm. The apparatus, consisting of conducting wires created to establish a communication between the right hand of the corpse and an electrical peal of bells, which the slightest movement set in motion, was attached to the young girl's body. Since that day, the grieving father visited the cemetery of Loyasse, accompanied by the doctor and Monsieur Delay. On descending into the vault each day, no sign of decomposition could be perceived, and the temperature of the body was the same as that of the vault, varying from 15 to 20 degrees. At last, after seven days without decided results, the physician went into the vault and took off the lid of the coffin in order to make a conclusive decision. The features of the girl were still unaltered but putting aside the white dress which covered the body, he detected a livid tinge characteristic of death, conclusive proof that the girl was now deceased. The question remained, however, as to *when* death had actually occurred.

In 1872, the Jews in London were about to open a new cemetery and also planned to construct a mortuary chapel for the deposit of the dead prior to burial. Although England is a much colder country, the Jews were still burying their dead as quickly as their ancestors used to in the almost torrid climate of Palestine, the climate which rendered a physical necessity for quick interment. However, at the time of the announcement for these plans, a terrible admission was made that several cases of premature burial had taken place. A Jewish paper stated that:

When a certain Jewish Cemetery in Budapest happened to be disturbed for reasons of state, coffins were opened in which there seemed evident proofs of premature interment. The bodies of the buried were found in a disturbed condition, as if consciousness had returned to the inanimate corpse after the body had been placed in its mortuary receptacle.

It was further urged that all subscribers to the proposed cemetery near London should insist on the establishment in the grounds of a mortuary house, in which the bodies of the dead, or supposed dead, should be placed for at least three or four days before they were consigned to their grave in the cemetery. This mortuary house was to be under constant surveillance, with unceasing supervision, so that the least signs of return to life would be noticed and immediate measures adopted.

However, whilst the London Jews were remedying their errors, a shocking case of premature interment was reported to have taken place in the burial ground of the Jewish community of Brody, in Gallicia. The city, now in western Ukraine, had the highest population of Jews in Europe in the nineteenth century and was formerly known as the 'Jerusalem of Austria.' The Jews were prohibited from keeping corpses in their houses for more than one day and, in accordance with this holy law, deceased Israelites were generally buried within twenty-four hours after death. As a result, in November 1874, a Jewish lady who was the wife of a wealthy merchant residing in Brody, was interred the day following her demise. After the week of mourning prescribed by Jewish law had passed over, the bereaved husband was taken with the desire of opening his wife's grave so that he might gaze upon her once more. The Rabbi granted permission and the widower was horrified to find that when the coffin was opened, the shroud in which the corpse was attired was completely covered with blood. There were all the signs of a premature interment and a fearful struggle for life.

Incidentally, seventy years earlier, in 1804, a number of the Jewish nation in Hamburgh (now known as Hamburg) resolved not to bury their dead before the lapse of three days to prevent the dreadful consequence of premature burial, which were so prevalent among their people. As the Hamburgh Jews were, in matters of religion, under the Chief Rabbi at Altona, they were required to procure a legal confirmation of their wishes.

Much was being said and written about cremation and the belief that people were still being buried alive in the late nineteenth century while in a state of trance. Without doubt there were numerous instances of individuals undergoing all the horrors of premature interment and a very narrow escape from which took place at Newcastle, Delaware, in the United States, in 1875.

A young girl, named Matilda Ruddick, the daughter of poor but respectable parents, had been suffering from a low, intermittent fever, which had reduced her to a mere shadow. Her life was despaired of, but she lingered for some time in a coma. Eventually, to all appearance, she breathed her last breath. The doctors pronounced her dead, and five full days elapsed before the last obsequies were performed. While the body was being conveyed to its last resting place, strange sounds proceeded from the hearse. The mourners looked vacantly at one another, but the sounds seemed to increase rather than diminish. The procession came to a halt, and the coffin, at the earnest request of the relatives, was withdrawn from the hearse and the lid wrenched open. To the infinite amazement of the mourners, Matilda Ruddick was found to be alive.

In February 1877, the body of a man who went to California to regain his health was shipped to his former home in the East inside a metallic coffin. When the Central Pacific train arrived at Ogden Junction, the corpse was consigned to the Union Pacific Express Company and placed under the charge of Express Messenger Frank Burgess. While the train was in the western part of Nebraska during the night Mr Burgess heard sounds coming from the coffin that led him to believe that the dead man had come to life. He was half asleep and dozing, but again he heard the sound, and his attention was soon riveted on the coffin. The horrible possibility that the man might actually be alive convinced the messenger to call the attention of other employees, but after a few minutes of listening and hearing nothing they merely laughed at him. However, Burgess' convictions that he had heard moans were so strong that he had the coffin inspected as soon as the train arrived at the next station. The weather was very cold, and a thin film of frost had accumulated on the inside of the coffin's glass plate, such as might have been deposited by the breath of a person confined in narrow quarters, with the face drawn up against the glass plate. While Frank Burgess had no doubt that the man, although dead at that point, had been alive in the coffin, the other employees present explained the frost on the glass as natural exhalations of the dead body, and the disturbances of the corpse as due to the movements in shipping. However, a private dispatch received from Chicago stated that when the coffin arrived at its destination and was opened, unmistakable proof of the terrible reality was discovered. The hands were clenched, the lips bitten, and the mouth filled with bloody froth. The man had been alive, and it was his moaning that had been heard but not recognised.

A tragic case where a man was buried alive caused grievous consequences after it occurred in May 1879, in Rochester, New York. Henry Garlin was the unfortunate man's name, and he was one of the most prosperous and respected men in the community. Early one morning he was found lying in a stall beside a horse in his barn. He had gone there a few minutes before to feed the cattle and the loud neighing of the horse attracted members of the family. The unconscious man was carried into the house and physicians hastily summoned. After working over him for more than an hour doctors pronounced Henry dead, giving heart disease as the cause.

Garlin had always expressed a wish to be buried in Albany, New York, where he was born, but as his wife was too ill to leave the home, it was decided to place Henry's body in a vault and carry out his request at some later date. Three weeks afterwards a grave was prepared in a cemetery in Albany and Mrs. Garlin went to the tomb to take a last look at her dead husband. The coffin was raised, and Mrs Garlin turned her pale face to look inside the rosewood coffin. There was a shriek, a heavy fall, and then all was still. Only the old gravedigger was left to gaze upon the sickening sight.

The flesh on the dead man's face had been torn in strips with his fingernails, and in his terrible death struggles Garlin's garments and the silk lining of the coffin torn to shreds. Doctors concluded from the appearance and condition of the body that Henry must have regained consciousness a few hours, or at least a day, after he was buried. These opinions were relayed to the grieving widow, and she was left to brood over the terrible fate of her beloved husband. She blamed herself for allowing the body to be placed inside the tomb so soon, and two months later Mrs Garlin was found dead in her bed. The doctors said, and all of her friends believed it to be so, that she had died of a broken heart.

Occasionally, the red tape involved in disinterring corpses could be detrimental to the well-being of a person who had been accidentally buried alive. One example is the horrifying case of a man in Samara, Russia. Comrade Tichonoff was employed as a writer in a machine depot and, on the day of his reported demise, in February 1883, Tichonoff drank heavily and suffered an epileptic seizure. For a long time thereafter he lay quite still, showing no signs of life, which led his wife and relatives to conclude that he was dead. This happened on Saint Silvester's Day, and to avoid keeping the supposed corpse in the house for three days, for on a Saturday preceding a festival no body could be buried, it was decided to lay Tichonoff in the ground that very night after Vespers. Arrangements were made accordingly, and the body was removed to the church where a local priest read the service for the dead. While this was going on, with the coffin being uncovered, some of the mourners noticed what appeared to be beads of sweat on the dead man's face. However, those in authority attributed this to snowflakes which had fallen during the journey from Tichonoff's house to the cemetery, and he was laid in the grave without further ado. By that time the hour was late and very little earth was thrown over the coffin.

Early the next morning, the gravedigger arrived at the cemetery to complete his work of filling in the grave. As soon as he had lifted the spade, the man heard a groaning sound and the noise of a struggle within Tichonoff's grave. However, instead of forthwith releasing the poor wretch, the gravedigger ran to the local priest to ask leave to disinter the body. The priest refused this request on the grounds that he dare not touch a corpse once buried without permission from the police. On this news, the sexton informed Tichonoff's wife of what had come to pass, and they went together to the chief of the local police. This gentleman said it was quite out of his power to give the required authorisation and referred them to the archimandrite who in turn professed to be equally powerless and told them to approach the procurator. Finally, the agonised wife procured the authorisation, without which nobody could act, and returned to the cemetery. It was too late. Five hours had elapsed since the sexton had first heard the groans and Tichonoff was now dead beyond the possibility of doubt. The poor fellow had succumbed only after a mortal struggle and had finally turned around in his coffin, with bitten fingers, torn flesh and ripped clothing. 'This fatality,' said the Viedmosti News, 'is due to no other cause than the senseless formalities which prevail in every branch of Russian administration.' It was later reported that Madame Tichonoff sued the priest who had refused to allow the gravedigger to disinter her husband for damages, on the grounds that he caused her husband's death by too slavishly obeying the letter of his instructions.

A story from Maine, United States, claimed that in 1884 Joseph Dyer was thrown from a wagon and killed. His remains were properly interred but, in November 1885, his parents received information that their son was alive. The coffin was exhumed and as it was about to be opened Dyer walked in and delayed further proceedings. It turned out that medical students had stolen Joseph's 'supposed' corpse and restored him to consciousness!

Martha Devine, a spinster, who resided with her nephew, Theodore Cook, at Allendale, New Jersey, suddenly became a curiosity and startled the whole neighbourhood in 1886. For several years Miss Devine had been an invalid and on 26 March her relatives were called to her bedside to bid the woman farewell, as she was evidently dying. Shortly after ten o'clock she closed her eyes and ceased breathing. A looking-glass was held over the mouth but no indication of respiration appeared on it. Martha Devine was prepared for burial. The undertaker, Mr Mitchell, noticed that although the dead woman's form was rigid, with the exception of her extremities, her body remained warm. Without notifying the relatives he placed her in a coffin without putting her on ice. For twenty hours Martha lay in the box and was viewed by several neighbours and mourned by her friends. Her relatives even opened and read Miss Devine's Will, thinking that she might have made some request regarding her funeral. On the evening before burial, while the family were at supper, Mr Cook heard a noise in the parlour where his aunt's remains were lying. He was horror-stricken to find her sitting up with her head and shoulders partly out of the glass covering over the coffin. She had been in a trance or coma. After getting out of the coffin, Martha Devine walked and appeared perfectly well. She afterwards related many curious things that she apparently saw while in the trance.

On the evening of 18 June 1886, George Wellington, an Indiana farmer, had a gathering of friends at his house. He was a man of 42 and of robust health, and on this evening, it was noticed that he was in particularly good spirits. After the guests had departed George remarked to his wife that he felt more like singing and dancing than going to bed. They retired about half past eleven and the wife was asleep before midnight. The farmer was always out of bed before five in the mornings, but on the following day Mrs. Wellington woke at six and found her husband still sleeping. When she attempted to rouse him a little later, she discovered that he was dead. A doctor was sent for and within an hour he had arrived and pronounced George dead from heart disease. He estimated that Mr. Wellington had been dead since around three in the morning. The undertaker came and prepared the body for burial, remarking that the corpse had retained a strikingly life-like appearance and that none of the limbs had grown rigid. Two more physicians were called in but combated the idea that George might be in a trance and could be restored to life. Nevertheless, Mrs. Wellington and her sons held a secret hope that George was not really dead and postponed the funeral until two days later. During this interval the body was constantly watched for signs of returning animation, but nothing occurred to delay the funeral arrangements.

The burial was to take place in a country graveyard, and most of the vehicles gathered at the house belonged to farmers. The usual ceremonies took place over the dead body and the coffin was then brought out and placed in the hearse. While the procession to follow the coffin was forming, a team of horses attached to an empty wagon came running away down the road and collided with the hearse, causing it to turn over and the coffin flung out. Four men raced to pick it up but before a hand touched the coffin, a voice was heard saying:

For God's sake let me out of this!

People moved back in fright at first but as the voice continued to address them the coffin was righted and opened, from which George Wellington was found struggling to get out. With a little help he walked back to the house and sat down in a chair. Within half an hour he had put his clothes on and was walking around amongst the mourners. He related his experience in the *New York Sun*:

I did not fall asleep until some time after midnight. When I awoke the clock was striking five. I made a move to get out of bed, but to my great amazement, I could stir neither hand nor foot. I had the full use of my ears, but I could not open my eyes. I argued at first that I was not yet wide awake, but when my wife shook me and called me by name, and I could not respond by even moving an eyelid, I became satisfied that I was in a trance. My mind was never clearer, and my hearing was painfully acute. I made effort after effort to throw off the great weight which seemed to be holding me down, but I could not bend a toe or crook a finger. However, it was only after the doctor pronounced me dead that I felt any alarm. Up to that time it had seemed to me that I could soon manage to get rid of the weight. Had a pistol been fired in the room I'm sure the spell would have been broken. After the doctor's ultimatum I felt that I should be buried alive. But was I alive? All of a sudden, this query flashed across my brain and I was troubled more than I can tell you. As I had never died before, how was I to know the sensations? Could the dead hear and think? Was the mind of a corpse in active operation? It was a problem I could not solve.

He went on:

I heard the people assemble for the funeral, and as I caught a word from this one or that one I identified them by name to myself. I listened closely to the sermon, but when the minister spoke of me I could not take it as personal. It was as though the name and person belonged to someone I had known years before. I knew when I was carried out and placed in the hearse, and I am certain that I heard the clatter of the team running away before anybody sighted them. When the people began to call out in a fright I felt that same fear of being hurt that any live man does. I heard them trying to back the hearse out of the way to let the team go by, but they were not quick enough. As the collision came my eyes opened and my speech was restored, and from that moment I was all right.

During the session of the Lutheran Evangelical Synod at Booneville, Indiana, Philip Gyer, a wealthy citizen from Mount Auburn, Ohio, who was present as a delegate, arose to make a few remarks. He had scarcely risen from his seat when he was noticed to stagger, and the next second fell on the floor apparently dead. A physician was called and pronounced it a case of apoplexy. The remains were hurriedly prepared for burial and ordered to be shipped at once to the home of the deceased. Ten hours after Gyer's supposed death his body arrived in Ohio by special train from Evansville. John Kuster, the baggage master, assisted by Clark Harvey, transferred the corpse from the Evansville and Terre Haute train to an Ohio and Mississippi train. Harvey declared that he heard the dead man kick against the lid of the box three or four times. Mr. Kuster said, 'I have handled more coffins than any other man about this depot, and I flatter myself that I am not superstitious. The sensation I experienced in lifting the coffin from one car to another was the same as lifting a crate having a live calf in it. The coffin seemed to be alive. There was no dead weight about it. We only had a few minutes in which to transfer the remains, and it was suggested by some of the boys that the box be opened, and an examination made of the corpse. To this a strenuous objection was entered by an unknown gentleman who accompanied the remains.'

Depot master Mechlin telegraphed from the station to Washington requesting that the coffin be opened on arrival and an examination made of the body. Once again, the man who had charge of the corpse interposed. Word was sent from Washington to the Chief of Police at Cincinnati, and a telegraph sent to instruct that the coffin be opened on arrival. As the lid was taken off, it was found that the man was lying on his face, his shroud torn and other indications to show that Philip Gyer had come to life after having been placed in the coffin.

Mrs Dicie Webb kept a grocery on Beale Street, Saint Paul, Minnesota, and was known to hundreds of people in the neighbourhood. In 1886, Mrs Webb's son, John, married Sarah Kelly, a remarkably pretty girl, to whom the mother-in-law became greatly attached. Before the first year of their married life had passed, Sarah Webb became stricken with consumption and in June 1888 became anxious to visit her parents in Henderson County. Two weeks after her arrival, a telegram was sent to John Webb announcing his wife's death and he started out to fetch her remains. Three days later he returned with the corpse. Dicie Webb pleaded so hard for a glimpse of the dead woman that it was decided to open the coffin. While looking at the placid face, Mrs Webb became almost paralysed with fright at beholding the eyelids of the dead woman as they slowly opened. Dicie was unable to utter a sound but fell back upon a chair, which was when the supposedly dead Sarah slowly sat upright and said quietly, 'Oh, where am I?' At this the weeping woman screamed.

Friends rushed into the room and were shocked, but one bolder than the others spoke to Sarah, who asked to be laid on the bed. Hastily she was taken from the coffin and cared for. The following day Sarah Webb related a strange story. She had been aware of everything that had occurred and did not lose consciousness until she was put aboard the train for Memphis. Soon after being placed in her mother-in-law's home Sarah regained her senses. She made a supreme effort to speak while Dicie Webb was looking at her and in that instant lost track of her surroundings which caused her to ask where she was. Sarah Webb lived a number of days and then died. The doctor pronounced her dead and she was once more placed in the same coffin and buried the following Sunday.

A gendarme was buried alive in January 1889, in a village near Grenoble, France. The man had become intoxicated on potato brandy and subsequently fell into a deep sleep. After twenty hours of slumber had passed, his friends considered the officer to be dead, particularly as his body had assumed the usual rigidity of a corpse. However, when the sexton was lowering the remains of the ill-fated gendarme into the grave, he heard moans and knocks proceeding from the interior of the coffin. The sexton immediately bored holes into the sides of the coffin to let air in and then pulled off the lid. The gendarme had, unfortunately, ceased to live, having horribly mutilated his head in his frantic but futile efforts to burst the coffin open. The correspondent from Paris commented, 'So terrible a case of premature burial has hardly ever before been reported in this country, where hasty interments are only too common.'

On 20 December 1889, a correspondent wrote to the 'Factory Times' to air his concerns of people being prematurely interred. He cites evidence such as the story of one of his own relations:

The lady was attended by a medical man who thought her to be dead and gave a certificate of death. In accordance with a desire she had frequently expressed, she was buried wearing her diamond rings, which were extremely valuable. The coffin was deposited – fortunately, as it turned out – in a vault. The story of the rings got abroad, and a man entered the vault and broke open the coffin to get the rings. Finding it difficult to remove them, he cut one of the fingers. The blood ran from the living limb and the 'corpse' moved in its coffin. The would-be thief ran away screaming with fright and was thus the means of attracting the aid of neighbours to rescue the buried lady, who lived many years to tell the tale.

This was just one case that the writer gave, but claimed to know of many more, all of people who had only escaped being buried alive by pure accident. He goes on to give details:

A woman had been extremely ill and had an infant only a few hours old and was said by the doctor and nurse to be dead. Her body was arranged, and the room set in order for the burial, which would take place in a few days. But it so happened that she was a poor woman and had not many rooms, so the husband, who was very fond of his wife, sat hour after hour, every now and then looking at her face, thinking she was gone forever. He put the candle where he could best see his wife's face when suddenly he felt sure that her lips moved. He at once called up the nurse, who was too frightened to do anything but scream, but some neighbours helped him to remove all signs of death, and set to work with rubbing and brandy, and the man had the delight of seeing his wife alive once more. The man died first, and the woman married again and served me for many years after that.

Another case was that of a gentleman, a friend of mine, in Paris, who was attended by a physician and was supposed to be dead. He was in his coffin when the guardian of the young man, in whose house he was, felt anxious that a certain young lady should see the deceased once again, and took her into the room where the body lay. The moment she looked at the body she exclaimed, 'He does not seem to be dead.' 'Not dead!' cried the guardian, 'Why, he died of poison, and I have the doctor's certificate! Why not dead? We must apply a test at once.' They took the body quickly out of the coffin and applied a test. The man lived, and, I believe, is still living.

It was often asserted by medical men of prominence and repute that premature burial was extremely infrequent in the late nineteenth century, if not altogether mythical, yet there were many authentic instances of cases where people escaped interment alive only by the merest accident. In early 1890 the young daughter of Mr and Mrs F.M. Bashelier, of Elkhart, Indiana, was pronounced dead and prepared for the grave. While her father was absent arranging the funeral details, a group of sympathetic neighbours called at the house and viewed the supposed corpse as it lay in an open coffin. As they gazed upon the features of the young woman they had known and loved, they were astounded to see Miss Bashelier raise herself up and look around. Recovering from their momentary panic, they raised the girl from the coffin and helped her to bed, where a full recovery was made soon afterwards.

This case is similar to that of Mrs Sorrich, who resided near Steubenville, Ohio. When still a schoolgirl of fifteen, she married against her parents' wishes and subsequent annoyance and anxiety brought on an attack of nervous prostration. One day the young woman fell down in a fainting fit from which she failed to revive. The attending physicians declared her dead and, to make the matter of her dissolution certain, opened a vein from which no blood flowed. Everyone except for Mrs Sorrich's twin brother were satisfied that she had passed away. He insisted that she was still alive and day after day refused to allow her interment. Finally, it was resolved to bury her despite his protests. In the struggle to remove the brother from the room, the bandage around the young woman's face fell off and her lips were seen to move. She called for water, and on being given this she was revived. By all accounts, the woman lived a very long and natural life thereafter.

Fred H. Leider, who took an overdose of morphine on 25 October 1890 and was supposed to have died, was buried two days later. His brother, who could not get to the funeral, arrived on 1 November and wanted to see the body. When the coffin was opened it was found that the supposed dead man had been in a stupor and had come to life in the casket. His face was scratched and the glass in the coffin broken. Everything evidenced a fearful struggle. A strained, terror-stricken look was in his eyes, which were wide open. In his agony and despair the poor victim had torn the front of his shirt. He had evidently tried to burst out through the side of his coffin, for his elbows were drawn out on either side and showed extensive skin abrasions. The shoulders were also bruised where he had tried to lift off the lid. Mr Leider's brother was vocal in his denunciation of the doctor who passed his sibling for dead and gave a certificate to secure burial.

In a similar case occurring the same year, Louis Brenner, an employee of the South Park railroad shops of Denver, Colorado, was supposed to be dead, and the funeral was conducted under the auspices of one of the local tribes of native American Indians in December 1890. The corpse was taken to Riverside Cemetery and interred. However, there were several incidents connected with his funeral which led to doubt surrounding the circumstances of Brenner's death. Accordingly, four days later, it was deemed advisable to investigate the matter by disinterring the remains and to their horror officials discovered that Louis Brenner had been buried alive. The coffin lid was split, the glass cover broken in and it was obvious that the poor man had struggled with mad desperation to free himself with utter helplessness. The body was lying face down, the lining of the coffin torn to shreds, hair pulled out of the man's head, arms bent and the hands so tightly clenched that the fingernails had been sunk into the flesh. Brenner's face was distorted from the awful struggle through which he had passed. Terror stricken at the discovery they had made, officials made sure that life was completely extinct before having the remains reinterred.

The following sad story was reported from Southern France in November 1891.

A young married lady, Madame Joffis, living in Mirabel, near Montauban, had a cataleptic seizure when in childbirth. Two days passed and there was no sign of returning animation, which indeed was not expected as the lady's friends all believed her dead. The funeral was arranged and carried out, and the mourners returned to the house to hold wake. Shortly afterwards, the undertaker casually remarked that when the corpse was put into the coffin, he noticed that the bed was slightly warm where the body had lain. On hearing this, Monsieur Joffis, the widower, instantly went to the burial ground and had the coffin taken from the grave and opened. To his horror, he then found the body turned over, the shroud torn and the fingers of one hand bleeding, as if from a desperate attempt to remove the coffin lid. But it was too late. Madame Joffis, who was undoubtedly alive when buried, had since suffocated.

A tragic incident was reported from the village of Proschovitsakh, in the province of Kielce, Poland, in January 1892, when in the cemetery of that village, a local physician was interred. The funeral took place in the morning and as soon as the ceremony was over the sorrowing relatives returned to their homes. In the afternoon of the same day a second interment took place, the new grave being in the immediate vicinity of the one which had been filled in a few hours previously. While the funeral service was proceeding, the mourners were horrified to hear a succession of strange subterranean noises. Before they could recover from their astonishment, these sounds were followed by a series of half-stifled shrieks, which plainly emanated from the adjacent grave. The officiating priest at once stopped the service, and the gravediggers, assisted as far as possible by the bystanders, set to work to reopen the grave. When the coffin was reached it was broken open and it was seen in a moment that the unfortunate doctor had been buried alive, and succour had come too late, as he had perished from suffocation while the work of rescue was actually in progress. The deceased was found to have turned upon his left side. In the agony of suffocation, he had bitten his fingers to the bone and had knocked his head against the sides of his terrible prison until his temples were covered with bruises.

Russia was a testing place for sanitary officers during the cholera epidemic in 1892 (see bottom image on page 2 of the plate section). The peasants persisted in associating the officials with spreading the disease they were endeavouring to combat. In one Polish province a party of sanitary inspectors which had been sent to check on the town of Lyssboki had a narrow escape from being massacred. A report had been circulated that the sanitary officers had intentions to poison the sick and bury them alive, and a furious mob locked them up in the local police quarters until armed forces arrived to protect them. Fighting cholera was sufficiently hard work, but with a bloodthirsty crowd thrown in, the task of the health inspectors became rather too much for human endurance.

In January 1893, a story came from Paris of a young man named Daubenesque, just twenty years of age, who was suffering from typhoid fever. On Sunday 18 December 1892, it was believed that he was dead, the funeral being arranged to take place the following Tuesday. As the time fixed for the interment arrived it was found that the family vault had not been finished, so the coffin was deposited temporarily in another one, and afterwards removed to the church pending the completion of the family vault. At midnight on the Wednesday the person appointed to watch the body thought he heard a noise proceeding from the coffin. After giving the alarm he had the coffin removed to the nearby rectory. The lid was forced open, and it was discovered that the young man had merely been in a trance and was not dead. Strong restoratives were immediately applied, and the hero of this ghastly adventure returned to consciousness, making rapid strides towards a full recovery.

A terrible case of premature burial was reported from Doussard, on the shores of the Lake of Annecy, in the Department of Haute Savoie, France, in May 1895. The coffin containing what was believed to be the dead body of a woman named Mme Rassat had been lowered into the grave, and the mourners had withdrawn from the cemetery after seeing a little earth thrown on the lid, when the gravedigger, occupied in filling up the hole, heard a knocking. It was just past nine o'clock in the morning. Calling one of his fellow workmen, the two men listened to the continued knocking in the coffin for half an hour before they made up their minds to do anything, and then, instead of breaking open the coffin lid to release the unfortunate person within it, they went to warn the authorities. The parish priest was the first to arrive, but even that enlightened individual was careful not to open the coffin, because the legal authorisation to exhume the body had not been given. All he did was to bore a few holes in the lid to let in a little air. At length, three hours after the noise in the coffin was first heard, all the legal formalities had been accomplished. The knocking had by this time ceased and the lid was finally removed. Whether Madame Rassat was alive or not at that moment does not appear very certain, but some of the persons present affirmed that her cheeks were flushed, and her eyes half opened. What was ascertained, by Doctor Estay who was finally summoned later, was that Madame Rassat had not been dead for more than six hours, which would put her death at around the time that the coffin was opened!

Fred Markham of Santa Cruz, California, received a letter on 1 December 1895, stating that his mother had died in Battle Creek, Michigan, as the result of a railroad accident, and that the remains would be interred before he could reach Battle Creek. A few days later he was astonished at receiving another letter containing the information that his mother was alive and would probably recover. The letter further stated that his mother's apparent death had occurred when the first letter was written. Arrangements for her burial were then underway, but while the funeral service was in progress the minister, relatives and congregation were horrified by a sound from the coffin. They were almost paralysed with surprise when a moment later the coffin lid was opened, and Mrs. Markham found to be alive. It appeared that she had suffered from concussion to the head and had lain unconscious for two days.

Medical men in Paris were very perplexed over the case of thirty-six-year-old Monsieur Poinsignon who died in April 1898 and was duly buried two days afterwards at the expense of the parish. The undertaker's men were surprised at the absence of rigidity in the corpse, which was also warm at the time of burial. One of them happened to mention this fact to an acquaintance of the deceased man, who thereupon related that only a year before his friend had fallen into a lethargic sleep and had remained so for a month. The undertaker's man communicated this information to the authorities, with the result that the body was hastily exhumed. It was found to be still comparatively warm. There were no traces of decomposition, neither was the 'corpse' stiff. Several doctors examined Monsieur Poinsignon, but hesitated to say whether the man was dead or alive, therefore he was kept in hospital until positive proof one way or the other was obtained!

At Moglia, a small village of some 5,000 inhabitants, in Mantua Province, Italy, the wife of a shopkeeper, named Lavinia Merli, was supposed to have died of epilepsy, and her death was duly certified by the physician who attended her. At the time of her death Lavinia was about to become a mother. The funeral took place, as was common in Italy, almost immediately after the death, and the coffin was deposited for the night in the mortuary chapel in the cemetery. The next morning when gravediggers went to entomb the body, they found that the coffin had been burst open. The woman was scarcely recognisable, while between her knees she held a newly born infant. She had been coffined alive, and in her struggles for liberty, and in her labour pains, Lavinia had torn her hair from her head and wounded herself in many places. As both mother and child were dead, the gravediggers, without apparently consulting anyone, closed the coffin and buried it. They then told their tragic story, to which the villagers became almost panic stricken with horror and fright. As soon as the authorities heard of it, they had the bodies exhumed and an inquiry into the tragedy was held in the village.

Finally, to close the nineteenth century, a shocking discovery was made at the Tonawanda Cemetery two miles north of Pendleton, New York, on 9 February 1899, when the body of James Rigley was exhumed for the purpose of holding an autopsy to discover the cause of his death. The glass covering the casket was broken and the distorted features of the corpse, the position of his hands and feet, together with a number of blood spots on his face, showed that the man had been buried alive. Mr Rigley was undoubtedly interred while in a trance, it was contended by physicians who viewed the body. On the previous Wednesday, Rigley had apparently died and Dr Monterey, the family physician, declared him dead. A few years earlier Mr Rigley had taken out several insurance policies on his life, and it was partly for this reason that it was decided to hold an autopsy to ascertain beyond doubt the exact cause of death. But for this, the discovery of the terrible mistake would never have become known. Mr Rigley was a prominent figure in the area and was considerably wealthy. He was survived by a widow and four sons. Naturally, the discovery that he had been buried alive was said to have greatly shocked the man's family and friends.

Chapter Three

Twentieth & Twenty-First Century Cases

O ne might assume that entering the twentieth century cases of premature burial might fade from the news. However, this does not appear to be the case, although admittedly with the advancement in technology and newspaper reporting, it is likely that hundreds of past cases were simply not brought to light or were yet to be discovered. Still, it does make the blood run cold to discover that there are, even now, cases of mistaken interment.

One of the very first recorded cases of premature burial in modern times occurred in April 1901 at Nola, Italy, when the local stationmaster collapsed and was judged to be dead of cardiac arrest. His body was coffined and taken to the cemetery chapel for burial the next day. During the night, however, the custodian heard groans proceeding from the coffin. Later, when the coffin was eventually opened, the stationmaster was found to have died from asphyxia and terror.

An extraordinarily tragic story was reported later the same year from Pauillac, France in November 1901. A Mademoiselle Bobin arrived at the port on board the steam ship *La Plata* from Senegal. She was supposed to be suffering from yellow fever and was transferred from the *Lazaret* by order of the health officers onboard. There poor Mme Bobin deteriorated and apparently died. Her body became rigid, her face ashen and corpse-like and, in that condition, she was buried. The nurse attending the young woman, however, had noticed that the body was not cold and that there was a tremulousness of the muscles and expressed the opinion that Mme Bobin had been prematurely buried. On this being reported to the young woman's father, he had the body exhumed. Shockingly, it was found that a baby had been born inside the coffin. An autopsy showed that Mademoiselle Bobin had not contracted yellow fever and had died from asphyxiation after burial. A lawsuit was actioned against the health officers and ship's Prefect, which resulted in a French court awarding the Bobin family the equivalent of £8,000 in damages against them.

A sensation was caused in Ohio, in January 1902, by the supposed death of Blanche Evans after a sickness of several weeks. Printed cards were sent out from Deerfield, a village a few miles north of Alliance, announcing the woman's death from typhoid fever. The funeral was set for the following Saturday after two physicians from Youngstown and one from Deerfield pronounced her dead.

An undertaker was called, and the body lain in a casket. Around three o'clock on the Friday afternoon, while a friend stood taking a look at the face of her dead friend, grief was turned to amazement, and then alarm, by a twitching of the face of the corpse. The family was called, and it was decided that Blanche might well still be alive. Doctors were summoned and resuscitation methods applied. After some time, the woman opened her eyes but seemed only partly conscious. By the Saturday morning, however, Mrs Evans had fully regained consciousness, and while unable to speak and still very weak at that time, she made a full recovery. The matter had been kept very quiet but was leaked to the press a few days after the incident.

A mad peasant woman living in the village of Kapustino, Russia, discovered a subterranean passage leading to a family vault in the churchyard, and decided to bury herself alive in August 1902. For fourteen days she sat in a polluted atmosphere surrounded by coffins without food or drink. Her presence was discovered quite by chance by the sexton, who heard groans and sighs, causing him to drop his spade in horror and scream for help. The woman had temporarily lost the power of speech and was almost blind. She survived her experience but only for a matter of a few weeks.

From Malmo, the picturesque Swedish town which faces Copenhagen across the Sound, came a ghastly story of premature interment in September 1902. A servant girl of the town, who suffered from severe toothache, had placed a small wad of cotton wool steeped in narcotic oil in the hollow of a decayed tooth before she went to bed. While she was asleep the cotton ball dropped into her windpipe and she was found the next morning, apparently dead. The master of the house, believing that she had taken poison for the purpose of committing suicide, and being anxious to avoid publicity of the matter, at once sent for a coffin. The body was placed in it and the lid screwed down. Later on, in order to obtain the necessary medical certificate, without which the burial could not take place, a doctor was sent for, and on his arrival the coffin lid was unscrewed. It was evident from the appearance of the girl's body that she had recovered her senses sometime after being enclosed in the coffin and had made violent and ineffectual efforts to free herself. These efforts had only finally ceased when death came to her aid.

A remarkable story appeared in the 'Club Chatterer' section of *Today* in April 1904. It would appear that a certain middle-aged gentleman, about forty-five years old, from Hampstead, London, had for a long time been suffering from general physical exhaustion. This man, David Brown, had been employed for many years as a clerk in a firm of brokers in the City, but the strain of the work, the increasing responsibilities of his family, and the inadequacy of his salary, less than three pounds per week, proved too much for his debilitated condition.

In late March 1903 he died, leaving his wife and children absolutely penniless, after the funeral expenses had been paid. Mrs Brown, who was deeply attached to her husband, was heartbroken. The couple's two children, a son and daughter, earned a small weekly sum but barely enough to keep body and soul together. The widow was so stunned by her loss and forebodings for the future, that as the day for the funeral grew near it seemed that it might not be long before she joined her husband. Then a very strange thing happened. On the day before the funeral, as the grief-stricken family were sitting in hopeless gloom in a room on the ground floor, they suddenly heard a cry from upstairs. The sound electrified them, as there was nobody else in the house. Again, it was repeated, and this time the voice was so wonderfully familiar that they all rose to their feet and rushed upstairs. There, in the chamber of death, they saw the figure of David Brown sitting up in his coffin, as much alive as he ever had been. Mr Brown made a speedy recovery with no traces of the cataleptic fit left behind.

Helen Fritsch, the daughter of a rich farmer from Egenszeg, Hungary, was buried on 27 April 1904 with great ceremony. At nine o'clock the same evening, there was a knock at the window of the sexton's house, and he was horrified to see the face of the girl he had just buried. Three fingers of her right hand were missing. Helen stated that she had been awakened by feeling great pain, and on opening her eyes saw two men climbing up a ladder from the grave. The top of the coffin had been smashed in by the men, whose intention it was to steal the rings that she wore. The thieves had cut off the girl's fingers and it was the pain that had roused her from the deathlike trance.

The above story is one of many similar tales that recur almost as urban myth when broaching the subject of premature interment. Some are more creative than others in their detail, but all have a theme based around grave robbery and some might pass them off as nothing more than fantastical tales. However, in the case of Helen Fritsch, the case was well-documented in international publications.

Occasionally, medics have doubted their own diagnosis of death in cases where the deceased has displayed indications of life well after rigor mortis should have set in. One such case was brought before an inquest at Crewe in February 1905, where Dr Wilson tendered some remarkable evidence as the result of his examination of the dead body of Annie Jinks, a married woman aged twenty-one. According to the account of the deceased's mother, someone knocked at the door of their house in Flag Lane not long after they had retired to bed on the previous Saturday night. Annie looked through the bedroom window, apparently to ascertain who had called, and almost immediately afterwards she fell in a faint and died within a few seconds. The doctor stated that there was no external appearance of death on the woman's body.

The Coroner asked, 'Are you sure she is dead now? We have heard so many extraordinary cases lately about people being pronounced dead and who have not been dead.'

Doctor Wilson said that Mrs Jinks was undoubtedly dead, but during the whole of his experience he had never seen a corpse so life-like. On looking at the body there was not a single sign of death. He had seen many living people who looked more like death than this one, he added. It was some time before the doctor could satisfy himself that the woman was really dead. He was of the opinion that the sudden getting out of bed caused a chill and produced syncope. The jury returned a verdict to that effect.

A distressing story of premature interment was published by the *Paris Journal* from St. Etienne, in the department of the Loire. On 3 January 1905, at the village of La Ricamarie, three or four miles from St. Etienne, a young man named Choveaux, just eighteen years of age, who had been subject to epileptic attacks, suddenly lost consciousness and lay, to all appearances, dead. In France a funeral was seldom postponed more than forty-eight hours and, in this case, the family and friends, being convinced that Choveaux was dead, at once began the funeral preparations. The interment took place without even a doctor seeing the body, but this sometimes happened in country villages. Some three days afterwards, when another grave was being dug near that in which Choveaux had been buried, the gravedigger thought he heard groans. It was asserted that the gravedigger had also heard groans on three consecutive days but said nothing until 12 January, nine days after the presumed death of Choveaux. It was only then, after this lapse of many days, that he told some neighbours about what he had heard. The mayor and the village gendarme went to the cemetery at once and had the coffin exhumed. On it being opened, Choveaux was found lying on his right side. He had nearly turned over on to his stomach and, during his agony, which was thought must have lasted at least three days, he had gnawed off a portion of his thumbs.

A Russian village priest was buried alive by a mob of peasants at Svino Krivza, in the Crimea, in August 1905. The people had blamed the prolonged drought which had ruined their crops on the death of a certain old man who had been regarded as an 'opyr' or wizard, no rain having fallen since his burial the previous March. According to popular superstition it was necessary, in order to appease the sorcerer's spirit, to exhume his remains at midnight and, after being sprinkled with holy water by a priest, replaced in the grave. Accordingly, one Sunday night a procession of villagers, headed by boys and girls carrying torches, and accompanied by fiddlers and flautists playing dismal dirges, set out for the cemetery. The body of the dead wizard was duly exhumed and placed in a sitting posture against a tree, around which forty or fifty of the peasants danced a weird jig to the accompaniment of a village musician. In the midst of this curious ceremony, Father Constantin, the village priest, arrived. The villagers, thinking that he had come to pour holy water on the corpse, hailed him with joyous greetings. To their surprise and disappointment, the priest not only declined to assist in the affair but upbraided them for their superstition and sacrilegious barbarity. The crowd grew very indignant on hearing this. Some amongst them, who were under the influence of vodka, shouted that Father Constantin was a real wizard, as the spirit of the dead man had entered his body. The priest was then seized and, despite his screams for mercy, was hurled by four men into the reopened grave, the remains of the opyr's corpse being flung in after him with earth and stones, burying the poor cleric alive!

James Milligan of Ioga, Wisconsin, United States narrowly escaped being buried alive on 23 February 1906. The funeral procession was slowly moving toward the church when the driver of the hearse heard groans from within, followed by the smashing of glass, which indicated plainly that Milligan objected to being buried alive. The casket was opened and Milligan, fully restored to consciousness, sat up and began to inquire where he was. He had lain in a trance for three days.

A month later, the danger of premature burial was illustrated in the case of Mrs William Sherwood, living near La Crosse, also in Wisconsin, United States, in March 1906, who, according to the *New York Herald*, had only been married a week and was taken down with pneumonia, to which she apparently succumbed. The absence of the embalmer from the village prevented her body from being filled with poisonous fluids, which would definitely have ensured death. Mrs Sherwood was placed in a coffin which, however, was not nailed down. Some hours afterwards, people in an adjoining room were startled to find the supposed 'corpse' sitting up. The woman was placed in a hot bath, and after having regained strength, stated that whilst fully aware of the preparations for her burial she had been unable to move or speak.

Mrs Thomas Chapman, aged sixty, was supposed to have died suddenly of a heart attack at her home at Ellis, Kansas, in October 1908. The body was prepared for burial, but was not embalmed, with the funeral planned for a few days later. However, a few minutes before the coffin was to have been sealed, a physician requested permission to see the body. After confirming his suspicions that the woman's body was made rigid by suspended animation, Mrs Chapman was removed from the coffin, placed in bed and revived. While her heart was still weak, she made a good recovery.

Tymko Novak, a peasant who owned a small farm in the village of Mackowica, in Austria, lived through the greatest tragedy of his life after his funeral, thanks to the criminal carelessness and stupidity of three people. Tymko, an elderly man, was thought to have died in his cottage home in October 1908, and was buried in the neighbouring churchyard with all the pomp and ceremony so dear to his Slavic traditions. His family and friends, having shed tears over their loss, went home. Only the gravedigger remained, and he hurried to fill up the grave before nightfall. Suddenly the man was horrified to hear a dull sound coming from below the earth that he had just thrown in. It stopped and, thinking that his nerves were getting the better of his reason, he went on with his work. Again, the noise began, and this time he felt sure that it sounded as if the dead man's soul were trying to get out of the coffin. Instead of uncovering the soil and opening the coffin, he gave a shriek of fear, threw down the spade and ran to the head of the village to ask what to do.

Sadly, the village elder, a man named Kusek, was as stupid as the gravedigger. All the advice he could give was, 'Nobody is allowed to open a grave except by special permission of the gendarmes. You must go to the gendarmes and ask them for permission. But our friend Tymko Novak must have committed a great sin if his soul cannot rest quietly in that coffin.' The gravedigger took Kusek's advice and set out to the gendarme station. By this time, it was dark, and the gravedigger hurried on thinking that he was being pursued by poor Tymko's soul, which had escaped from the coffin. When he passed the local inn, he met Jan Wenger and relayed the circumstances to him. Wenger, without waiting to hear the theory of Tymko Novak's soul, pulled the gravedigger along to the cemetery and began to uncover the grave as fast as he could. When they finally got the coffin up and opened it, a terrible sight met their eyes. The corpse now lay on one side. The left arm, instead of being crossed with the right over the breast, was under the head. The face was distorted with agony, the clothing torn to shreds and the flesh cut from Novak's efforts to get out of his living grave.

Whether the following tale is more myth than fact, it is difficult to ascertain, but certainly makes for interesting reading. A photograph featured in *The Sketch* on 21 June 1911 (see top image on page 3 of the plate section), illustrates a curious legend of Cologne. There was once a burgermeister of the town whose wife died and was buried. In the evening, thieves seeking to take jewels from the dead, opened the coffin. Now, it happened that the woman was not dead, but in a trance, and when the thieves broke into her burial place she awoke, climbed out of the coffin, and went home. There she called a servant, who ran in fear to his master and told him what had happened. The scared burgermeister replied to this, 'I would sooner believe that my horses were looking out of the top-floor window than believe that such a thing could be.' Scarcely had the words left his mouth than he heard horses galloping up the stairs. In memory of this, and the return of his wife, he had two horses' heads made in stone and set in a top-floor window of his house, where they remain to this day.

In December 1911, recluse James H. Magee was lowered into a grave in Hopkins, Missourri, for the second time in a quarter of a century. Twenty-five years earlier, in Burlington, Iowa, Magee was stricken with cholera. He was thought to be dead, placed in an old board coffin and was being lowered into the ground when a friend stopped the proceedings, declaring that he believed the man to be alive. The coffin was raised, a doctor sent for, and Magee was revived and nursed back to health, despite doctors claiming that there was no doubt of his death when he had 'passed away' earlier that week. Magee was best known as 'Old Mack' in the vicinity of Hopkins, although he was born in Ireland and emigrated to America with his parents at the age of three. Mack originally lived in New York and New Jersey in his youth and learned the trade of plasterer, later moving to Bushnell, Illinois. In 1862 he married Hester Ann Pierce, the daughter of a wealthy landowner. After his wife died, Mack became a wanderer and travelled a great deal. He took up the work of a contractor and built a number of the Harvey eating-houses along the Santa Fe, between Newton, Kansas, and Albuquerque, New Mexico. Although he was an avowed free thinker, shortly before his death James Magee asked that a minister be called, and he died praying that his sins be forgiven.

It is not given to everybody to attend his own funeral feast, but this was the experience of a Cossack named Ivan Chourtenko at Karpovskaja, near Tsaritzin, in Russia. Chourtenko, his death having been duly certified by the local authorities in January 1914, was buried after his body had lain in the morgue for two days. When the coffin had been lowered into the grave and the customary spadeful of earth had been thrown in by the mourners, repeated knocking and muffled cries were heard from the grave. A panic arose among those present, the majority of whom fled from the scene with superstitious terror. Some of the closest relatives summoned the courage to descend into the grave and the coffin was lifted to the surface before being opened. The 'dead man' then related that he had been deprived of the power of speech for some days, but not of his hearing, the consequence being that he had been cognisant the whole time during the preparations for his burial and funeral. Chourtenko was carried back to the village in triumph. There he had the rare satisfaction of partaking of his own funeral feast, which was spread out in the customary style at the house of the military governor. Among those present were the two doctors who had attended Chourtenko in his illness, as well as the police inspector who had certified his death. This official proposed a toast 'to our lively deceased friend,' to which the latter responded in humorous terms.

One of the most talked about cases of premature burial of the twentieth century was that of Essie Dunbar, an active member of the African Methodist Episcopal Church, in South Carolina. In 1915, Essie suffered an epileptic fit which was thought to have killed her. Aged just thirty years old, Mrs Dunbar was pronounced dead by local Blackville physician, Doctor Briggs. Essie was duly placed in a wooden coffin and the funeral arranged for the next morning. The supposedly deceased woman's sister lived in a neighbouring town and didn't receive news of her sibling's demise until the following day. Rushing to attend the ceremony just in time to see the coffin being covered with dirt, Essie's sister begged the preacher to allow her to see the corpse. After some persuasion, the minister agreed, and the coffin was lifted back out of the grave. As soon as the lid was lifted, onlookers witnessed Essie smiling at her sister with a healthy glow. The case became so notorious in the town that the local mayor launched a full investigation and had several cemetery workers replaced with new staff. As for Essie, she lived for another forty years, finally dying in 1955, at the grand old age of ninety-seven.

Renowned stage actor Edgar Vincent saw a great deal of the world during his time serving in the First World War and had a weird and wonderful story to tell of his time in the East. The following was relayed to a newspaper in 1922:

One day in Malay two Chinese beggars were carrying away an old man to bury him when they heard a noise in the coffin. On investigation they found that the old chap was not dead, so they took him out and gave him some of their rice to eat. Then they told him he must get back in the coffin for burial else they would not get payment for the job. Naturally the old man protested against premature interment, so the beggars killed him to save further trouble, and duly buried him. Whether they got their money, Mr Vincent was unable to say.

A report from El Paso, Texas, in August 1934, shed light on an unusual medical condition suffered by Juana Ramirez. Three times in her life the woman was thought to be dead, dressed in burial clothes, and placed in a bed with candles and mourners standing around. Each time she 'came back to life' to the terror of those attending. Juana lived in constant fear of being buried alive, for since childhood she had suffered from fainting fits which lasted for many hours. Miss Ramirez was afraid that one day she would faint when none of her close friends were near and that she would not recover until it was too late!

Faint knocks coming from inside a tiny coffin in a corner of the Cantonese Benevolent Society's mortuary, Shanghai, in May 1935, attracted the attention of an attendant. Snatching the lid off the coffin, he found a three-year-old boy inside, who had been certified dead by a local doctor the previous day. The child was gasping for breath and beating his fists on the side of the coffin. The attendant took him to the hospital, where he was found to have pneumonia. The boy recovered, completely cured, and was duly returned to his parents.

Doctors were studying the strange case of a young woman discovered to be alive in her coffin just as her mourning family were about to bury her in January 1950. Medical authorities said that the woman, Anita Souffrant, aged twenty-six, from the rural district of St. Michel, Port au Prince, Haiti, had lost consciousness after a six-month illness during which she was dosed with medicines recommended by sympathetic friends. On 14 December 1949, Anita's family decided she was now actually dead and arranged a funeral. On the way to the church mourners were startled to hear noises coming from Anita's coffin. They looked inside and found her breathing. The local priest ordered that the woman be rushed to the General Hospital at Port au Prince. Dr Paul Desmangles, head of the hospital staff, said that Anita Souffrant gained full consciousness three days after her 'funeral' and was able to talk intelligently. He said her illness had been diagnosed as a type of malaria. Her condition was reported as fair.

On 2 August 1969, fifty-four-year-old Joseph Ramosch, from Graz, Austria, was pronounced dead as he lay in bed at the city's university clinic. Paralysed after a stroke, Joseph could neither see nor speak, but could apparently hear everything that was going on around him. The Austrian heard a nurse call for a priest and the doctor saying, 'There is nothing we can do for him.' Then later, in the mortuary, Ramosch heard another doctor saying, 'This corpse will have to stay here until Monday, because the pathology lab is booked up.'

Joseph later contemplated the consequences, saying, 'If it hadn't happened at a weekend, they would have performed the post-mortem there and then.' The following Monday, a nurse saw the middle finger of Ramosch's left hand move and called in a doctor who told her that it was just the corpse twitching. Joseph tried desperately to crook his finger again and his gesture was seen by the nurse. When the doctor finally went over to look, he asked for a sign of life, and Joseph was thankfully once again able to bend his finger. Oxygen and a blood drip were immediately administered and, after twenty days in hospital, Joseph Ramosch was finally able to return home.

On 13 March 1993, a man was declared dead after a traffic accident in the township of Sebokeng, south of Johannesburg, South Africa. Sipho William Mdletshe was placed inside a metal box at the mortuary and, according to his own testimony, spent the next forty-eight hours drifting slowly in and out of consciousness. Eventually the poor man became alert enough to start screaming for assistance and was rescued by mortuary workers. Sadly, Sipho's fiancée believed that he had returned to life as a zombie and refused to continue their relationship.

So, we ask, is it possible for a person to be mistakenly certified as dead in the twenty-first century, with modern technology and medical advances? The answer is clearly yes, as these cases prove.

Following a heart attack in 2011, forty-nine-year-old Fagilyu Mukhametzyanov from Kazan, Russia, collapsed at her home and was pronounced dead. As she lay in her open casket surrounded by mourners a few days later, Fagilyu was woken up by the sound of people crying loudly and saying prayers. Realising what was happening, she began screaming and was rushed to the local hospital. Sadly, Fagilyu lived only twelve minutes before dying in intensive care, this time for real. Her cause of death was recorded as heart failure caused by shock.

In 2014, in Peraia, on the island of Thessaloniki, Greece, children were playing near a cemetery when they heard screams from below the earth. Police discovered that a forty-five-year-old woman had been buried alive and had died of asphyxia after being declared dead by a private hospital in the area. The family successfully sued the facility involved. A separate incident in the same town, in the same year, concluded with a police investigation proving that a forty-nine-year-old woman was prematurely interred after being declared dead due to a prognosis of terminal cancer. Her family reported hearing screams shortly after burial but sadly, by the time the coffin was reopened, the poor woman had died of heart failure. It was later discovered that medicine given to the patient by her physician as part of the cancer treatment had slowed the woman's heart rate and was the cause of her being pronounced dead.

On 23 August 2020, the family of Timesha Beauchamp found her collapsed and unresponsive at home in Southfield, Michigan, United States, and immediately dialled 911. Paramedics arrived and confirmed that the girl was not breathing. Cardiopulmonary resuscitation was administered for thirty minutes without response and Timesha was pronounced dead by the doctor on duty at the emergency department of the local hospital, based on the information provided by the paramedics. Resuscitation was ceased and Timesha was taken to a funeral home in Detroit. However, as funeral staff prepared to embalm the new arrival, they found that the girl was still breathing and transferred her to the Michigan Children's Hospital without further delay. Sadly, Timesha died there on 18 October of the same year.

As we close the cases of the twenty-first century, up to date in 2023, let us take a look at those fortunate enough to escape the confines of their coffins, although still enduring a near-death experience in the mortuaries and funeral homes of today, many of them resulting from accidents.

In September 2007, Venezuelan man Carlos Camejo, from Caracas, woke up on the dissecting table of a morgue in excruciating pain. Medical examiners had just begun their autopsy into the cause of his supposed death following a traffic accident and realised that something was wrong when Camejo's body started bleeding. They quickly stitched up the incision and moved Carlos to a side room to recover, where his grieving wife later found him alive and well.

In November 2021, an electrician from Moradabad, India, was taken to a private hospital after suffering an internal head injury following an accident. Sreekesh Kumar, aged forty, was later taken to the district hospital to see a specialist but was pronounced dead a short while later. The body was then placed inside the mortuary freezer until a 'panchnama', the document signed by relatives to agree to an autopsy, was filed. By this time seven hours had passed and when Sreekesh was pulled from the freezer his sister-in-law noticed that he appeared to be breathing. It was ascertained that Kumar had slipped into a coma due to the injury and, as soon as it was discovered that he was still alive, he was put on a ventilator. Sadly, doctors were unable to operate due to a bleed on the brain and Sreekesh died five days later.

In February 2023, a sixty-six-year-old woman from Iowa, United States, was transported from hospice care inside a cloth body bag to a nearby funeral home. However, when a staff member unzipped the bag, it was found that the woman was breathing and desperately gasping for air. Glen Oaks Alzheimer Special Care Center was fined $10,000 for failing to 'assume the responsibility for the overall operation of the residential care facility.' Sadly, the woman died in hospice care just two days after her terrible ordeal.

On 13 June 2023, retired nurse Bella Montoya frightened mourners by knocking on the lid of the coffin during her own funeral in the city of Babahoyo, Ecuador. Relatives rushed the woman to hospital where she was treated for a suspected stroke and cardiopulmonary arrest. Sadly, Bella was unresponsive and was soon pronounced dead for a second time.

Chapter Four

Societies, Lectures & News

In 1746, a book entitled *The Uncertainty of the Signs of Death* was published in London, its author J.J. Bruhier d'Ablaincourt. It contained directions for preventing such accidents and repairing the misfortunes brought upon the constitution by them. It gave many striking instances of persons who had been restored to life from their grave, or when about to be buried, and of others who were found to have reclaimed consciousness in the grave and were later found with gnawed fingers or torn flesh. Shortly before the publication date, on digging in a churchyard, a coffin was opened. The corpse was reduced to a skeleton, but an observer noticed that the corpse was lying on its face, the back part of the head and heels uppermost, and when he commented, the gravedigger said that he had found several persons turned in their coffin over time. This account shows the general concern at that period. It was noted that perhaps ministers should make enquiries as to whether gravediggers across the country observed such things as this in their daily routine and perhaps ought to carefully raise coffin lids in order to check if the position of a body had turned. The book argued that persons ought not to be buried until three full days, at least, after they were pronounced dead, or until they began to smell of natural putrefaction.

Several years later, in 1774, doctors William Hawes and Thomas Cogan founded the Royal Humane Society after concern at the number of people being wrongly diagnosed as dead, and in some cases, having been buried alive. The main aim was to share their advancements in resuscitation and the medics even offered money to anyone rescuing an 'undead' corpse from burial. The medical men invited fifteen friends to join them, and the first meeting was held at the Chapter Coffee House in St. Paul's Yard, London, on 18 April 1774. At first named the 'Society for the Recovery of Persons Apparently Drowned', they set out five key objectives:

- To publish information on how to save people from drowning
- To pay two guineas to anyone attempting a rescue in the Westminster area of London
- To pay four guineas to anyone successfully bringing someone back to life

- To pay one guinea to anyone – often a pub owner – allowing a body to be treated in his house
- To provide volunteer medical assistants with some basic life-saving equipment

Proud of their efforts and advancements in preventing premature interments, many prominent advocates for the cause celebrated their achievements. Tuesday 22 March 1785 was the anniversary festival of the Humane Society (see bottom image on page 3 of the plate section). This most virtuous institution dined together at the London Tavern, the Earl of Stamford in the Chair. After dinner, the fruits of their noble charity were introduced – a procession of men, women and children, whom they had rescued from a premature grave, afforded a spectacle which was unequalled for its time.

In September 1803, Doctor Hayes, Treasurer to the Royal Humane Society, published the following hints concerning the prevention of premature burial:

Under the proper restrictions no danger can possibly aim to the living, as the first stage of putrescence is always distinguished by a perceptible clamminess of the skin, and an acid gas, which marks the earliest time for interment. In the second stage of putrescence, an alkalescent vapour escapes, attended with an offensive odour. It is these alone which prove noxious to the attendants and survivors. The reality of Death, in all cases, may therefore be thus known from its semblance. By an earnest attention to these important circumstances, premature interment will be prevented, and an immense number of our fellow creatures restored to life, provided the resuscitative process of the Humane Society be assiduously employed. If the least doubt remains, relatives &c, should consult the faculty, as they will readily form an accurate discrimination of the exudations &c, on which the absolute criteria of life and death depend.

The following observations on the subject of premature interment were taken from Mr Belinay's book *On the Sources of Heath and Disease* in 1832:

The record of who have been buried alive, in all countries and ages, would form a fearful volume, and strongly guard us against a too hasty presumption of death. Bodies have been found in burial vaults, which have turned upon their faces or sides, which have bled, which had marks of self-inflicted violence upon them etc.

Surgeons have, through inadvertence, opened bodies which have only parted with life at the application of the scalpel. In 1763, a clergyman, supposed to have died from apoplexy, emitted a groan at the first incision of the knife by a surgeon deputed to investigate the cause of his death. La Place, being informed of the circumstance, and asked what was to be done, replied, '*Gemir et setaire*' (Weep and be silent).

As early as 1866, the French Senate discussed a petition calling for further precautions against the possibility of people being buried alive on the supposition that they were dead. The petitioner asked for the adaptation of a system prevalent in some parts of Germany, the application of the test of electricity and the deposit of the coffins for a certain time, before the final interment, in vaults open to medical inspection. Viscount de la Guerroniere, who presented the report of a committee on the petition, said that the subject of premature burial had been very often considered, that the precautions prescribed by the code were quite sufficient, and that the proper course on the petition would be to pass to the order of the day, i.e. to reject it.

However, Cardinal Donnet, the Archbishop of Bordeaux, opposed this conclusion, and in a speech which made great sensation adduced many instances within his own knowledge of people certified dead by authority who turned out to be alive. He remembered a case when he was a young priest, of an old man who lived twelve hours after the legal warrant for his burial was issued. In another case, at Bordeaux, a young girl was pronounced dead. He, Monsieur Donnet, providentially arrived at the house just as the coffin lid was about to be screwed down. The priest conceived doubts about her dissolution, spoke to the child in a loud voice and, in his own words, 'had the inexpressible happiness of hearing her answer.' The girl, he said, belonged to one of the most respectable families in Bordeaux and was still alive, now a wife and mother. Cardinal Donnet then concluded with his most striking report yet.

In 1826, a young priest preaching on a hot day in a crowded church suddenly fell down unconscious. He was taken home and laid out for dead. A medical certificate of his death was given, and preparations were made for his funeral. The bishop of the cathedral in which the young priest had been preaching came to the foot of the bed and said '*de profundis*' (from the Latin, meaning 'from the depths', when one expresses great sadness or misery). The measure of the young man's coffin was taken, and he, quite alive all the time, heard the orders given for his burial but was not able to protest against them. At length the voice of a childhood friend produced a magical effect upon the man and he awoke.

'That priest,' said Cardinal Donnet, 'is now, at the distance of forty years, alive; he is here among you, a member of this Senate, and he now supplicates the Government to frame better regulations so as to prevent terrible and irreparable misfortunes.' There was great sensation amongst those present and several other senators mentioned cases of suspended animation and asserted that the number of corpses found in coffins which had unquestionably moved after burial led to the conclusion that burial of living persons must be far more frequent than supposed. The Senate voted that the petition should be referred, as worthy of consideration, to the Minister of the Interior.

At Neustrelitz, Prussia, in 1827, Herr Counsellor Hesse underwent a rather extreme experiment to test an apparatus for preventing injury to persons who may have been buried alive. Hesse had himself buried two feet underground in a closed coffin, to which tubes were attached, one for breathing and another for communicating with his assistants by means of a bell. He remained in this situation for two hours and was disinterred in good health, except that he claimed to be feeling very hot. The thermometer which stood at twelve outside, rose to nineteen inside the coffin. However, the device was deemed impractical for common usage and thought to be an invention aimed only at wealthier families.

By 1829, many efforts had been made by philanthropists in France, to induce the French Government to alter the regulations which ordered that the interment of dead people should take place within forty-eight hours of their demise. The late Dr McNab, who was physician to the Duke of Kent, collected a variety of information for the purpose of showing that many persons had been buried alive under these regulations. The facts collected were considered to be so important by the then Prime Minister of France, the Duke de Cazes, that he sent McNab's manuscript to the Faculty of Medicine and earnestly recommended them to immediately report upon it. They did so. The report was unfavourable, chiefly from the circumstance of the would-be reformer being an Englishman, but also partly from the aversion to reform of every kind generally felt by that body.

Attempts were then made to create a strong interest in the subject of premature interment in France, and a society was formed for the purpose of collecting the necessary information. In addition to the facts stated by McNab, they added many interesting accounts, among them one from a German paper. This paper, after citing several instances of persons having been buried alive under the regulations of that country, similar to those in France except that the time was limited to four days, it gave the following example:

In 1824 a chambermaid was struck by lightning near a village. She was buried the next morning. Eight days afterwards, when doubts were entertained, the body was exhumed. It was found the unfortunate creature had lived in the grave. Her nails were bitten to pieces, her left breast was mutilated, there had been flowing of blood at the mouth, four of the left-hand fingers were thrust in the mouth as far as they could be. The unfortunate creature had doubtless suffocated herself. She was lying on the left side, her eyes were open, and the grave clothes torn to pieces and stained with blood.

In another instance, the daughter of a weaver, who was said to have died of apoplexy, was buried on the fourth day according to custom. Four hours after her interment, a sportsman discovered that he had lost his dog, which had followed him close to the little town on his return from shooting. The next morning the animal was found on the grave of the young girl, scratching away at the earth and howling very loudly. The local officials insisted on waiting two days until the arrival of the district doctor before they would have the grave opened. The unfortunate young girl was then found lying on her forehead, covered in blood and torn in several places. It was presumed that the dog had heard the girl's groans and that, if she had been exhumed immediately, her life would have been saved.

In 1829 it was reported that in apoplectic and fainting fits, when opium or spirituous liquors had been taken in too great quantities, the appearances of death were often mistaken for reality. In these cases, the means recommended by the Humane Society for the Recovery of Drowned Persons should be persevered in for several hours – bleeding used with great caution, but every effort used to excite vomiting by introducing tartar emetic through a proper tube into the stomach. The same method was to be adopted in regard to children who died of convulsions. In such cases, it recommended, Volatiles, Eau Deluce, or any very strong preparation of that sort ought to be rubbed to the temples, applied to the nose, and sprinkled about the bed. Hot flannels moistened with a strong solution of camphorated spirit, applied over the breast, and renewed every quarter of an hour were another restorative.

In the same newspaper it gave the instance of a lady in Cornwall, over eighty years old, who had seemingly expired in the morning. As she had desired not to be buried for two days, her friends were determined to fulfil the request. All who looked at her perceived the old woman to be dead, a mirror had repeatedly been applied to her mouth, but some of the servants said they felt a degree of heat in the middle of her back. In the evening the heat increased and at length the woman breathed normally.

A letter from Dresden, Germany, dated 15 October 1833, contained the following:

In one of the last sittings of the first chamber of our States-General, a motion was made by Count Bruhl, calling for an increase of punishment for certain crimes. He proposes a new punishment for incendiaries; that the culprit should be buried alive, and a guard stationed over the earth that covers him. He proposes the penalty of death, simple it is true, for the parents of the condemned, who, by neglecting his education, facilitated the development of his vicious inclinations, and who ought therefore to be considered his accomplices. The chamber did not think proper to adopt Count Bruhl's propositions, which were rejected by a great majority.

In January 1846, a communication to the London Academy relative to premature burial in France was received. Its attention was directed to a paper on the subject from Monsieur Le Guern, in which he pointed out the danger of enforcing the regulation for interment within the short period of time allowed. The author said that he ascertained that since the year 1833, no less than 94 premature burials were prevented by accidental causes. Thirty-five of the persons supposed to be dead had awoke from their lethargy at the moment when their coffins were about to be nailed down, thirteen had been recovered by care, seven by the upsetting of the coffins in which they had been placed, nine by incisions or punctures in pinning their shrouds, nineteen by accidental delays in the ceremony of interment, six by delays which had been created purposely by their friends and five by other causes. Monsieur Le Guern supposed, with much reason, that the number of persons prematurely buried must have been very great. His estimate was twenty-seven a year at the least. This, of course, was merely conjectural, but from the number of authenticated cases which he gives of persons who were saved by chance from a horrible fate, the Academy were inclined to think that, when he took an annual average of only 27 premature burials, he was very much below the truth!

Several cases of premature burial occurred in France in the summer of 1867, causing the Minister of the Interior to issue a circular to the prefects, accompanied by a code of instructions to be made known by them to the medical officers whose duty it was to report deaths, and contained a series of tests to be applied to any case in which there could be possible doubt. It stated that such cases rarely arose, especially when death resulted after sickness and has pursued its usual course, but sudden deaths arising from nervous affections, hysteria, lethargies, etc, required particular care and attention.

In 1868, a German gentleman living in the State of New Jersey claimed credit for one of the most extraordinary inventions ever brought before the public. Franz Vester was well known, and his idea tried in the presence of six hundred spectators. Filled with the idea that many persons were buried alive, Herr Vester constructed what he called a 'safety coffin.' Larger than an ordinary coffin, the top held a receptacle for refreshments and restoratives. The top part of the lid was moveable and a box about two feet square was attached to it and reached to a foot above the ground, where it appeared like a chimney. The top of the tube or pipe was covered with a lid opened by a spring inside, and just below that was a bell connected with a cord. If the cord was pulled, the bell would ring, and the spring threw back the cover of the chimney. Cleats were nailed to the side of the box and, if the person in the coffin needed to get out, he could mount a sort of ladder to get out into the open air. 'Or otherwise,' said the description of this wonderful contrivance, 'the individual can rest at ease, munch his lunch, drink the wine, and ring the bell for the sexton to come and assist him out.' Herr Vester tested his invention by permitting himself to be buried alive. A grave six feet deep was dug, and the inventor got into the coffin. The band played a dirge, wreaths of flowers were laid upon the coffin lid and within a quarter of an hour Herr Vester was effectually buried. He was supposed to have remained in the grave for two hours, but the crowd became impatient and, after a lapse of an hour and a quarter, the signal for his reappearance was given by one of Vester's assistants. A minute later Herr Vester stepped unaided out of his living grave, 'with no more perceptible exhaustion than would have been caused by walking two or three blocks under the hot sun.'

On 12 March 1884, the *St. James's Gazette* reported that cremation was making progress on both the continent and in England. The French Chamber of Deputies had before it a Bill, introduced by Monsieur Casimir-Perier, giving French citizens the option of being buried or cremated. The Belgian Chamber of Representatives also had before it a petition from the Town Council of Brussels praying for the legalisation of cremation. The International Cremation Association, which had its headquarters in Milan, was at the same time carrying on an active propaganda in both France and Belgium. The agent whom the society had sent to Belgium was a close relation of the late Papal Nuncio at the Court of Brussels, and he was charged to obtain permission to erect an experimental crematorium in 'the gay city of Brabant' at the expense of the association. In Italy at the time, a considerable number of priests had been cremated. In Europe, where funerals usually took place within forty-eight hours of death, there existed a morbid fear of being buried alive, and this may explain the favour into which incineration was rapidly rising on the other side of the channel.

During the summer of 1887, several more instances of premature burial were recorded in France. In order to attempt to prevent the recurrence of such deplorable calamities, the proposal of safety coffins was renewed in the form of coffins provided with an India-rubber tube through which air from above ground could reach the person below. The latest case of that fateful year was that of an old lady who fell ill and, as those present thought, died. The heat being great, the funeral took place the following day, but as the gravedigger was beginning to throw earth on to the coffin, he thought he heard moans issuing from inside it. In France, the administrative routine did not permit anything to be done in a case of this kind without the sanction of the mayor, so the gravedigger, leaving the coffin in the care of the mourners, hurried off to find an official. The rural dignitary, having put on his scarf and knocked up the village doctor, proceeded to the cemetery and, after all the delay this caused, the coffin was opened, leading to the horrible discovery that the poor woman, who had awakened from a trance or lethargic fit to find herself enclosed in the narrow box, had just succumbed to fright at her terrible situation. Possibly, had the coffin been opened more promptly, her life might have been saved, but the presence of the mayor was considered indispensable, and pending his arrival the flickering lamp of light went out!

An article written by George Sims in the *Referee* periodical, dated July 1888, mentions an epidemic of cases of being buried alive in Britain. He said, 'In London, the matter of fact and utterly unromantic House of Commons has actually had a burying alive case before it, and we have had a Home Secretary gravely replying to a query about a corpse giving three knocks on the inside of its own coffin, and the local coroner has been ordered to look into the matter.' He went on to comment that 'burials alive are far more common in hot countries, where the burial takes place within twenty hours after death, than they are in England, where one gets, as a rule, a week's grace.'

A few years later, in July 1894, an article was published in the *Newcastle Daily Chronicle*, reporting how astonishing it was that 'The Terror of Burial Alive', impresses itself on some people's imagination. It stated that a number of those who ordered that their remains should be cremated were simply influenced by the conclusion that cremation was the best sanitary method of disposing of human remains. The late Edmund Yates, a well-known journalist and proprietor of the *World*, whose body was cremated, seems to have been actuated by a livelier fear. According to his will the details of which were made known publicly, he gave instructions for the opening of his jugular vein immediately after death, and directed that a fee of twenty guineas should be paid to the surgeon for the operation. This was clearly to guard against the terrifying possibility of coma being mistaken for death.

The fear of being buried alive was also held by millionaire John Rose, of New York, who died in December 1895. In accordance with his earnest entreaties, his coffin was not closed, but laid in the family vault at Roseton and guarded day and night by two men who were instructed to watch for signs of reanimation. The doctors who attended Rose in his last illness asserted that his death was hastened by the 'condition of nervous prostration' into which the fear of being buried alive had caused him to fall!

A book published by Franz Hartmann, MD (London, Swan Sonnenschein & Co. Limited) in 1896 cites 64 cases of premature burial – and its author scouts many of the so-called tests of death. By way of safeguard, the establishment of a species of probationary mortuary chamber is suggested and the ultimate symptom of putrefaction is pleaded for. Hartmann claimed that no efforts could be superfluous that would prevent even one case of premature burial. He cited Bruhier's calculations, 'that among 80,992 persons who apparently died in one year, there were 154 buried alive.'

Later that year, in an article printed in November 1896, it was stated that 'people who have a haunting fear of being buried alive will no longer need to have electric bells in the family vault, or get some death-compelling operation done to them before they are buried.' It went on to say that the Rontgen Ray, created by German mechanical engineer and physicist Wilhelm Rontgen, would settle matters. It was found that the hands of the living and the dead, taken on the same plate by the X-ray, showed a decided difference. The bones of both were equally well-defined, but the soft parts of the dead hands were noticeably darker. Chicago physician Dr Carl Brown stated that this method would determine positively whether death had occurred or whether the patient was in a trance, since dead flesh offers more resistance to a passage of the rays than living.

Arguments raged on in England, and the following resolution was unanimously passed by the Executive Committee of the London Association for Prevention of Premature Burial in October 1897:

> That the unsatisfactory state of the laws relating to burial calls for legislation so as to provide better securities than now exist against premature interment, and that the electors throughout the country should immediately call the attention of their members to this unsatisfactory state, and instruct them to support a Bill which will be introduced to the notice of Parliament next session on the subject of death verification.

The horror of being buried alive resulted in the formation of a society in New York in 1900, known as the 'American Society for the Prevention of Premature Burial.' Medical men, the promoters stated, issued certificates of death without subjecting the body to a thorough physical test in order to ascertain absolutely the absence of life. The proposed charter of the society provided that physicians certifying the death of persons in the state of New York should sign a certificate prepared by the society stipulating that the following tests, or as many of them as may be decided upon, had been applied to the body of the supposed corpse without having produced any indication of life:

> Two or more incisions in an artery; the palm of the hand exposed to the flame of a candle; a mirror or crystal held to the lips and no sign of respiration; a hot iron or steel placed against the flesh without producing blisters.

Murmurs of the formation of such a society had already been circulated in America in 1890, and questions such as, 'Are men and women frequently buried alive?' and 'Are our laws such as to permit of too hasty interments of persons supposed to be dead, but not dead at all?' were raised amongst medical professionals seeking reform. At this point the society was only in its formative stages, but many prominent men showed interest in it being extended throughout the United States. Dr Leo, the chief mover in this new society had about as many opportunities to judge the different methods of treating persons supposedly dead as any other man that could be named. A student in Heidelberg, an observer in Paris, a practitioner at St. Bartholomew's Hospital in London, and a medical expert employed by the City of New York for fourteen years, he had chances that few medics had to acquire knowledge on the particular subject of premature burial. Dr Leo was most decidedly of the opinion that people were too frequently buried with a degree of haste and carelessness that was scandalous, if not criminal. He suggested that in every case where a person died, or was supposed to have died, a competent physician should at once be called in. No undertaker should be allowed to handle the body before this was done. He was also of the opinion that the body should not be placed in an air-tight casket where life, if not extinct, would be smothered out, nor placed in an ice box, where it would be frozen out. Such treatment of a body before it had been thoroughly examined, he claimed, was not only barbarous but absolutely criminal. Now as to the tests, he remarked:

> The best way to determine the absence of life would be to attach the muscles of the various parts of the body to an appliance connected with electric batteries, so that the very slightest movement of the body would cause a bell to ring and thus occasion alarm. You know it is a very difficult thing to determine or state definitely just when the spark of life becomes extinct. The matter has been much discussed, and again and again valuable prizes have been offered for some means by which this important fact might be definitely determined. However, the test as to whether there is life in the body that I mention is about as sure as any that can be named.

The matter of premature burial was one that interested a very large body of people from all walks of life. It was this fact that led the physicians and lawyers belonging to the New York Medico Legal Society, who were interested in the new organisation, to believe that it would be successful.

A gruesome fascination always surrounds the discussion of the subject of persons being buried alive, but a recurring question raised at the society meetings was '*how many such cases occur?*'

There is no shape in which death can come to us which is dreaded more. Edgar Allen Poe's description of the man waking in the darkness of the night upon a vessel, and finding wood above him and by his side, by which he is impressed that he is in a coffin is a blood-curdling story. Suspended animation, catalepsy etc, resembled what we call death so accurately that in 1900 when the Society was formed, there did not appear to be one actual test which was universally accepted as an unfailing indication that life had departed. Huge rewards were offered for the discovery of some simple method to prove that life was extinct.

From a leaflet on 'Premature Burial issued by the United Templars Society the following extracts are taken:

The increasing number of cases that are coming to light of persons carried to the grave before they are dead, and still more, it is feared, actually buried alive, is a matter of grave anxiety to all but the thoughtless and self-satisfied.

Bruhier collected the details of 52 cases of persons buried alive, of 53 who recovered after they were placed in their coffins, of 72 who were falsely reported dead.

Dr. Franz Hartmann, of Vienna, has collected over 700 cases well authenticated, and of those he has given the details of over 100 cases.

In Holland an average 5 out of 1,000 recover before burial, or as they are in their coffins. In New York the average is 6 in 1,200. In Paris it is 4 in 1,200, the low temperature being less favourable to recovery. Taking the average of 5 in the 1,000 and applying it to England and Wales, with a death-rate of 550,000 yearly, 2,700 would be the probable number consigned to the most horrible of deaths that can be well conceived, through the carelessness of the survivors, doctors, undertakers, and the incompetent persons who are by the present state of the law allowed to certify deaths in all parts of the country. And be it remembered, the figures given above, with regard to Paris, Holland and New York do not include the numbers who are actually buried alive and unable to tell the tale. In England the case is worse, for out of 550,000 burials we have but an average of five cases in the year, and the entreaties of friends or relations are unavailing.

Let the body be buried without any coffin at all, in a shroud, as was formerly the custom, and is still done in religious communities in the Church ; or else let it be placed in a wicker cradle (which can be had for 15s), without any hood or cover to it ; or else in a perishable coffin, without any cover whatever, but only a layer of dry earth, carbolised if need be (or crumbled charcoal), to cover the body and prevent any odour or infection.

In this, and no other way, let it be buried, and that only when it has been kept sufficiently long to be in an advanced stage of decomposition, for this is the only infallible sign of the absolute departure of life. In *Premature Burial* by Colonel Vollum, Med Depart. U.S.A. (Allen Ave Maria Lane), Sir Benjamin Richardson, M.D., enumerates eleven signs which point to death, but not one is an absolutely infallible test but the one of advanced decomposition.

Scheider says that even the beginning of decomposition is not sufficient, as many have actually recovered and been restored to health, whose bodies exhibited the blue marks with the strong and overpowering odour of putrefaction. This being so, in order to prevent being buried alive, the body should be kept in all cases in a temperature of 84 deg. Fahrenheit till advanced decomposition sets in.

It will be seen that there are two stages – burial alive, and the waking to life in a closed coffin, with all its revolting horrors. The means we have pointed out to prevent the former may not always be easy of adoption, but the means we suggested for the prevention of the latter is always easily procurable, and the neglect of it is the more criminal.

The correspondence which this momentous subject elicited in the Press shows how common the belief was that under regulations at the turn of the century many persons were buried with a suspicion, on part of friends and relatives, that they were not dead. The cases brought to light in England were nearly all those who had either been discovered at or before burial by the undertaker and his assistants when preparing the body for the grave, or strange and gruesome stories brought from the dissecting table by medical students. In America similar discoveries were made under like circumstances, and also those when professional embalmers began their process upon the supposed dead.

From the 1850s it was the custom in the United States to build cemeteries on the outskirts of new settlements, and the rapid increase of the population had in many instances made it necessary to remove these burial grounds to further out and, whenever exhumation and examination of the corpses was made, the most awful discoveries were revealed. In one notable instance these cases amounted to 6 out of 1,200 cases, or 0.5 per cent, but it must be conceded that in many cases of suffocation or starvation, the corpses would fail to exhibit those unmistakable signs of an agonising struggle as the six registered and the belief was that the percentage was actually much higher.

According to the *Chicago Herald*, several gentlemen well known in the city were seated in the rotunda of the Leland Hotel after supper in April 1891, when someone brought up the subject of persons being buried alive. Two of the men were undertakers and one a physician.

'It's all "bosh" about people being buried alive,' said one. 'You read in the newspapers once in a while of such a case, but I never yet saw a man who had ever seen such a case. I think the changes in the position of a body, as is frequently described after a resurrection, are brought about by the careless handling of the coffin, which causes the body to be rolled around and disarranged.'

'Never will any of the bodies buried by me come to life,' remarked one of the undertakers. 'I have a perfect horror of such an idea. I always fix them so that there is no danger of such an occurrence. No one will ever say that I buried a live person. I started in business in a little town in Minnesota, and one night I was called to arrange a body for burial. The body was that of a young girl. We fixed everything all up nicely and I went home to bed. The funeral was to occur the next day, because it was during warm weather and they wanted to get the body underground. At about three o'clock in the morning I was called again, and what I saw made me creep. The girl had come back to life and was the liveliest dead person I ever saw. She was a very nervous person and had gone into a trance, during which she seemed to be dead.'

He went on, 'The body had looked exactly as though in death, and the attending physician had declared that life was extinct. The girl completely recovered and the last I heard of her she was married and the mother of a large family. I shudder when I think of the consequences if she had been buried and afterwards came to life. To think of her agony and suffering in finding herself confined in a narrow box with several feet of earth and the solid box cover between her and continued life. How she would have endeavoured to free herself from the place only to find her efforts unavailing. Now, whenever I have a body to prepare for burial, I arrange it in the proper manner and embalm it. After a body is embalmed there is no danger of its ever coming to life again. I do this for the sake of the dead person, its relatives and my own personal feeling in the matter. The embalming process is very simple. An incision is made in the body, generally in the abdomen, and the fluids are drawn off. The arteries of the heart are opened in some cases and all the blood drawn off. This is done with a suction pump. Then the embalming fluid is injected into the veins, and this preserves the body. The embalming fluid is composed principally of arsenical properties, arsenic, you know, acting as a preservative of the body.'

'Yes, in cases of a man dying from the effects of arsenic the body lasts longer and is found in a better state of preservation if resurrected after some time,' replied the doctor, 'In post-mortem examination we find this always to be the case.'

'Well, I don't believe that people are buried alive,' said the other undertaker. 'I never yet heard anything definite of such a case. But I used to have a man work for me when I was in business in New York who had a horror of such an occurrence. He was a Spaniard and was one of the best men I ever had work for me. One day he was arranging a body for burial when I noticed a queer movement which he made. It was as though he were striking the body. When he left the room for a moment I turned the sheet down from the body, and right over the heart was a tiny round red spot. I examined it closely and saw that an incision had been made with some instrument. We dressed another body that night, and I watched him very closely to see what he did. Finally, I saw him draw something from his breast pocket, and, with a thrust, press it against the breast of the corpse. I sprang and seized his arm, which startled him so that he dropped what he had in his hand. It was a dagger, the blade being no larger than a needle. It was about five inches long and had a beautifully jewelled handle. I asked him what he did that for, and he replied that he always pierced the hearts of the bodies he prepared for burial. When in Madrid, where he learned his trade of undertaker, he had become involved in trouble, as one of the persons whom he had prepared for burial had been proved by a later disinterment to have been buried alive. The authorities made trouble over the matter, and he nearly lost his life as the result. He made a vow that he would never again run such a risk, and he made it a point ever afterward to pierce the heart of any body he prepared for burial. It had become a second nature to him, and he always carried it out as a part of the business. It may have been the proper thing in Spain, but it was too cold blooded for me, and I had to let him go.'

'I had a patient once who had a great terror of being buried alive,' said the doctor, 'and one day he made me promise that after his body was ready for burial I would plunge a knife into his heart, so that he would not run the risk of waking up in his coffin. The poor old fellow nearly had a fit over the idea, and I promised to do as he requested. The day for the funeral came, and I was present to carry out the last wish of the old man. Several members of the family entered the room with me to watch the commission of the deed. I had a slender dagger which I had used as a paper knife. It was a relic which I had picked up in the East. I opened the clothing on the corpse, put the point of the knife over the place where the heart was and struck the handle of the dagger with the palm of my hand. My hair stood right up on end, and I felt as faint as though I had received a sunstroke. I pulled the knife out, arranged the clothing and we left the room. When I got outside, I found that I was wet with perspiration.'

'Didn't you feel like a murderer?' asked the undertakers.

'Why should I?' was the reply, 'The man was as dead as a nail. He was a man no longer. I felt just as though I were handling a piece of lifeless clay. That is all it was, anyhow.'

In the late 1890s many persons still lived in fear of being buried alive. In the United States physicians had concluded that it was now easy to distinguish death, at least they thought that the case in their country. In Italy, however, it was very different. The doctors there declared that up to the present time, 1897, no infallible test for distinguishing apparent death from real death had been discovered, in consequence of which, horrifying cases of persons being buried alive occurred from time to time. 'Who told these doctors that these persons were buried alive?' argued the Americans. 'The victims could not possibly live long enough in their coffins to do so themselves, and even if it had been found that a few of them turned over in their graves it is no sign that they were alive when they did so.' There was such a thing as post-mortem contradiction in Italy as well as in America. However, Italian medics and laymen were, at the turn of the nineteenth century, engaged in preparing a report, with exhibits, on the subject of the 'Apparent Death and Premature Burial', and this report was to be the main feature of the medical department at the national exposition opened in Turin in April 1898. The Italian government, through ambassadors and ministers, then extended an invitation to other nations to take part in this branch of the exposition.

New York physician Dr George F. Shady gave an interview upon the gruesome subject of persons being buried alive in December 1897, his intention being to highlight the fallacies of stories. When asked to talk about premature burial and more especially how to distinguish apparent from real death, Dr. Shady said:

It is really astonishing how many persons fear being buried alive, and more astonishing the number who have their dead disinterred to see if they have been buried alive. This is done quietly and does not reach the ears of the public. A child takes a notion that its mother has been buried alive or a husband concludes in his hopeless grief that perhaps after all, his wife was not dead, and the bodies are taken up to satisfy distorted imagination.

There is little if any danger of a body being buried alive. All of these horrible stories about premature burial are on a par with the ghost stories told in the nursery, the more improbable they are the more readily they are believed. These stories are circulated usually in times of an epidemic, when bodies have to be disposed of quickly. Many of them do seem to have a foundation in truth, because frequently after death bodies show a muscular action. Especially is this true of victims of cholera. And sometimes one would think that an epidemic of premature burials was in progress, stories of them are told so often, and retold and told again, being added to with each telling.

Dr Shady went on to say that:

The greatest danger of premature burials, if there is any at all is in cases of sudden death at times of epidemic. Over a century ago several mortuary chambers were established in Germany. The first was at Weimer and the second at Munich. Dead bodies were brought to these places and watched closely by medical men. During the first forty-eight hours after death a bell rope is attached to the hand of the corpse so that in case death was not real the slightest movement will ring the bell. In all these hundred years only once has the loud sound of a bell been heard in any of these mortuary chambers, and then it was due to the relaxation of the stiffened hand of the corpse.

He explained,

Not all persons when they die are absolutely cold. Different diseases produce different temperatures. The higher the temperature has been the longer it takes the body to cool, and young persons hold heat much longer after death than old ones. A corpse often has the appearance of breathing to those looking at it. This is the association of the habit of vision with life. All this talk about death, apparent death and premature burials brings us down to one vital question. How long could life be maintained in a coffin? An experiment on a dog in a coffin showed that the animal lived five or six hours. A body in an ordinary coffin gets only three or four cubic feet of air, and that would keep one alive only fifteen or twenty minutes. So those who trouble themselves about being buried when only apparently dead may rest assured that if such an improbability were realised, they would not live to hear the last hymn sung at their funeral.

Hardly an encouraging thought to end his conviction with, is it?

In England, burial places were considered far too sacred to be dealt with in this summary fashion, and the terrible experiences of those who had been committed to earth while in a state of lethargy, trance or catalepsy, remained a profound secret. On 23 November 1901, an article appeared in *Jackson's Oxford Journal*, outlining the beginnings of the London Association for the Prevention of Premature Burial. Described as a 'philanthropic and humane society', it had, in 1901, been established for five years. So, what prompted such a group to form? Jas. R. Williamson, explained:

In May 1895, a child was discovered apparently dead in Regent's Park, London, and was conveyed to the Marylebone mortuary, where it was laid out for dead. Later, however, the child showed signs of life and was restored to its family. Just at that period, several other instances of narrow escape from premature burial were reported in the Press, and extensive correspondence, with editorial comments, appeared in newspapers throughout the country, exciting much attention and interest in the public mind. The important question of premature burial was also discussed in Continental and Colonial journals, and practical measures for its prevention were urged by numerous able writers, both medical and lay.

Renewed interest in the subject exhibited itself in the United States, where an attempt to obtain legislative precautions against burial alive had been made as far back as 25 January 1871, when Dr Alex Wilder, Professor of Physiology and Psychological Science, delivered a public address before members of the Legislature at the Capitol, Albany, New York. A Bill to provide surer guarantees before interment was presented to the Senate by the Hon. A.X. Parker. The address was reprinted in London in 1895 and published in a six-penny pamphlet by E.W. Allen, under the title of *The Perils of Premature Burial*. Shortly after, a monograph entitled *Premature Burial*, by Dr Franz Hartmann appeared, the first edition of which had been published in America. This volume had originally been issued in German, under the auspices of the Cremation Society. Two independent investigators, one in England, the other in the United States, had for many years given special attention to the phenomena of apparent death and premature burial, unknown to each other, and had collected in the course of their research a considerable amount of authentic evidence of the reality of the danger of burial alive in Europe, the United States, and India.

In the search for reliable information a personal acquaintance resulted, and in the early part of 1896 a treatise of 400 pages was published on *Premature Burial and how it may be prevented*, with special references to trance, catalepsy, and other forms of suspended animation, by W. Tebb FRGS and Colonel Vollum MD, of which the first edition was almost exhausted. This comprehensive work revealed in its pages much patient labour and research into a subject which interested everyone, considering that under the haphazard laws at that time, anyone could be mistaken for being dead whilst actually still breathing, and meet with one of the most appalling of deaths without the faintest hope of rescue. There existed an almost unanimous consensus of opinion that the authors' contention as to the urgent need of legislative reforms had been abundantly proven and were urged to be carried into effect without further loss of time.

Reforms, however, are never brought to fruition without a long, continuous and arduous struggle. It was therefore considered expedient to form an association, which, in addition to spreading information as to the perils of premature burial, would protect its members by means of a system of careful verification of death by experts against the terrible possibility of a person being buried alive. The society issued a considerable amount of literature, which was widely distributed, but was hampered by lack of financial support in carrying out its philanthropic efforts.

It was little comfort to those who feared being buried alive to reflect on the words of one French physician. In his work entitled, *Des Inhumations Precipitees*, Dr Leone Lenormand observed in 1904: 'It is a mistake to think that a living person, enclosed in a narrow box and covered with several feet of earth, would succumb to immediate asphyxiation.' This authority on death also showed that air percolated through the earth, that the air in the coffin was thereby renewed in part, and that a man could live in a coffin underground for many hours, the time depending on the depth and frequency of the respirations!

In 1904 the British Home Secretary admitted in Parliament that, in England and Wales, 10,000 persons were buried each year without death certificates. In response, the London Association for the Prevention of Premature Burial pointed out that death certificates were not only frequently granted by medical men without careful inspection of the body, and without the use of any special tests to ascertain whether or not life was extinct, but often simply on the information of some relative or friend, without seeing the body at all. With a view to remedying this the Association drew up a draft Bill enacting that no certificate should be give without a personal examination and inspection of the body and requiring the local sanitary authorities to provide waiting mortuaries in their respective districts. In an appendix of the association's annual report a number of instances of narrow escapes from premature burial were reported.

Some uncomfortable statistics were also given at the annual meeting of the London Association for the Prevention of Premature Burial in May 1905. Dr Hadwen said that in his recently published book he had cited, from medial sources alone, no fewer than 384 instances of horrible conditions relating to premature burial, viz: buried alive 149, narrow escapes from burial alive 219, dissected alive 10, narrow escapes from dissection alive 3, embalming alive 2, and burned alive 1. There were thousands of more or less authenticated cases which he had to wade through and reject for want of space.

In August of 1905, it was reported that a new method had been invented for ascertaining, on the eve of burial, whether life existed in a body or not. The agent being used was fluorescine in solution, which could be injected deep into the tissue of the supposed corpse. In the event of circulation having ceased, the skin and mucous membrane would become very yellow and the eyes assumed the colour of emeralds. If death had not yet taken place, the injected fluid cased no harm and no discolouration took place.

'I do not consider such a test, in itself, sufficiently reliable,' said Mr H.W. Denton-Ingham, Secretary of the London Association for the Prevention of Premature Burial, 'There is always a chance that the test might fail occasionally, and in such a serious matter as the risk of premature burial one should chance nothing. The only really infallible test of death which has been discovered so far is the presence of decomposition.'

The fear of premature burial oppressed a very large section of the public at the turn of the century, and there was abundant proof that they had good reason for their dread. The Association for the Prevention of Premature Burial held its annual meeting in January 1905 and numbered among its members a woman who had narrowly escaped being buried alive on three separate occasions! Mrs Heigham, the woman in question, was living in London and could hardly bear to recall the terrible ordeal that she experienced. Her extraordinary case was well known to the medical secretary of the association, and among her possessions was her death certificate signed by her own family doctor. Mrs Heigham, who was subject to cataleptic seizures, had been regarded as dead three times. On each occasion all the details connected with the preparation of the body for interment were gone through, the unfortunate lady remaining fully conscious of what was passing.

On the first occasion there was all the rigidity of death after two hours. For forty-eight hours the unhappy woman remained as one dead, unable to move a single muscle, while weeping friends and relatives took what they believed to be a last farewell. In speaking of her terrible experience, however, Mrs Heigham described the arrival of the undertaker's men as the worst of the many horrors that she had to endure.

'When the undertaker's men came to measure me, I tried to shriek aloud, but not a sound came from my lips,' she said, 'The final agony came when my coffin was brought into the house. At the sight of that gruesome object placed by my bedside I felt as if my brain would break under its futile efforts to assert itself.'

At midnight on the second night of the sleep that counterfeited death, Mrs Heigham's daughter was overcome with a fear that her mother might be buried alive. She went to the death-chamber and, looking down at her mother, the daughter thought she detected a faint flicker of the eyelid. At first, she believed it was some curious effect of light, but again the lids seemed to move and when a minute later she held a bottle of volatile salts to the nostrils, the 'dead' woman sat up by the side of her coffin. Twice after this, when similarly seized, Mrs Heigham was declared by the doctors to be dead, but precautions were taken by the family to delay burial with the result that the lady recovered.

The possibility of paupers being buried alive was discussed by the Hexham Board of Guardians at their meeting in February 1905. Mr Henry Straker asked what the practice was regarding deaths in the workhouse and contended that the medical officer should testify that life had gone before any person was placed in a coffin.

'I know it is not done,' he added. 'When persons are apparently dead they are taken to the mortuary, put into coffins, and screwed down. No medical examination is made.'

The clerk pointed out that there were no special regulations. The workhouse medical officer was governed by the same rules as those applying to medical men in private practice.

'That I do not dispute,' said Mr Straker, 'But that some persons are buried alive in their coffins is beyond doubt. It is a horrible thing to think of.'

'There cannot be many cases,' said the chairman. 'There may be one here and there. The medical officer is satisfied, and the master and matron are satisfied before dead persons are put into coffins. It would be an unreasonable thing to ask our medical officer to see every corpse.'

It was pointed out by the clerk that in every case a certificate was given by a medical man and the doctor who gave that did so on his own responsibility.

Discussing the possibility of burial alive in 1905, the *Medical Press* pointed out that no single instance of incontrovertible proof of live burial existed. They found it inconceivable that death could not be ascertained by the careful examination of a skilled medical man. However, the faculty of correct observation and logical reasoning was not always guaranteed by the possession of a medical degree or diploma. In the case where a woman was resuscitated after having been laid out for dead, it was shown that the death certificate had been filled out by the medical attendant on the strength of the friends' report. The *Medical Press* pointed out that the fact that a person was not actually buried alive 'scarcely warranted the wholesale revival of a mischievous and foolish scare.'

In 1906, by request of the London Association for the Prevention of Premature Burial, Miss Lizzie Lind, of Hageby, gave a lecture at the Agricultural Hall in Stockholm on a subject entitled 'Is There Any Danger Existing of Being Buried Alive?' It attracted a crowded audience. The speaker began by remarking that nobody could take an interest in this question from pleasure. It was a question of great importance and Miss Lind had taken it upon herself to show some facts and the results of investigation related to the topic. She said that foreign testimonials on that point were numerous. For example, Dr Franz Hartmann had collected over 700 cases of such burials and, in a pamphlet from London, it was stated that 2,700 persons were buried alive every year, whilst a French author claimed the figure to be 8,000 yearly over there.

Miss Lind went on: 'The English Association before mentioned works to examine scientifically these cases of apparent death, to distribute among the public knowledge of the different kinds of trance, and to prevent premature burial of its members twelve doctors are engaged for the use of the Association. A state of trance can last any time almost – weeks, months, or longer – and all the different signs of death can be noticed with a person in this condition.' The speaker related several cases from abroad of persons being buried while in a trance or cataleptic state, all of the most distressing kind, and yet Miss Lind declared that she had, on purpose, avoided the most heartrending cases. She claimed: 'There has been far too much indifference on this subject. During plague or cholera or other epidemics the danger of premature burial is great, and during war it is not at all uncommon that many of the wounded who are only unconscious are buried with the dead.'

The speaker also showed by a few examples that they could not be sure of their friends being dead in Sweden either. Among the most important inventions to prevent this danger, Lizzie Lind referred to a mechanism invented by a Russian, Count Karnice-Karnicki. It was to be fastened to the coffin and consisted of a tube about three and a half inches in diameter and ended by a hermetically shut box. The tube was screwed into a hole in the cover of the coffin, and on the chest of the deceased was put a glass ball which was in connection with a very sensitive spring. At the slightest movement of the 'dead', the faintest beating of the heart, or breathing, the glass ball would move, a flag raised over the grave and an electric bell rung. This apparatus cost twelve crowns (13 shillings and 4 pence). The speaker also described the 'houses for the dead' in Germany, where the dead were kept until decay set in, and she considered that something of that kind ought to be introduced in other countries. So what were these 'House for the Dead' that Lizzie Lind referred to?

Archdeacon Colley, rector of Stockton, Warwickshire, was a surprising old gentleman. In 1906 he startled a gathering of highly respectable ladies and gentlemen with the statement, 'For two and a half days I was regarded as dead, laid out, and coffined.' The occasion was the annual meeting of the Association for the Prevention of Premature Burial, at Frascati's Restaurant, London.

'Yes,' declared the archdeacon cheerfully, 'I myself am an instance of a narrow escape from premature interment. I was nearly buried alive when a child. I don't remember many of the circumstances, but I'll just report what I felt as a child about two and a half years old.'

'I remember,' he went on, 'having leeches upon my breast, the marks of the bites of which are still to be seen. There was a glass or something placed over them, and I was held by my father. Then, in reward for my suffering, I was placed upon a couch and given a peal of bells. I remember it dropped from my hands as something seemed to go right through from my right ear to my left. I don't remember the resuscitation, but was told afterwards that for two and a half days I was regarded as dead, laid out, and coffined. When the nurse found some indications of life, a doctor was called in, and I was restored to consciousness, to be before you this afternoon.'

In the same year, Father Henry Flood contributed an article to the June edition of the *Irish Rosary*, saying that he would like to see more attention paid to the danger of premature burial by the medical men of England and Ireland:

'A great number of the medical profession are either sceptical or apathetic as to the danger of living burial. Some do not believe in the existence of death-trance or death-counterfeit, while many of those who do believe in it declare that it is of very rare occurrence.'

After giving several cases in which premature burial took place, he concluded:

According to the legal form of death certification, a doctor is not bound to see that the patient is dead. A space is left for him to write 'As I am informed'. Is it not curious that although the law protects the citizen's property and life, and the disposition of his property after death, it does not protect the same citizen from the most ghastly danger of being buried alive.

In many of the towns in Germany in the eighteenth and nineteenth century, there was a building at the entrance of a cemetery called the 'Deadhouse,' where, at the request of families, bodies could be deposited for a few days before interment. By this plan, the danger of a person being buried alive was prevented. The 'Deadhouse' in Frankfurt was the best constructed place of its kind in the whole of the German Confederation. It consisted of a central room, which looked, from a dozen windows, into twelve smaller rooms. In each of them stood an iron bedstead on which the open coffin was laid. Over the head of the corpse was suspended a small cord, to the end of which ten brass thimbles were attached by wires, with the thimbles being placed on the ten fingers of the body. If the slightest movement was made, a bell would be rung and alert the person stationed in the central room. Staff would work on a rota system and be forced to stay awake for the duration of each shift by a special mechanism. Between 1833 and 1862, however, no instance ever occurred of the bell being rung. Medicines, baths and other remedies were always kept in readiness, but were apparently never used, and yet during that time thousands of bodies had thimbles placed on their fingers.

Of course, the most thrilling account of a German deadhouse was given in novelist Wilkie Collins' book, *Jezebel's Daughter*, which contains a scene in which an English widow, poisoned and supposed to be dead, sits up and confronts her enemies. Incidentally, Collins also had a fear of being buried prematurely!

Horrors of premature burial had become so impressive to two justices of the Supreme Court of the United States that in 1908 they engaged Dr John Dixwell of Harvard University to guarantee that they should not be buried alive. Dr Dixwell also told the committee on legal affairs of the Massachusetts legislature that many years before he was himself pronounced dead by distinguished physicians and barely escaped a horrible fate. Witnesses told the committee that by estimate, two people out of every thousand were buried alive. Numerous terrifying instances were cited in an effort to have the committee report a bill making proof of death compulsory. There was currently no such law in the state of Massachusetts. The bill provided that local boards of health should be notified within six hours of the death of any person and that as soon as possible they should cause an examination to be made of the reported deceased. It added that the certificate of death should only be issued after ten tests had been made for heart action, respiration, muscles and use of subcutaneous injection of ammonia to ascertain dissolution, the purpose being to prevent burial alive. They specified that suitable rooms should be set aside for these tests if not made at the domicile by three, and not less than two, physicians. The bill provided a penalty of one thousand dollars fine or a year's imprisonment for violation of the act. Dr Dixwell urged that the state should endeavour to relieve the deadly and widespread worry caused by fear of premature burial.

A notable case showing the difficulty of knowing whether a patient was really dead was told of a Natick man who was laid out for two days, presumed dead, but who was entirely conscious and afterward complained of an undertaker who lifted his head by the nose.

Frederick W. Briggs, member of the state embalming board, opposed the bill and resented aspersions upon doctors and undertakers. Judge Lloyd E. Chamberlain of Brockton made a forceful argument for the bill.

'If there is a single case where a person has been declared dead and prepared for burial before the life has left his body,' he said with earnestness, 'that ought to be enough for the passage of proper legislation. And we have none on the books today. The physician too frequently takes the word of friends or of the undertaker.'

Judge Chamberlain contended that the state, in the exercise of its parental duty, should take up the matter.

'The only way to do it in the light of science is to provide that there shall be positive proofs from positive tests. Undertakers will tell you that they embalm,' he continued. 'Yes, they do embalm; but if they do the embalming that will kill, if life is there, is it any more than murder?' The judge said that his own mother had had a bitter experience in her youth, and it followed her throughout life.

'I came very near being buried alive myself in the early 1870s,' said Dr Dixwell, 'Very eminent physicians determined that I was dead and gave me up, but after an hour or so I thought I wouldn't die and so I am alive today, while they are all dead. Dr Henry I. Bowditch was the chief of the consultation at my bedside, and I will never forget how surprised he was to find me alive next morning. The horror exists as a fact, and it can't be disputed. I have two justices of the Supreme Court of the United States whom I promised I would see they should not be buried alive. I recall a case at the General Hospital of a woman sent there with bronchitis. After a time, it was decided that she was dead and she was sent to the morgue. There she suddenly woke up and is alive today.'

'Worry kills,' said the doctor, 'as well as disease. It becomes a regular monomania with some natures, and they go wild over the fear of being buried alive. If the state should stop that I believe it would be a wise thing to do.'

A minefield of interesting information was elicited in the course of the evidence taken before the Departmental Committee in August 1909. It was appointed by the Home Secretary to inquire into the law relating to coroner's inquests. One of the most interesting points touched upon was the danger of being buried alive, on which the medical witnesses were widely at variance.

Doctor Walter Hadwen, vice-president of the Society for the Prevention of Premature Burial (see top left image on page 4 of the plate section), mentioned three specific cases. All these, he said, occurred in his own experience and he told the Committee that he had mentioned them because they were all entered into a book that he had with him, enabling him to furnish those present with the 'exact facts.' Firstly, he referred to a girl, aged seventeen, who suffered from catalepsy in 1895 after having spent practically the whole of the previous day listening to music and singing in special services in Wells Cathedral.

Dr Hadwen said:

On arrival at the house, I was informed by the weeping relatives that I was too late – she was dead. The poor girl had fallen into a swoon while sitting in a chair, soon after arrival at home, and though every effort had been made to rouse her, they all proved ineffectual, even then I heard her distracted friends shouting her name in her ears without effect. I had lifted the wrist from the bed in order to examine the pulse, and was struck by the fact that upon releasing it the forearm remained suspended, and continued in a state of suspension for some considerable time. I then put other limbs in various positions, placed the body in absurd postures when, to the amazement of onlookers, such positions were maintained and apparently would have been maintained indefinitely. At the close of the sixth day I noticed a slight sign of consciousness, I told her to sit up, and she did so, and opened her eyes vacantly.

In reply to questions, Dr. Hadwen said: 'Here was a case in which a girl was supposed to be dead by the friends, and they could make no impression whatever upon her.' He emphasised the need for a doctor seeing the body after death before giving a certificate.

Dr. Hadwen proceeded to narrate a second case. Seven years previously, he had been attending a three-year-old child who had suffered from convulsions for some time, followed by exhaustion. He said:

There seemed, no hope of recovery, and I left my little patient one night fully believing I had seen him for the last time alive. I was late on my country rounds next day, and when I arrived at the cottage I noticed the blinds were drawn, and, upon entering, my eyes at once fell upon a couch pushed into a corner of the room, and covered by a white sheet, while the broken-hearted parents were weeping by the settle. I sat down and tried to comfort them, and finally left directions as to the hour when they might send for the death certificate. Before leaving I walked towards the couch, and drew back the covering from the pale, waxen face. The jaw was fastened by a band in the usual way, coppers had been placed over the eyelids, and all was in readiness for the shell, which the undertaker was expected to bring in a few minutes. As I stood looking intently at the child I fancied I detected the slightest movement of the chest. It could but be imagination, I thought, nevertheless instinctively I felt for the wrist, but failed to detect any pulse. Still, I watched, there again was that tremor. I applied my stethoscope to the region of the heart without response, but feeling dissatisfied, I undid the nightdress and applied the instrument to the bare skin. I could hardly believe my ears – there was undoubtedly a beat! I shall never forget the shriek which the mother gave when I said: 'Mrs W----, your child is not dead!' I at once applied hot flannels to the feet, and gently massaged the body for two or three hours and had the satisfaction before I left – long after the undertaker had come and gone – of seeing the child taking nourishments in its mother's arms. He is now a fine, strong, healthy lad. That boy was in Gloucester only last week.

At the annual meeting of the Society for the Prevention of Premature Burials in February 1910, Mr Barnard, a Paris surgeon, certified that in the parish of Riol he himself saw a monk of the Order of St. Francis (a subject of catalepsy), who had been buried for three or four days, taken from his grave breathing and alive, with his arms lacerated near the swathes which bound him. An account of this was drawn up by public authority. The doctor added that it would appear to be quite possible for a person to live forty to sixty minutes in a closed coffin, and what a century of time would be compressed into that brief space!

In 1910 legislative action in the United States was discussed as the widely prevalent dread of gruesome accidents continued to grow. Sometime before, Assemblyman Marks of Hudson County, New Jersey, introduced a bill providing that all cemeteries be equipped with a receiving vault, the interior of which should be in view of a person outside and subject to frequent inspection by a physician. In this vault bodies were to be kept until it was proven beyond any doubt that life was extinct. In the interior of the vault were to be placed mechanical devices which would enable the supposedly dead person to give an alarm in the event of a return to consciousness. Somewhat similar provisions were contained in a bill introduced in the house at Albany by Assemblyman Redington. It provided that each cemetery should have a mortuary to be used for the disposal of the dead. Each body so received was to be kept under observation for a certain period of time before interment or cremation.

While the subject of premature burial was, and still is, a most distressing one, certain occurrences occasionally arose serving to reawaken the widely prevalent dread of being buried alive. Medical science, the legislature and inventors all endeavoured to obliterate that dread by providing means whereby premature burial and its gruesome consequences might be effectively prevented. It was suggested that to this end waiting mortuaries, vented and lighted, furnished with pleasing surroundings and replete with every apparatus for resuscitation, should be provided by urban or rural cemetery authorities, where every person dying within their respective areas could be deposited until such time as the official death verifier appointed for the purpose, certified that the signs of decomposition in the body warranted interment.

Meanwhile, Doctor Vaillant, chief of the radiographic service of La Riboisiere Hospital, Paris, was experimenting with a machine which, he asserted, would provide an absolute test of death. It involved the use of x-ray photographs on the internal organs, which Dr Vaillant declared, differed in the cases of subjects alive or dead. 'Death tails show clearly in the case of a corpse,' he said, 'but not if life is present.' Radiographs of bodies taken even a few minutes after death could clearly reveal the outlines of all the organs, whereas if the radiographs were taken during life the organs were not revealed.

In Pittsburgh, Hubert Devan, a French-Canadian, announced the invention of a device he called a 'grave signal' and had it protected by patents. The device consisted of a piece of ordinary gas pipe, six feet long, with a glass globe about the size of an incandescent lamp on one end. The pipe was arranged to pass through a brass plate at the head of the coffin, leaving the lower end within a fraction of an inch of the forehead of the corpse. Through the centre of the pipe ran a plain, smooth stick, one end of which rested on the forehead of the body in the coffin. The other end was in the glass globe, with a red cloth attached to it. Should the person have come to life in the coffin, the stick would be forced through the pipe and the red cloth signal displayed. At the same time, a number of small apertures would open at the base of the globe and fresh air forced down the pipe into the nostrils.

A startling statement was made in March 1924 by Professor Jellinek, head of the Electro-Pathological Institute in Vienna, Austria. Speaking on the theory that electrocution did not permanently kill all victims, he shocked the medical and electrical world by announcing that, in his opinion, many victims of electrocutions had been buried alive. He maintained that electric shock only drove a victim into a trance, and that hope of saving them should not be abandoned unless physical decay had started. He believed that hundreds of people had been buried alive whereas if they had been 'worked over for a day or more' they would have been revived!

'Once buried, twice shy,' was the motto of Angelo Hays, a Frenchman who took the unusual step of creating himself a coffin with mod cons in 1979. However, Angelo had good reason to fear premature burial, as at the young age of eighteen he was injured in a motorcycle accident and was pronounced dead. For two days, the 'body' lay inside its coffin and was visited by close relatives. However, when Angelo's Uncle Marcel insisted that the coffin lid be removed for one last glimpse of his nephew, the supposed corpse's hands were found to be warm. Within six weeks, Angelo Hays had fully recovered from the concussion that had caused the village doctor to believe him deceased. Apparently, the severe head injury had cut body functions so low that he needed hardly any oxygen to survive. This experience prompted Angelo to ensure that the same mistake could never be made again. Inside his 'safety coffin' Monsieur Hays arranged oxygen, blankets, a reading lamp, books, canned food and a large quantity of wine. The coffin was also fitted with a sophisticated alarm system which would be triggered by the slightest body movement, thus being connected to bells and flashing lights that was capable of sending a signal to his local village police station near Bordeaux, in western France. When news of Angelo's creation got out, others began to contact him to provide a 'safety coffin' for them, his most optimistic customer being a woman of ninety-three!

Chapter Five
Children Buried Alive

Although all cases of premature burial are tragic, there is undoubtedly something more unnerving about cases involving children. Perhaps it is the inability of youngsters to shout loud enough about their plight as fragile air is expelled within the coffin, or the lack of strength in a babe to bang on the lid of their wooden tomb. The following cases are both tragic and unsettling.

One of the earliest documented newspaper reports tells of a cruel mother who refused to heed concerns after the burial of her daughter in Enfield, Middlesex, in 1729. As reported in the *Caledonian Mercury* of 21 January, the milkwoman's daughter was accidentally buried alive. Just as the girl was about to be interred in her coffin, some funeral attendees commented that they thought she looked 'fresh.' One concerned person took up a looking-glass and applied it to the young girl's lips, noting that there was a slight dew on it, as if from her breath. However, the mother of the girl mocked and reviled them, insisting that her daughter should be buried without further delay. Reluctantly, the body was sealed in, lowered into its grave and covered with earth. It wasn't long before the incident came to the ears of a near relation, who got the grave dug up and the coffin opened. Tragically, the girl was found with her knees drawn up and the nosegay of flowers in her hands bitten to pieces as she had struggled for life. A surgeon was sent for to let the young female's blood, but it was too late, and she died within a very short time.

Another very sad case came to light in July 1740. Mary Powell was apprehended in Southwark, London, on suspicion of murdering her female child, of which she was delivered the previous week. She confessed before the Justice that the child was born alive and that she had buried it in St. George's Fields. In regard to her very weak condition, Powell was sent to the workhouse in St. Mary Overy's.

The death of a young woman named Susan Rudson was reported on 25 May 1811, in the small village community of Mill Hill, her complaint being termed as the general condition of galloping consumption. The illness arose after the woman took a concoction of poisonous medicines at different times over a prolonged period, procured, she claimed, by her seducer in order to produce a miscarriage. Sadly, the unfortunate offspring of Susan's last pregnancy was her fifth child. For several days prior to her demise, Miss Rudson struggled with violent convulsions and unendurable agony. However, a short time before her death, the young woman closed her eyes and declared that she could not die without unburdening her conscience. A clergyman was sent for, but Susan refused to say a word to him, calling out instead for a Mrs Mackay, a neighbour who had cared for her during the final days. Susan then related how she had falsely accused an innocent man of fathering her two surviving children and how she had disposed of three babies since. The first child, a little boy, she smothered at birth, burying him under a tree in a garden near Dors Lane. The second was a girl who met with a similar fate and was buried behind the Adam and Eve public house in Mill Hill. The last child, also a girl, she confessed to burying alive in a field near Totteridge. After the final disclosure, the unhappy woman appeared to be at peace and took her final breath almost immediately afterwards.

Sadly, in a time of scant contraception, illicit affairs and unwanted pregnancies, the discovery of newborn babies which had been abandoned was no unusual occurrence, least of all in a predominantly Catholic Ireland.

Information was given to William Lobdell of Athenry, Ireland, that a child had been buried alive near the town in March 1820, by its 'unnatural parent.' Being an active magistrate, accompanied by the Reverend F. Pendergast he immediately repaired to the spot and, from a faint cry, they were fully convinced of the truth of the matter. The unfortunate child was placed under an old ditch, the upper part of which the cruel mother had thrown down on it for covering, thinking it would be instantly smothered. Fearing detection, she ran away, leaving the poor innocent slightly covered with earth. Fortunately, not long afterwards, a person coming that way was drawn towards the infant's cries. It was he who gave the information and brought the two men to witness the scene. The baby was instantly removed from its intended grave, where it had been consigned totally naked. It was incredible that the babe was unharmed. The child was found to be a female of about fourteen days old, who had been baptised that very day by Reverend Pendergast, who recognised it and gave the name and description of the mother. A diligent search was made and towards evening she was found and taken back to town where the woman acknowledged her guilt. She was committed to the County Gaol in Galway the next day by Mr Lobdell who, at the same time, humanely ordered every necessary requisite for the infant, which was said to be likely to do well.

A similar report, yet without repercussions for the mother, was discovered on 3 May 1870, when a patient of Greatham Hospital, near Hartlepool, was walking in a field. He suddenly stepped on a small mound of newly turned earth and heard a child's cry proceeding from it. Removing the soil, he discovered a female child of a few months old, decently dressed but bleeding from the nose and mouth, no doubt caused by the pressure from the man's foot. He promptly conveyed the little one into the village where a local surgeon saved its life. The police were also sent for, and an active search was made for clues as to the identity of the guilty person or parties. The event caused great excitement in Greatham village, but the identity of the child's mother was never discovered.

Of course, not all child burials bore murderous intentions. In January 1871, Mr Price, coroner for Salford, held an inquest at the Duke of Lancaster public house, located near the town hall, concerning the death of Mary Josephina Kate Mounslow Tarbuck, a child of seven-months-old, which was nearly buried alive along with the corpse of her father, at the Salford Cemetery. Witness Rebecca Butterworth stated that she was a widow and resided at Wimpole Street, Ashton-under-Lyne, and had attended the wife of the late Joseph Tarbuck for a week after her confinement following the birth of Mary. She commented that the baby was very delicate. On the Tuesday, Mrs Tarbuck sent for Mrs Butterworth a second time and asked if she could procure a nurse for her baby. Mrs Butterworth replied that she would ask her daughter, Mary Ann Pennington, to take it. The latter consented to do so, and the baby was taken to her house. The evening of the next day, being Wednesday, Joseph Tarbuck died.

The witness said that she did not see baby Mary again until the Saturday, when she was at the Tarbucks' house making arrangements for Joseph's funeral. Her daughter sent a messenger, who said that the baby was in a fearful way, and that Mrs Butterworth was needed immediately. She proceeded to her daughter's house and found the child very ill. Mr T. Cooke, surgeon, was sent for. He stated that nothing could be done for little Mary and that she was dying. Mr Cooke stayed for about half an hour, during which time Mrs Butterworth asked him if, in the event of the child dying shortly, it could be buried with its father, whose funeral was to take place that day. He replied that it would be rather quick, but he would leave them to make their own arrangements. Someone mentioned that it would save a deal of expense to have the child buried together with Mr Tarbuck. Mrs Butterworth then went and consulted Mrs Tarbuck on the subject, who agreed that it would be wise to have a joint funeral and, that if her husband could speak, he would only be too glad to take the baby with him.

About one o'clock the child's breathing became very heavy, and ultimately it ceased altogether. The witness thought it was dead and loosened its clothes. She felt Mary's chest, which was as cold as if it had been dead a week. Mrs Butterworth washed the baby, put on clean clothes, and took it to Mrs Tarbuck. In the meantime, Mrs Butterworth had instructed a young woman to go to Mr Cooke to obtain a certificate of death, which was taken to the registrar and a burial order obtained. The latter was given to Mr Booth, the undertaker, who unscrewed the lid of Joseph Tarbuck's coffin and placed the child inside. Several people saw the baby before she was placed with her father about five minutes past two in the afternoon. The funeral cortege left for Salford about twenty minutes later, with everyone perfectly satisfied that Mary was dead.

In court, Jane Waterhouse, residing in Newton Street, Ashton, said that she was at Mrs Pennington's house on the Saturday and saw the child. She corroborated the evidence given by Mrs Butterworth and said she had no doubt that the baby was dead. However, she also said that Mrs Pennington had told her on the following Monday that she had given the child the 'rinsings' of a laudanum bottle on the Friday afternoon, the day before it died.

Mary Ann Pennington told Coroner Price that, at the suggestion of her mother, she took the deceased child in to nurse at one shilling per day. When she received Mary, she found the skin to be raw on her neck and other parts of the body. Its clothing was dirty, and she felt that it had not been attended to as it ought to have been. She fed the child with milk, bread and sugar but on the Friday afternoon the infant became very restless. Mrs Pennington confessed that some months before she had obtained a bottle of laudanum for her mother's toothache and when the baby became cross, she put some warm water into the empty bottle and gave it to her. On the Sunday night, Mrs Pennington remembered giving the baby some laudanum and informed the Chief Constable, telling him she had thrown the empty bottle into the ashpit the previous day.

Mr Booth, the undertaker, stated that the funeral cortege arrived at Salford Cemetery at about quarter-past four in the afternoon. He immediately went to the registrar's office to conclude some business connected with the interment and, when he returned to the chapel, he found a couple of people unscrewing the lid of the coffin. The child was found to be alive, in exactly the same position as it had been placed inside the coffin. Mr Hamilton, surgeon, was called into attendance and was under the impression that the child was labouring from exposure to the cold. However, his treatment having no effect, he realised that it might be suffering from poisoning and altered the medication, administering warm coffee and cordial, trying to rouse the child, but sadly Mary gradually sank and died later that afternoon. He made a post-mortem examination the following day and found the baby's brain to be healthy. In his opinion the cause of death was debility. The jury returned a verdict of death from natural causes but expressed their disapprobation of the indecent haste manifested by Mrs Butterworth to have the child buried, and of the conduct of Mrs Pennington in administering laudanum without informing the doctor.

Misdiagnosis of death was also becoming commonplace across the Atlantic. Mr and Mrs William Sperinfogle, living on Fetter Avenue, Louisville, Kentucky, were taking their two-year-old child to the St. Louis cemetery for interment on 26 January 1887, when they were startled by peculiar noises issuing from the coffin. At first the parents were dumbfounded, but the father placed his ear against the coffin lid and heard the cries of what he thought to be his dead child. He tried in vain to force open the coffin lid, so placed it on his shoulders and hurried to a neighbouring grocery store, where he took up a hatchet and burst the lid. With outstretched arms and the faintest of cries, the child held its tiny arms out to him. The infant was taken back home and although very ill, was said not to be beyond the hope of recovery. The strangest feature of this case is that the child was supposed to have died early the day before when a physician pronounced it dead. Since the moment of its demise the body had been closely watched by the grief-stricken parents and no sign of life was evident. The child was icy cold and was as stiff as a corpse. There were no signs of breathing, and the eyes were set 'as if in death.' Several doctors, attracted to the case by its peculiarity, seemed to think that the youngster was in a trance. The funeral procession was near the cemetery, and if the cries of the child had not been heard so timely it would have been buried within a few minutes. The attending friends gathered around the now joyous parents and the funeral cortege was turned back.

In 1901, while friends and relatives of Mr and Mr C. Harrington of Orange, near El Paso in Texas, United States, were assembled to attend the burial of a 2-month-old child which had been declared dead, the baby moved in her tiny coffin. The mourners were immediately dismissed. Apparently, after the child had been certified as deceased by physicians, she had been prepared for burial, but it was postponed for three days owing to Mrs Harrington suffering from shock. Thankfully, this was enough time for the baby to come round from its coma. After the incident, the child was pronounced out of danger. The coffin was sent back to the undertaker and the period of mourning gave way to one of joy.

While temporarily insane as the result of the birth of an illegitimate child, Katie Busch, a nineteen-year-old Polish girl, buried her newborn baby alive in the barnyard near her home at Franklin, United States, in July 1904, causing its death. Coroner Hoye, who went to Franklin to investigate the report of infanticide, returned to Seattle with the girl who was placed under supervision in Providence Hospital. The intention was to charge her with the child's murder. Katie admitted the birth of the baby but claimed not to remember anything that happened on the day of its death. She was the step-sister of Stanley Smith, a coal miner, and lived with him and his wife. The case was placed in the hands of prosecuting Attorney Scott, who considered releasing Busch from custody in view of the strong evidence that she was not mentally responsible for her unnatural crime.

Katie was reported to have been acting strangely for several days prior to the birth of the child. On the Tuesday morning she left the house and was gone nearly half an hour. On her return, the young woman refused to explain her actions. Mrs. Smith then went out to investigate. Her attention was attracted immediately by the barking of a dog over a little mound of fresh earth at the back of the barn. Probing around in the dirt she found the baby, which was still alive. Horrified at what she had seen, Mrs. Smith ran back into the house and asked Katie what she had done but the woman denied that the child was hers. Mrs. Smith then ran to the mine and fetched her husband to the scene. The pair carried the baby into the house and summoned Dr. McCormick, the mining company's surgeon, who worked on the dying baby but could not resuscitate it.

Three years earlier Stanley Smith, the girl's step-brother, was living at Scranton, Pennsylvania, and sent for Katie to emigrate to America. She refused to travel at the time and Smith moved west to Franklin. A year later Katie Busch left Poland and landed in New York, although she was alone and drifted from place to place for the next couple of years. In the meantime, Smith had written to relatives in Poland and found out that the girl was in New York. Stanley immediately communicated with her, and she arrived in Franklin four months before the birth of her child. Katie spoke little English and was said to be laying in the hospital in a stupor, from which she only roused to answer questions. She was described as pretty and innocent looking. What Kaite did manage to tell authorities was that the father of the baby was a man who ran a tailor shop in New York. She was employed by him for some time but claimed not to know his name. Coroner Hoye said he believed that she really was ignorant of it, and the nature of the crime did indeed show a great deal of naivety.

In rare instances, the false declaration of a child being pronounced dead put a fear into those tasked with the burial of minors, which is exactly what happened when a child named Willie Allsop was about to be buried at South Normanton. Four days after his supposed death in April 1905, signs of life were detected, but sadly the efforts of doctors to restore life failed. A final examination was made the following day to decide if the child was really dead, and the interment subsequently took place at Selston Church. Before the funeral, however, the vicar of Selston had the coffin reopened to make certain that Willie really was deceased.

Murder charges for infanticide were no uncommon scenario at the turn of the twentieth century. Mary Aiken, who was confined in the county jail at Carlsbad, United States, on a charge of murder in the second degree, signed a confession that she buried her child alive on the night of 7 January 1906. She did not show any emotion when telling of the horrible crime and gave the reason that her husband had deserted her and she could therefore no longer afford to support the infant. Aiken also said that neighbours taunted her because her husband had left her. The grand jury at Carlsbad indicted Aiken on a charge of murder in the first degree and returned a 'no' bill in the case of Arthur Aiken, her husband. Arthur deserted Mary three weeks before the crime was committed and was arrested at the home of his father at Gate, Oklahoma. Mary Aiken claimed that a stranger had taken her child but the next day it was found by neighbours near the house in a roughly made grave. When disinterred, the hand of the seven-month-old boy was clutched to a mesquite root. When arrested and shown the hand of her child, the woman did not wince and claimed innocence until later when she gave a written confession. Mary Aiken did not explain why she did not kill the baby before burying it. She was described as thirty years of age, attractive and stylish. Aiken was tried and the verdict of insanity was recorded, with her being sent to the territorial insane asylum.

The corpse of a baby but a few days old was exhumed from the grave at noon on 15 September 1910, at Pierce County, Nebraska, United States. The child, belonging to the Georgii family, had died on the previous Monday, and was buried without a doctor's certificate and was not taken to an undertaker. The case immediately aroused suspicion in the neighbourhood. Gossip became so strong that information was sent into Coroner Macy, who went to Pierce to have the body removed from the grave. The baby's corpse was in a perfect state and there were unmistakable signs that the infant was buried alive. The doctor attending to the baby in its 'last hours' was placed under arrest.

Sadly, some cases of child cruelty also involved the recipient of abuse being interred whilst still alive. In November 1912, the father of a seven-year-old boy at Kiyosu, Japan, punished him for disobedience by burying the boy in a hole for twenty-four hours, leaving only his head above the surface. It took four men to dig him out. Thankfully, the boy survived and the father was taken before magistrates to answer for his actions.

The mother of an illegitimate child, following an ancient German superstition from heathen times, deliberately buried her baby alive near Oppein, Germany, in December 1922. Those who believed in the old ritual did not believe it a crime to do away with a child born out of wedlock, provided the baby was buried by moonlight in a cemetery. The superstition was that the shadow of a cross, thrown by the moon, must fall over the body of the infant as it was lowered into its grave. Consequently, Apollonta Poser, a simple woman from Oppein, acted when she found herself burdened with a 6-week-old child and carried out the ancient burial rite. Seeking the body of her child, the police discovered the bodies of three other babies buried behind the same cross where the moon cast its shadow each month. The strong supposition was that these children were done away with in accordance with the same beliefs.

A black mother who buried her 6-week-old daughter alive in 1950 was sentenced to ten years in prison. Fortunately, the baby survived the ordeal, having been rescued from an untimely grave before death occurred. The defendant, Gracie Lee White, pleaded guilty to murder and her sentence was imposed on 6 March by Superior Court Judge Lee Carr of Burlington, United States. The child, 4 months old at the time of the trial, was rescued six hours after she was buried in a two-foot grave. Gracie showed police officers where the grave was after an older child told investigators she saw Miss White taking the crying baby to the woodshed and place her in a grave. The child was found in a covered hole at the home of Grace White's parents and was turned over to the Vance County welfare department for adoption under court order.

One of the most bizarre cases of children being incarcerated underground was that of the 1976 abduction of a school bus driver and twenty-six children, aged five to fourteen, in Chowchilla, California. Kidnappers demanded a huge ransom of $5 million after hijacking the bus and holding their captives in a box truck buried in a quarry in Livermore. Thankfully, those imprisoned were tough and after sixteen hours underground they managed to dig themselves out. Everyone survived. The quarry owner's son and two of his friends were eventually convicted of the crime (see top right image on page 4 of the plate section), each receiving a life sentence. Frederick Newhall Woods, instigator of the crime was repeatedly denied parole until August 2022 when, at the age of seventy, he was granted full parole. The other two convicted men were James and Richard Schoenfeld, aged twenty-four and twenty-two respectively at the time of the kidnapping, were paroled in 2015 and 2012.

A more recent case of a child cruelty and burial alive happened in Waynesburg, Greene County, United States. In September 2022, social workers were alerted to bruising on the body of John Kaft's daughter and decided to interview the child and her sibling. It was then that they discovered how the girl had been buried alive in a hole in the backyard overnight, which left her smelling like sewage. Kaft's daughter said that it was her father's punishment when he thought that she was lying to him. The children were immediately placed in foster care, while their father faced charges of aggravated assault, strangulation, reckless endangerment, false imprisonment and simple assault (see bottom image on page 4 of the plate section).

Cases of utter medical negligence involving children have also resulted in near loss of life, such as that of a baby girl who was born to Shamemma Begum in Bankoot village, India in May 2022. Jammu Hospital staff were quick to pronounce the child as stillborn and prepared it for local burial in a cemetery. However, residents in the area protested and insisted that the baby be taken to a traditional ancestral site. The family duly dug up the little girl and found her to be still breathing. Two hospital employees in the gynaecological department were duly suspended. Sadly, further reports from India show a trend owing to deeprooted superstitions. Another baby, named Radhika suffered from acute malnutrition when her father and uncle tried to bury her alive in May 2012. Apparently, the chid was being used as a sacrifice to protect the health of the family's other children. Thanks to vigilant locals, the little girl was rescued and received treatment at Meerut Hospital in Uttar Pradesh State, fifty miles east of Delhi.

Chapter Six

Cases from War

Cases of war victims being buried alive have been recorded during many conflicts, some instances being reported as a means of torture to enemy soldiers, others purely accidental when injured fighters were mistakenly thrown in with dead comrades in hastily dug graves.

One of the worst periods of bloody repression in Vietnam took place between 1857 and 1862 during the reign of the Annamese Emperor Tu Duc, who was violently anti-Catholic, despite the fact that his father had won his throne with the help of a French missionary, Bishop Pierre Joseph Pigneaux. From the onset, Tu Duc's reign was plagued with trouble. In the summer of 1849, just one year after the new emperor's coronation, a cholera epidemic struck Vietnam and Cambodia, in which over 600,000 lost their lives. This was followed by a plague of locusts which ravaged crops in Son Tay and Bac Ninh provinces in 1854. Continuing to follow in the footsteps of his ancestors, Tu Doc refused to allow Vietnam to be exposed to the outside world, oppressing foreigners living there and raising conflicting policies with Europe. During those years 10,000 Catholics were imprisoned, with over five thousand of them dying for their faith. Some had a court trial, after which their heads were cut off, while others were burned to death, buried alive or drowned. There were also 117 foreign missionaries and 100 nuns murdered and 115 Vietnamese priests martyred, which amounted to one-third of the native clergy of Annam. The persecution was only brought to a close when French armed forces intervened.

Not long afterwards, rebellion was raging in China. The following interesting extract from a letter of Dr Charles M. Scott, dated 3 September 1863, was sent from Swatow, Double Island (now Shantou, Guangdong Province):

Swatow is the most lawless part of China. The people here have little or no respect for mandarins, or even Europeans. Many attacks have been made upon the houses of Europeans, and, though no one has ever been killed, they have been very much frightened; so much so that now in all houses you find no end of revolvers and guns always ready for use. But things are much more quiet now than formerly. At present one village goes out to fight against another.

He continues,

> A new mandarin was sent here a few months ago from Canton, to see what he could do to put down the disturbers of the peace. He was given unlimited powers of life and death, which he has been using in the most fearful way, but with great success. One of his modes of punishment is burying people alive with their heads down and their feet sticking out of the ground. They dig a number of holes in the ground, then lash the unfortunate man to a stick and put him in head foremost, and then fill in the earth, leaving the feet over ground. I have seen a row of such feet sticking up out of the ground. There are other modes of punishment too terrible to be told, which those people who have a morbid taste for such horrors can see every day in the week.

In another harrowing report from the Far East in 1900, the persecution of Catholic missionaries in China highlighted a period of upheaval in society with many members of the Church laying down their lives for their faith. A few non-Catholic Europeans perished in the tumult instigated by the Imperial authorities, but the heaviest blows fell in terrible succession on Catholic bishops, priests and their native converts. One Belgian priest, Father Joseph De St. Nicholas, after undergoing many tortures, suffered a most cruel martyrdom, by being buried alive by his relentless persecutors on 24 July by order of the Sub-Prefect of Lan Pin Hsien.

The following year, in 1901, shocking details came from the Schent Fathers mission in Mongolia. In the eastern vicariate six residences, fifty-five Christian villages, several oratories, fifty schools and four orphanages were destroyed. Father Seghers was buried alive by order of the Mandarin and hundreds of Christians were slaughtered at Sa-Hu. In the central areas, Fathers Heirman and Mollet were slain, it was said cut into pieces, before a tribunal, and three other missionaries were burned to death by Chinese soldiers at Hupa. In the south of the region, Bishop Hamer, after an apostolate of thirty-five years, was cruelly tortured and burned alive, with one of his fellow priests being thrown into the Yellow River. Fifteen missionaries managed to escape by taking forty-two days to cross the Gobi desert, finally reaching the Russian Trans-Siberian railway.

A much more uplifting case was that of George Coleman, an eighteen-year-old from Chicago, who ran away from school to go to war, and was laid out for dead in a military morgue near Manila in the Philippines the year after and came close to being buried alive. His name was entered upon the death roll in the War Department in Washington, but young Coleman was very much alive. George died, to all appearances, of typhoid fever and was removed from the hospital to the morgue. After placing the young soldier in a coffin in preparation for burial, an army surgeon suddenly discovered a spark of life in the young man's body. In their excitement the doctors must have used drastic measures to resuscitate Coleman, for they burned the flesh off his knees and ankles to the bone, presumably with electricity. The joints were left stiff, and the otherwise stalwart boy thereafter hobbled about with the use of a cane and was crippled for life.

Coleman ran away during the summer of 1898. He was then sixteen years of age but so large in build that the recruiting officers accepted him into the United States service without question. Young Coleman made his way from Chicago to Fort Snelling during the organisation of the Forty-Fifth Regiment, US Infantry, by Colonel Dorst. He was assigned to 'A Company' and travelled with the unit when it moved to San Francisco and later to the Philippines. George remained in good health until after a march of forty-eight miles, which he made with his company to meet a provision train that had been sent out of Manila for the relief of the regiment. His shoes had worn out and Coleman wore a pair of native slippers during the long trek. These were so thin that they afforded little protection. One night after their arrival, Coleman fell sick and went to his bunk and later lost his mind completely. Like many who return after reaching death's door, the young soldier had no story to relate of strange visions, but only the information that the doctors and morgue keeper related to him. The following is George Coleman's own account:

They could have buried me alive, and I never would have known it. I did not know how close they had taken me to the grave until a week after I was returned from the slab to the hospital. Then I opened my eyes with a feeling that I had been asleep. The doctor who had pronounced me dead told me the story afterward, when most of the fever had left me and I was quite myself again. He said that after passing through a night at a very high temperature my heart apparently stopped beating. He pronounced me dead and they lugged me off to the morgue, which was a small building convenient to the hospital, where many poor fellows die. A cloth was tied around my head and jaw, to keep my mouth closed and prevent small insects from crawling in. They left me on the slab all that day and night. Next morning, I was lifted into a pine coffin.

A guard was there to accompany my body to the grave. The soldiers had their guns with which to fire the regular military salute. It was at this juncture – it makes me shudder now to think of it – that a little spark of life that was left in me signalled to the surgeon bending over my coffin. Hence, I am here today to relate this strange story which other people told me. So far as consciousness was concerned, I was dead at that time and probably I would have passed away without suffering had they buried me. While I was lying in the morgue word was sent to my company that I was dead and in the reports of the lists of death my name was sent on to this country. I don't think my old comrades know I am alive now, as they were transferred during the period of my sickness. October 2nd, 1900, I was carried to Manila and treated there in the hospital until November 1st, when I took the transport to San Francisco. I stayed in the hospital there until I was honourably discharged from the army. Then I came home to surprise the folks.

George Coleman had grown so tall in two years that his father, John, a policeman living at Shields Avenue, Chicago, hardly knew his son when he limped into the house a cripple in March 1901.

Meanwhile, the trial of Cornelius Broeksma, a Dutchman, and formerly Public Prosecutor in Johannesburg, South Africa, began in September 1901 during the Boer War. The charges brought against him were breaking the oath of neutrality, treachery and treason. The President of the Court was Colonel Bull, of the Welsh Regiment. The evidence consisted wholly of documents found in the house of the accused, and included a long, printed pamphlet in Dutch for distribution among the Boers who were fighting. The contents comprised long and repeated comparisons between the War of American Independence and the Boer War, and also falsehoods about the treatment of the inhabitants of refugee camps. It further included elaborate arguments to show that oaths taken to the British authorities were not binding, and also copious abuse of those Boers who had taken office under the British Government, recommending hanging or burying alive as a punishment for them when captured as spies and traitors. The pamphlet also recommended all Boers in the field to take an oath to continue shooting Englishmen as long as God gave them breath.

There's nothing like being prepared and, possessed with the firm belief that he would be killed in battle during the war in the Far East, General Kuropatkin, commander of the Russian forces in Manchuria (see top left image on page 5 of the plate section), insisted upon carrying his coffin into the field with him. The information was contained in a letter received by Adam Bantro, editor of a Polish newspaper, from Brunslau Kobylanski, who returned to Russia from Baltimore, United States, in 1904 and was evidently impressed with the Russian Army. According to Kobylanski the general's casket bore a silver plate with the full name Alexei Nikolayevich Kuropatkin engraved on it. Some time before, General Kuropatkin had a dream that he was killed in a battle and that his body was so badly mangled that he was not identified and was buried in a trench with the privates. This dream was so vivid that when he went to the front, he told family and friends that he would not return alive. The coffin accompaniment to headquarters, the writer said, had a disheartening effect on the troops, but nothing could change the general's mind. However, Kuropatkin's fears were unfounded, as he lived until 1925, dying at his home in Petrograd.

That same year, a telegram from the war correspondent of the *Russkye Slovo* stated that a frontier guard near the Sungari River on the Russia-China border stopped a Chinese funeral as it emerged from a neighbouring village in October 1904. The officer questioned one of the principal mourners, who declared that the corpse was that of a Chinese dignitary. The officer was unconvinced and decided that the coffin must be opened. At this the mourners attempted to escape. Instead of a dead Chinaman the coffin contained a live Japanese spy, who was supposed to have had orders to blow up the Sungari Bridge.

From disclosures made in January 1906, it became evident that many soldiers were buried alive in the burial ground at old Fort Hayes, in the United States, during the cholera epidemic. Coffins were dug up that gave evidence of frightful struggles, some bodies turned over, others having the legs drawn up to the neck, others grasping at their own hair. In the epidemic, health laws required the immediate burial of the victims, and the ghastly discovery indicated that a large number of cholera patients were actually still alive when buried, the medical auxiliaries being in haste to rid the area of supposedly diseased corpses. After the discovery, the bodies were moved to Leavenworth and the fort was abandoned as a military reserve.

On 26 April 1906, the ruling Amir returned to Kabul, Afghanistan, after a prolonged tour. He was accompanied by a British agent. Sirdar Nasrullah Khan, his brother, and Sirdar Inayatullah Kahn, his son, went out to receive him together with all the civil and military officers and salutes were fired as he entered the city. With it being the hour for prayer, the Amir went to the Jama Masjid to offer up his prayers and then proceeded to the Palace. He was greatly concerned to hear of the price of grain in the capital and immediately ordered grain to be issued at cheap rates from the State Granary at Bamain. His Highness expressed his high appreciation of the manner in which Nasrullah Khan had managed affairs of the Government in his absence and held daily meetings to go through cases that had been dealt with during his tour. One of the cases brought forward was one of three muftis, Islamic jurists, who were brought up for trial for taking bribes and maltreating the poor. The Amir gave orders to the Governor that the three men should be buried alive, and the sentence was duly carried out after the Amir's departure to Purwan.

Stories of almost incredible barbarities practised by Arabs and Turks were contained in dispatches received by the Italian Embassy in Washington in

November 1911. In a message from Rome, the Italian Minister of Foreign Affairs described alleged atrocities practised on the Italian wounded, which included crucifixion and burial alive. Women, it was said, took part in the perpetration of the cruelty. The dispatch, signed by Signor San Gulliano, read:

> Near the mosque of Hani, where the medical post of the Twenty-Seventh Battalion of Bersaglieri had been located, and in its vicinity, 28 bodies of our soldiers were found. They were horribly mutilated, crucified, with their throats cut open, impaled, torn to pieces and dismembered. Among them was the body of a surgeon lieutenant. In the Arab cemetery, near the place where the Fourth Company of Bersaglieri was located, seven bodies of Bersaglieri were discovered. They had been interred alive, with the heads out of the earth. The body of one of them shows that he had been terribly tortured. It showed many shots and dagger wounds. The eyes had been pulled out and threaded and the eyelids sewn to the brows. This body shows terrible spasmodic contractions. Another one had one arm out of the earth, from which the hand had been cut off. A captain's cap has been found and its owner was identified by the corporal, Pasqui, who escaped miraculously after remaining four hours in a ditch. He testified that among the ferocious ill-treating hordes were Turks and women. The military engineer corps took photographs.

The dispatch also confirmed the withdrawal of the Italian troops from Horni. This, it said, was necessary because the Turks had polluted the wells.

The *Revue des deux Mondes*, in its January 1915 edition published an article by Monsieur Pierre Nothomb, in which were reproduced parts of reports laid before a commission appointed by the Belgian Minister of Justice to investigate the violation by German troops of the customs of war and international law. The reports constituted a most terrible indictment of Germany. They gave long lists of acts of violence committed on prisoners, such as the quartering of a wounded French officer of high rank, the burning alive of wounded men, the murder of priests and Red Cross male nurses, the burying of civilians alive, driving women in front of troops about to make an assault, and the killing or torturing of little children. The article recounted the shocking destruction of Louvain, Termonde, Dinaut, and the Ardennes generally, and told of atrocities carried out by the order of high German officers, including one of the emperor's sons. Monsieur Nothomb concluded: 'When German criticism ceases to be blind it will, of necessity, shrink with shame at the open page of this record.'

Monsieur Ludovic Nadaul, a special correspondent for the *Journal*, gave a sensational account of the cruelties committed by the Germans in Poland in July

1915. Farmers were tortured, while soldiers and officers committed outrages on daughters. Several girls drowned themselves to escape. A priest who intervened, was brutally thrashed and buried alive.

A thrilling account of the battle of Neuve Chapelle was received by Mrs George Tansley of Woburn, in April 1915, from her brother, Sergeant A. Drage, who was in the 2nd Northamptonshire Regiment and described himself as 'one of the lucky ones.' Part of his letter home reads:

> You could see the earth heaving with Germans buried alive, so my men started to dig them out! The first one was an officer, and when we got him out he tapped me on the shoulder and also the man that dug him out. He gave him a gold watch and then he gave me a silver watch, which I am keeping as a souvenir. After that we received an order to retire, but only to take up another position and deliver a counterattack on the Germans. Another of their regiments got practically annihilated, so that gave us good heart, but still not a man of the old 'steelbacks' funked, and off we went, trampling over wounded Germans and our own comrades as well. We could not stop them, but when the first halt came, we lay at full length, not knowing when our turn would come.

On 12 June, during the Verdun battles of 1916, one hundred men, comprising the last remnant of a French company, were waiting in their trench for the order to go over the top toward Duoaumont, north-eastern France, where a German artillery regiment was stationed. The French soldiers had been ordered to stand ready. Their guns were poised, bayonets fixed and held upward, each soldier ready to spring at the word of command. The field through which the trench ran was being churned up with German shells. Overhead, daring the rain of shrapnel from the German artillery, flew American aviator Gordon Rand, son of the wealthy New York banker George Rand. As the young American hovered over the trench, ready to guide the attacking company to its objective, he saw the ground below heave suddenly in one mighty surge. Before he could warn the men below, the two sides of the trench rolled together, completely engulfing the hundred soldiers between them.

There had not been time for the men to throw up their arms, or even to cry out, so sudden was the catastrophe. Not one of those hundred soldiers escaped, each remaining upright with the tip of their bayonet protruding through the ground. The American pilot dipped his plane but knew the regiment was beyond help and flew back behind allied lines to await orders.

That night in his hangar, the pilot drew a cheque upon his French bankers for 500,000 Francs and sent it to General Headquarters with the request that the money be turned over to the proper agency to ensure the erection of a lasting memorial to the soldiers who had been wiped out so completely and suddenly. GHQ had not even heard of the incident. Nobody had witnessed it except for the pilot and no officer had survived to make a report, only the battalion major had reported that one hundred men were 'missing in action.' The cheque remained in the hands of the society in Paris until after the armistice, when investigation disclosed that pilot Gordon Rand had been killed in a flight over Verdun.

From Rand's closest companions in his squadron, members of the society learned of the horror of which the pilot had spoken after seeing the regiment buried alive and why he wished to commemorate it. A commission was then sent to the vicinity of Duoaumont to search for verification of the story. It was a dramatic moment when the investigators suddenly came across a straight line of gun barrels, bayonets pointing upwards, protruding from the ground.

Rand's relatives were sought in New York and, although his estate had already been divided among heirs, it was agreed that the cheque should be cashed in order to fulfil Gordon's wishes for a memorial. Monsieur Andre Ventre, an eminent French architect, was engaged by the society and it was eventually decided that a monument should be erected over the very spot where the hundred skeletons still stood, forever 'Ready for the Charge.' The ground was to be permanently preserved, with a marble slab placed above the site. Sadly, only thirty of the hundred were identified, and their names were engraved on an imposing cross to mark the place where an American watched from above as a trench engulfed a regiment of brave soldiers.

In May 1917, it was reported from Berne that the Austrian losses amounted to 35,000 killed, wounded and missing. The casualties were caused by the deadly effects of the heavy artillery which bombarded the trenches and dug-outs, many of which collapsed, burying the occupants. In one huge cavern a whole battalion was buried alive.

Later that year an official report on Austro-Hungarian atrocities was made by Professor R.A. Reiss of the Swiss University of Lausanne. The crimes were verified by the professor himself and were backed up by indisputable evidence, with actual photographs of the horribly mutilated bodies of the victims. According to Reiss, when the Austro-German armies hacked their way through Serbia, they went not only with the intention of defeating the Serbian army, but with the further purpose of largely exterminating the Serbian nation. They used explosive bullets, burned down houses and pillaged stores, homes and banks. But worst of all they made war upon the civilian inhabitants. It made no difference whether the age was three or ninety-three. Here are some of the forms of death and torture that were meted out to the unfortunate Serbs quoted directly from Professor Reiss:

Victims shot, bayonetted to death, killed with knives, arms lopped off, torn off or broken, legs broken, noses cut off, ears cut off, eyes put out, victims stoned, women violated and killed, breasts cut off, persons hanged, victims burned alive or buried alive, one child thrown to pigs, victims clubbed to death with rifle, victims impaled upon stakes, victims whose skin was cut in strips.

Professor Reiss went further. He gave the statistical tables showing the kinds of death and mutilation that were suffered by the victims in three Serb districts. Thus, thirty-five men and ninety-six women were buried alive. Thirty men and thirty-eight women had their eyes gouged out. And so on in sickening detail. He told of a massacre at Leshnitza where the Austrians executed one hundred civilians between eight and eighty years of age. They were taken to a spot where a pit had been prepared. The people were pinioned together, and a volley was fired at them. Everybody fell into the pit which was immediately filled with earth without any trouble being taken to see whether any of the victims were still alive. Professor Reiss had the pit opened. He found some of the bodies still pinioned. From the positions of some he could see they had been alive when buried and that they had struggled against smothering to death. He estimated that at least half of the party had perished in this way. Reiss said that the Austro-Hungarians tried to defend their actions by saying that their troops were in many instances shot by guerillas.

However, to quote the professor: 'Among the victims tabulated there are eighty-two children under ten, eight of whom were not even one year old, there are three hundred and six women, and a very large number of old men over sixty. It is impossible to suppose that babes of two and three months or old men of ninety-five should be francs-tireurs.'

The report gave a list of some hundreds of men and women victims of the Austrians whom he personally interviewed and whose wounds he examined. He also told of an incident that was never published in Great Britain. According to Reiss, in the early days of the invasion of Serbia, the Austrians shelled Belgrade, the capital. The Russian and British legations were hit by Austrian shells although the American and Spanish flags were hoisted above them. In other words, long before America was to war with Austria, that nation had fired upon the United States flag.

The *Petit Parisien* published shocking details brought to light by an inquiry into the Armenian massacres of 1918 to 1919, which established that the victims of Turkish brutality numbered no fewer than a million and a half. The newspaper gave an account of numerous atrocities, a particularly horrible case being that in which two thousand women who were suspected of having concealed their jewellery by swallowing it were saturated with petrol and burnt, the cinders being passed through a sieve in order that the avaricious Turks might recover the jewels. At one place seven thousand children perished from hunger, and one hundred women were beaten and thrown half-dead into ditches which they themselves had been made to dig. At Erzerum twenty children were buried alive. German officers caused the massacre of fifteen hundred persons at Keman. The *Petit Parisien's* correspondent demanded the hanging of Talaat Pasha, Enver Pasha, and Djemal Pasha, as well as the German General Liman von Sanders, who were all, he declared, responsible for the horrors.

Indisputable evidence of the massacre of more than two thousand civilians by the Russian Bolsheviks was reported by American Red Cross agents in May 1919. Dr Rudolph Teusler, returning from Perm, in the Osa district, claimed that there had been approximately 500 killed at Osa and 1,500 in the surrounding districts. In addition to securing verbal and documentary evidence, the Red Cross officials witnessed the exhumation of scores of victims from trenches, where they were buried sometimes several deep in graves revealed by the digging of dogs. The murders were without provocation and the victims were largely of the intelligent classes or servants of the church, which the Bolsheviks had announced it their intention to destroy. The evidence disclosed almost unthinkable atrocities.

A man was shot simply because he lived in a brick house. All attorneys and jurists were killed, and doctors, whose services were not required at the time, were disposed of in a similar manner. A woman whose husband and two sons were seized, applied to the commissar for information as to their fate and was told that they had been taken to Perm. After repeating her visit several times, she was told that if she bothered the commissar again, she would be shot.

Apparently, the Soviet officers called a meeting and prepared lists of those to die. The houses proscribed were visited by squads, the doors smashed in, and the victims dragged to the edge of town where they were forced to dig their own graves. Those who resisted were shot in the street. A survivor testified that he had seen men thrown into a pit and buried alive. This testimony was confirmed by bodies exhumed, the clenched hands of the corpses clinging to the mud at the bottom of the pit. The only spark of humanity discoverable was that in confiscating the belongings of the residents. In some instances where there was a family with small children, they were permitted to retain one cow. Occasionally a peasant was allowed to keep his worst horse. The Bolshevik attitude toward the church was uncompromising. Priests were hunted unmercifully. The evidence showed that men were slain whose only offence was that they worked as sextons or caretakers of churches.

The effects on an individual of enduring premature burial could have a profound effect on their mental well-being. One such case was that of Frederick

Green, aged thirty-eight, who was charged with obtaining money by false pretences and was placed on remand at Westminster in August 1923. It was stated that Green, a temporary clerk and messenger at the War Office, had been blown up by a shell and buried alive during the war. He had represented himself as an inspector of meat, and called on traders, pretending that he was authorised to invite tenders for contracts. He obtained a few pounds by asking for fees and tips and by other means. Green's plea after arrest was that he hardly knew what he was about, as he had taken a quantity of drink to overcome his shell-shock and depression. The Magistrate said that Frederick appeared in a terrible state when first brought before the court, and one could not help feeling sorry for a man who had undergone such an ordeal during the war. The judge reasoned that Green had punished himself by the loss of a good situation and character, and stated that a lenient course would be taken in binding him over for judgment.

In December of the same year, an official report on Austro-Hungarian atrocities was made by Professor R.A. Reiss of the Swiss University of Lausanne. Copies were sent to the US State Department. According to the verified evidence, when Austro-German armies hacked their way through Serbia, they went not only with the intention of defeating the Serb Army, but with the further purpose of largely exterminating the Serbian nation. They used explosive bullets, burned down houses and pillaged everything from stores and homes to banks. Worst of all, they made war upon the civilian inhabitants, regardless of age. Here are some of the forms of death meted out, quoted directly from Professor Reiss:

Victims shot, bayonetted to death, killed with knives, arms lopped off, torn off or broken, legs broken, nose cut off, ears cut off, eyes put out, victims stoned, women violated and killed, breasts cut off, persons hanged, victims burned alive or buried alive, one child thrown to pigs, victims clubbed to death with rifle, victims impaled upon stakes, victims whose skin was cut into strips.

Professor Reiss went on further. He gave statistical tables showing the kinds of death and mutilation that were suffered by the victims in three Serb districts. Thus, thirty-five men and ninety-six women were buried alive. Thirty men and thirty-eight women had their eyes gouged out. He told of a massacre at Leshnitza where the Austrians executed one hundred civilians between 8 and eighty years of age. They were taken to a spot where a pit had been prepared. The people were pinioned together, and a volley was fired at them. Everybody fell into the pit which was immediately filled with earth without any trouble being taken to see whether any of the victims were still alive. Professor Reiss had the pit opened. He found some of the bodies still pinioned. From the positions of some he could see they had been alive when buried and that they struggled against smothering to death. He estimated that at least half of the party had perished in this way.

At a meeting of the Society for the Prevention of Premature Burial at Caxton Hall, in July 1930, Major Reginald Austin stated that, 'I am of the opinion that many soldiers were buried alive during the war.' He cited the story of an Irish soldier who, while carrying out burial operations, approached his superior officer in a state of agitation. 'Sor,' he exclaimed, tremblingly, 'that German soldier says he is not dead.' 'Go back,' said the officer, who was also an Irishman, 'and tell him he's a liar.' Examination proved, however, that the soldier was indeed still alive.

In 1946, Majlech Elencwajg, a Displaced Person from Radom, Poland (see top right image on page 5 of the plate section), became a medical student at the University of Marburg in Germany, by grace of an UNRRA scholarship and freak of fate. According to a dispatch from UNRRA'S Central Headquarters in Germany, where they took care of 850,000 'Displaced Persons', the youth was executed in 1944 by a Nazi firing squad and was then buried under a thin layer of dirt. The bullet, however, had glanced off his skull and did no more than knock Majlech out temporarily. Regaining consciousness, he dug himself out of the grave and was concealed by other prisoners until the SS guards changed shift and he was able to resume his role of just another prisoner. In 1946, together with some other 90 DPs to whose rehabilitation UNRRA pledged, Elencwajg was working hard at the university. He was a man with a future in medicine, and a bullet scar on his forehead as a grim reminder of the past.

According to a report in the official Communist newspaper, *Peking People's Daily*, in June 1954, twenty counter-revolutionaries were executed in China and thirty others jailed after trials in Hubei Province. Those executed had formed a murderous gang who, during Nationalist rule in China, buried alive nineteen Communist Party leaders. The gang had been secretly re-formed by Han Yu Shu in 1950 and infested the areas of Peking (now Beijing) and Tientsin (Tianjin) pillaging seventeen different districts. Among those jailed were members of the 'Hopei Anti-Communist National Construction Army' led by Yank Ping Li, a former Nationalist Army Commander who had plotted a riot. Some elements of the gang had even infiltrated Communist ranks.

One of the longest and bloodiest battles of the Vietnam War was that of Hue. It began on 31 January 1968, and lasted for twenty-six days. During the months and years that followed, dozens of mass graves were uncovered in and around the Hue district. Victims included men, women and children, with an estimated death toll amounting to between 3,000 and 6,000 civilians and prisoners of war. The mass murders were perpetrated by the Viet Cong

(VC) and the People's Army of Vietnam (PAVN) during their capture of the Hue city during the Tet Offensive. Victims were found bound, tortured, and sometimes buried alive. The killings were part of a purge of the social stratum, which included anyone friendly with American forces in the region. Many foreign professors, missionaries and doctors were also victims of the atrocities. Two French priests, Fathers Urbain and Guy, were seen being led away and were executed. Father Urbain's body was found buried alive, bound hand and foot. Father Guy was stripped of his cassock and forced to kneel down on the ground, where he was shot in the back of the head. His corpse was discovered in the same grave as Father Urbain and 18 others. It is evident that these cases were by no means isolated incidents, neither were they confined to foreigners. In his book *The Viet Cong Massacre at Hue*, Dutch Canadian doctor Alje Vennema, recounts numerous murders, such as:

A forty-eight-year-old street vendor, Nguyen Thi Lao, was arrested on the main street. Her body was found at the school. Her arms had been bound and a rag stuffed into her mouth; there were no wounds to the body. She was probably buried alive.

Not all cases of war ended in tragedy. A remarkable incident followed a massive terrorist blast in Beirut, Lebanon, in December 1981, when rescue workers found a man alive after being buried for a week. Mohammed Fleih had managed to survive on a diet of chocolate and minerals in the wrecked kitchen of the Iraqi Embassy. He was said later to have put on seven pounds in weight!

The US Army division that burst through the Iraqi front line in the final days of the Gulf War used tanks and earthmovers to bury thousands of enemy soldiers in their trenches, some of them alive and in the action of firing their weapons, according to a report in September 1991. Colonel Lon Maggart, who led the 1st Brigade in the assault during the first two days of ground fighting told a New York newspaper, 'I know burying people like that sounds pretty nasty, but it would be even nastier if we had to put our troops in the trenches and clean them out with bayonets.'

Several years later, in May 1998, it was reported that Iraq's security forces had buried alive around one hundred detainees the previous month. A statement by the Supreme Council for the Islamic Revolution in Iraq, the country's biggest Shiite Muslim opposition group, said:

A group of detainees in Radwaniyah prison, estimated at about 100 young men, were taken in two big trucks to the Faluja district in Ramadi province in western Iraq. The security members dug a hole with a bulldozer, the detainees were thrown in it, then sand was put on them, and they were buried alive.' However, there was no way to independently confirm the claim by the council, based in neighbouring Iran, a longtime enemy of Saddam Hussein's government. The statement, sent by fax to the Associated Press in Cairo, said the incident took place on the night of 17/18 April. Radwaniyah is around 37.5 miles west of the Iraqi capital of Baghdad. Iraqi opposition groups said that in the past Iraq's security forces, headed by Saddam's younger son Qusai, had executed hundreds of prisoners. Independent human rights groups made similar statements.

Chapter Seven

Ritual & Superstition

T
he annals of Eastern nations furnish abundant examples of people being buried alive under many different circumstances. The practice was employed for the purpose of extinguishing life or maintaining life for a prolonged period without food or drink. A common form of being buried alive was leper burial (jamadh) which was frequently resorted to in India, often at the request or urgent entreaty of the victims of the disease. A pit was dug by relatives and the unfortunate was cast into it and smothered with earth. In some cases, the wretch was burned to death before being thrown into the pit. Opium water was freely drunk by executioners and this cruel rite lingered in Kashmir and some parts of Rajputana until the late 1800s. Lepers were known to commit suicide by jumping into pits in the extremity of their distress. Homicidal burial alive has been used as a means of punishment of crime, torture, revenge, and murder.

All over Europe you find stories of children, maidens, and matrons being buried alive in the foundations of castles and bridges in order that the local spirit might be placated and the building rest on a base which is secure and firm. When human sacrifice ceased, animals were buried instead, horses, dogs, and especially lambs. With a further advance in civilisation, inanimate articles took the place of these unfortunate animals, and documents, coins and newspapers began to be deposited in the cavities of foundation stones. However, centuries ago, in the foundations of cities, city walls, and houses, a human victim was often sacrificed in order that his blood might be used as cement and his soul be built into the very stones of the fabric, after which he became the tutelary deity of the house or city. It was believed that burying a person alive under large-scale structures, such as bridges, dams and castles, would act as a prayer and prevent the building from being destroyed by natural disasters or enemy attack.

The primitive ceremony of laying the foundation of a town or village consisted of killing, burying alive, or building into the wall a human victim and planting a tree close by to commemorate them. In Rome there is not only the legend of the death of Remus, a prince of the blood royal of Alba Longa, connected with the building of the city wall, but there is also the sacred fig tree of Romulus in the Forum, which was held in great veneration. It is also said that to the present-day London preserves her foundation god in the shape of the London

Stone, now enclosed in a railing or iron grill just opposite Cannon Street Station – one of the many relics of paganism in England (see bottom image on page 5 of the plate section). For ages proclamations and other important business was announced from its top, and the defendant in trials in the Lord Mayor's Court was summoned to attend from the London Stone, as though the stone itself spoke to the wrong-doer with the united voice of the assembled citizens.

In a note to Chapter XVI of a translation of the *Koran* it is said that the only occasion on which Ottoman (Sultan of the Turks) ever shed a tear was when his little daughter, whom he was burying alive, wiped the dust of the grave earth from his beard.

It is recorded that during the building of the wall of Copenhagen it sank for a time while still under construction. Then architects took an innocent little girl and set her at a table with toys and food. While she played and ate, masons closed a vault over the top of her. Descriptive of one of those cruel superstitious ceremonies where, in order to make the Castle of Leibenstein fast and impregnable, a child was bought from its mother and walled into the building before her eyes, is part of the *Legend of the Foundation of the Castle of Leibenstein*:

Stern, hoary-headed men stood round, with trowel, plum and line,
To lay the stones of the moveless walls of the Castle of Leibenstein.
And aged priests in their sacred robes were there in princely train
To bless the stones, to appease the gods with a human victim slain.
The little maid, in girlish pride, was lured away from her mother's side
To a sculptured niche in a massive stone, a living grave by workmen hewn,
And as she stood in the narrow cell that fitted size of her body well,
They slowly closed her little door of stone, that opened to her nevermore.

Faithless nuns were so immured in Europe during the middle-ages, and Rider Haggard, writer and adventurer, stated that he saw in the museum at Mexico bodies similarly immured by the Inquisition.

In Borneo a slave girl was crushed to death under the first post of a house. In October 1881, the King of Ashanti put fifty girls to death, that their blood might be mixed with the mud in the repairs of the royal buildings. It is said that Saint Columba consecrated his monastery in the Isle of Staffa in a similar manner. St. Ornan voluntarily became the victim and was forever after honoured as the patron saint of the monastery. In 1885, on the restoration of Holsworthy Church, in Devon, a skeleton with a mass of mortar plastered over the mouth was found embedded in an angle of the building.

The cultural practice of human sacrifice by premature burial was performed throughout East and Southeast Asia. It was known as *hitobashira* in Japan, *da sheng zhuang* in China, *myosade* in Burma and *tumbal proyek* in Indonesia.

An interesting legend in connection with *hitobashira* came to light in the late nineteenth century. In olden times, when the larger part of the present city of Yokohama was marsh and quagmire, it was decided to convert it into cultivatable land, but project after project failed. At length, a man named Yoshida Kambei appeared upon the scene, and he planned a strong dyke, of 21,300 feet in length, to enclose the marsh, his intention being to fill it in with earth brought from a neighbouring hill. His first attempt failed, and the second also, but he did not give up. Kambei tried and failed over and over again, until the eighth time when he called together his friends and employees to have a long consultation on the matter. At length they came to the conclusion that the spirits of the earth and sea were angry at the audacious attempt to build the dam, and to appease them it was necessary to erect a *hitobashira*, or human post. The way they intended carrying this out was by putting a human being into an air-tight box, burying him alive in the marsh, and erecting a post over him.

'But who will be the victim?' was asked. The whole assembly were dumbstruck and shook their heads.

Kambei was willing to offer himself but, if he were buried, there would be no leader to undertake the work, and his death would be no better than the death of a hungry dog (*inujine*, or dog's death, as the Japanese termed it). The miserable contractor was sorely grieved. At this juncture a young woman, O San by name, aged eighteen, stepped into the gathered assembly to the surprise of all, and walking to Kambei's seat, bowed down before him and said,

> My lord, I have been at the back of the assembly, and heard all your consultation. I cannot bear to see you in sorrow, so I offer myself. Make me the victim. I was an orphan child when you were in Mikawa. It is you who saved me and brought me up as your servant. The life I have lived since has been your gift. You are my second father. My own parents gave me birth, and you my life, I am glad to offer it for your sake, and for the good of all. Your sorrow is more painful to me than death, and your joy my heaven. Do not hesitate to bury me but complete your work.

Yoshida Kambei, whose eyes were filled with tears at the noble offer of the maiden, lifted her up by the hand and tried to express his sorrowful thanks. He worshipped her. Then his friends and employees thanked and praised her and told the woman that her name should be sacred to them and their children forever. After the terrible deed was done, the *hitobashira* complete, Kambei erected a shrine in the young woman's honour and named it *O San-no-Muja*.

The earliest archaeological evidence of *da sheng zhuang* in China was discovered during an excavation in Zhengzhou, Henan Province, where the remains of an infant used in the foundation of the Erlitou culture city were found. During the construction of a levee at Dahu Park in Taiwan, it is said that an elderly beggar was buried alive. A temple called *Laogongci* (literally translated from Mandarin as 'this old man') was set up in his honour.

A very unusual story, that of a self-burial which occurred locally, was documented by the *Derby Mercury* on 4 May 1753. A man who lived at the side of a common in Galgate buried himself alive. Having dug his own grave a few months previously, the man told a resident of the area of his intention, whereby the strangeness of the story spread around the area and induced many people to visit the site. Over the weeks the kerfuffle subsided, and people's curiosity waned, until a gentleman who had already seen the grave decided to go back to take a second look in order to show a friend. To their great surprise, they found the old man dead in the hole, wrapped in a blanket with his face downwards. A large wreath of thorns had been laid over him. It was uncertain how long he had been there, but the old man had not been seen for three weeks before he was found. Locals commented that the deceased was a miserable fellow who had always lived like a hermit. At an inquest no evidence of foul play was found.

Some curious facts about the crime of 'Sumadh' or burying alive, as practised in Rajputana, India, were brought to light in 1868, when the Political Agent of Serohi furnished a list of instances in the course of six years that came to his knowledge, chiefly in the neighbourhood of Motagoan, a border village. He also stated that the practice was carried on in the adjoining state of Marwar. Out of nine cases of Sumadh reported, eight of the victims were lepers, the other having been sacrificed at his own desire, on account of old age and poverty. Following the report, the Rao, or King, of Serohi issued a proclamation forbidding the practice of burying people alive, under the penalty of ten years' imprisonment. His Highness tried to do everything he could to enforce the prohibition but there were great difficulties in carrying out the order. In many of the cases the persons who dug the pit and covered up the unfortunate wretch were themselves lepers, and to them death itself was a welcome relief. It was also presumed that the Rao would not actually care to introduce any of these lepers into his prisons due to the nature of their disease!

Lieutenant Colonel Carnell told a story illustrative of the barbarous custom that prevailed on the State of Rajpootana, India, in 1876:

A man named Bhugga, for many years the sufferer of leprosy, having become so wasted and wounded, his fingers and toes even dropping off, that his life was a burden to him, determined to commit *sumadh*. He told his son Bija that when he (the leper) died, no one would touch or bury his body, and that therefore he (the son) was to dig a pit in the jungle. If not permitted to become *sumadh* the leper further threatened to jump into the village well. Under these persuasions the son, assisted by an uncle, dug a pit in the neighbouring jungle, in which the leper sat, and the son and uncle then filled in the earth. No one else was present at the time, but on the way to the pit the leper told several persons of his intentions, and no one interfered to prevent the sacrifice. On inquiry, it appeared the disease was hereditary in the family. The father of Bhugga also committed *sumadh*, and a brother and two daughters also died from leprosy. The son and uncle who dug Bhugga's grave were sentenced to two year's imprisonment with hard labour, and those who heard of his intention without interfering got three months each.

A much earlier article published in the *Oriental Annual* of November 1835, highlights the Indian superstition of burying a woman with her husband, a tradition commonly known as *suttee*:

It is the custom, when a woman of the weaver caste sacrifices herself to the manes of her husband, to descend with his body alive into the grave, which is dug near some sacred river. It is dug very large and deep, and after a number of initiatory rites, as unintelligible as they are fantastical, the widow takes a formal leave of her friends, who are always present upon these melancholy occasions, and descends into the chamber of death. It frequently happens that she is so stupefied with opium as to be scarcely conscious of what she is about but goes through the necessary forms with mere mechanical insensibility. As soon as she reaches the bottom of the pit, to which she descends by a rude ladder, the latter is withdrawn, and she is left alone with the body of her deceased husband, generally in a revolting state of decay. This she embraces, clasping it to her bosom without the slightest expression of disturbance at the effluvia it emits. Having finished her disgusting caresses, she places it upon her lap, and gives the signal for the last act of this shocking scene to commence, which is even more dreadful than immolation upon the funeral pile. The earth is now deliberately thrown upon her, while two persons descend into the grave to trample it tightly round the self-devoted sacrificant. During this tardy but terrible process, the doomed woman sits an unconcerned spectator, occasionally caressing the corpse, and looking with an expression of almost sublime triumph, as the earth embraces her body, at the anticipated honours which await her in the paradise of her god. The hands of her own children are perhaps at that very moment heaping around her the cold dust into which she is soon to be resolved. At length, all but her head is covered, when the pit is hurriedly filled in, and her nearest relatives dance over her inhumed body with those frantic gestures which, whether they betoken ecstasy or madness, it is difficult on witnessing them to decide.

Suttee (from the Sanskrit *sati* meaning good woman or chaste wife) or *sati* (widow burning) whereby a woman would either immolate herself on the funeral pyre of her late husband or in some other way soon after his death, such as being buried alive in the ground next to him (see top image on page 6 of the plate section) is one of the most difficult Indian customs to understand and was the way in which a wife would show her devotion and was upheld by certain Brahman and royal castes. Women were indoctrinated to believe that their destiny lay in committing their lives to their husbands, even after death. The origin is sometimes linked to the myth of the Hindu goddess Sati, who burned herself to death in a fire created by her own Yogic powers after her father deeply insulted her husband, the god Shiva. However, in the original tale, Shiva remains alive and goes on to avenge Sati's death. Numerous *suttee* stones and memorials to the women who died in this way can be found across India, with the earliest dating back to the sixth century. A law amongst Brahmans in Bengal (the Dayabhaga System) which gave inheritance to widows, was thought to have encouraged women to commit *suttee* in order to make their wealth available to other relatives. It became a central issue under the British Raj, who finally outlawed suttee in 1829, although rare instances of it continued to be reported years later.

To get an indication of the scale of this terrible ritual, there was an abstract statement of the number of Hindu widows who were burnt, or buried alive, in the several Zillahs and cities of Bengal etc during the year 1800, from the papers presented to Parliament:

Calcutta 370, Patna 42, Dacca 51, Moorshedabad 21, Bareilly 20, Benares 93.

During the years 1818 to 1819 it was considerably more:

Calcutta 421, Patna 40, Dacca 55, Moorshedabad 25, Bareilly 17, Benares 92.

The total numbers for 1820 and 1821 were 597 and 654 respectively.

The following first-hand account was communicated via *Missionary Intelligence* on 12 January 1814, by Mr Johns, a missionary who had recently returned to England from his posting in India:

On Thursday last (in March 1813) at nine o'clock in the morning, a sick man named Beechanaut was brought by his relatives to the river side, and was laid on the wet mud in expectation of his soon expiring: in this situation he remained, exposed to the scorching rays of the sun, till about four in the afternoon, when he was immersed up to the breast in the river, and whilst in this position one of his relatives vociferated in his ears the names of Hurri, Ram, Krishna, Ram. After some time, on finding that he was not so near death as they had apprehended, he was again replaced on the wet beach.

The next morning (Friday) the same ceremony commenced, of immersing the sick, and repeating the names of their deities: this was continued till five o'clock, when the man expired, being literally murdered by his near relations. It being the custom of this sect (the Yogi) to bury their dead, preparation was made for the interment of the deceased, as also, shocking to relate, of his wife, who was not more than sixteen years of age, she having signified her intention of being buried alive with the dead body of her husband. At six o'clock they repaired to the place of interment, a little way below our bungalow at the water side. At nine I went to the place and found a large concourse of people of both sexes collected: some were employed in digging a circular grave, which when finished was about thirteen or fourteen feet in circumference, and five and a half in depth.

I could scarcely believe that persons in their senses could voluntarily be brought to terminate their existence in such a horrid manner and had suspected that on these occasions something of a narcotic nature was used to deprive the victims of their reason; but on conversing with her I found her free from any such effects. All efforts to dissuade her from the desperate purpose of rushing as a suicide into the presence of her Creator, were unavailing. On asking her mother, who stood by her, how she could divest herself of that feeling which is discernible even amongst the most ferocious inhabitants of the jungle, who risk their own lives to save their offspring? Her reply was, it was her daughter's determination, and what could she do? She was then asked if a person saw his child about to eat some poisonous fruits, would he not use his authority and wrest him from it? Life was given us by God, and we have no right to take it away, but to submit when he calls for it. Remonstrances, however, being ineffectual, I remained a silent spectator of this horrid scene.

The dead body was now placed in a sitting position, at the bottom of the grave: the young woman was then brought forward. She held a small basket having betel leaves in it with one hand, with the other she distributed, during seven circumvolutions about the grave, *koee* (sugar plums) and cowries (shells used for money); all were anxious to catch some of this consecrated donation. The seventh time that she walked round the grave, she stopped, when a Brahmin repeated some words to her. She now lifted up her right hand above her head, with her forefinger erect, she waved it in a circular manner, pronouncing the words *Hurri bole, Hurri bole*, in which the surrounding multitude joined her. She then without any reluctance or dismay descended to the bottom of the grave, placed herself behind the dead body of her husband, her left hand round his waist, the other over her own head, which she reclined between his shoulders. In this position the mother was called (as I supposed) to resign her daughter, or to sanction her conduct, by applying a wisp of lighted straw to the crown of her head for the space of a second or two. The grave was now gradually filled by the bystanders, whilst two men trod the falling earth around the living and the dead, as a gardener does the mould around the newly transplanted tree, and this deliberately proceeded till the earth rose to the surface, leaving the bodies about three feet beneath: when the multitude dispersed.

The late Captain Ebeneezer Chapman Kemp, who in 1816 commanded the *Moira* which sailed to India, related a painful instance of self-immolation which occurred within his own family. A young woman in his service lost her husband and resolved without any hesitation to bury herself alive with the body. Both Captain and Mrs Kemp were shocked to hear of her determination and represented to the woman both the dreadful character of the crime she was about to commit, and the utter uselessness of the sacrifice to the departed spirit of her husband. Sadly, all the arguments and entreaties of Christian principle and feelings of humanity were urged in vain. The woman had been taught to believe that, by voluntarily dying with her husband, she would expedite his transit to the next life and herself bear him company. Every attempt to persuade the infatuated woman to live, whether for the sake of her family, or her own soul, appeared only to cause her to become more resolute to die. Captain Kemp continued his exertions to the last, even while the ceremony was proceeding, but without avail.

When the pit was dug, and the dead body lowered into it, the widow walked around several times, repeating the formalities which the priest dictated to her, all the while scattering sweetmeats, parched rice, flowers and other trifles for which the spectators scrambled. When these preliminary rites were finished, she descended into the grave, amid the din of barbarous music and deafening shouts of applause. Having taken her seat and placed the head of the corpse in her lap, she gave a signal to throw in the earth. For some time, the grave filled slowly, as the deed of death was perpetrated with appalling deliberation, and the relations continued to throw in garlands, sandalwood and other items, with the mould that was gradually covering the bodies. When it rose to the widow's breast, the woman raised her left arm and was seen to turn round her forefinger as long as it was visible, even after her head was covered. That, however, was a very short time, as the earth was thrown in hastily as soon as the head disappeared, and her relations jumped in to tread it down and smother their wretched victim.

In the following year, 1817, the government succeeded in issuing orders and instructions for the abolition of the practice of burying and burning people alive. These orders were to be carried into immediate effect, although as we shall see, the ritual ceremony of self-immolation was actually to continue for many more years.

Another case was reported in the *Bombay Gazette* on 12 August 1818:

We observe, from a letter in one of the papers of the week, that a woman was lately buried alive with her deceased husband, near Isherah, within a few miles of Calcutta. The ceremonies accompanying this shocking spectacle, as they are detailed by an eyewitness, bespeak an inhumanity and cruelty truly deplorable. We had imagined that this mode of immolation was not required and scarcely countenanced by the Hindu Law; but happening so close under the eye of Public Authority, we must conclude that it is according to law and usage. The bodies were placed upright in a hole dug for the purpose, and the earth was thrown in by handfuls around them, and trodden down by the woman's oldest son, a youth of about 19. When it reached above the head of the miserable victim, a shout of joy and exultation was raised by the unfeeling multitude.

A regulation for declaring the practice of *suttee*, or of burning or burying alive the widows of Hindus, illegal and punishable by the Criminal Courts was passed by the Governor in Council on the 4 December 1829. The Abolition of the Suttee Rite, partially laid out here, declared:

The practice of *suttee* is revolting to the feelings of human nature, it is no where enjoined by the religion of the Hindoos as an imperative duty; on the contrary, a life of purity and retirement on the part of the widow is more especially and preferably inculcated, and by a vast majority of that people throughout India the practice is not kept up or observed. In some extensive districts it does not exist. In those in which it has been most frequent it is notorious that in many instances acts of atrocity have been perpetrated which have been shocking to the Hindoos themselves, and in their eyes unlawful and wicked. The measures hitherto adopted to discourage and prevent such acts have failed of success, and the Governor-General in Council is deeply impressed with the conviction that the abuses in question cannot be effectually put an end to without abolishing the practice altogether. Actuated by these considerations, the Governor-General in Council, without intending to depart from one of the first and most important principles of the system of British government in India, that all classes of the people be secure in the observance of their religious usages, so long as that system can be adhered to without violation of the paramount dictates of justice and humanity, has deemed it right to establish the following rules, which are herby enacted to be in force from the time of their promulgation throughout the territories subject to the Presidency of Fort William.

2. The practice of *suttee*, or of burning or burying alive, the widows of Hindoos, is hereby declared illegal, and punishable by the Criminal Courts.
3. First. All Zemindars, Taloodars, or other proprietors of land, whether Malguzaree, or Lakherraj; all Suder farmers, and Under-rulers of land of every description; all dependent Talookdars; all Naibs, and other local agents; all Native Officers employed in the collection of the revenue, and rents of land on the part of Government or the Court of Wards; and all Munduls, or other head men of villages, are herby declared especially accountable for the immediate communication to the officers of the nearest police station of any intended sacrifice of the nature described on the foregoing section; and any Zemindar, or other description of persons above noticed, to whom such responsibility is declared to attach, who may be convicted of wilfully neglecting or delaying to furnish the information above required, shall be liable to be fined by the Magistrate, or joint Magistrate, in any sum not exceeding 200 rupees, and in default of payment confined for any period of imprisonment not exceeding six months.

Second – Immediately on receiving intelligence that the sacrifice declared illegal by this regulation is likely to occur, the Police Darogh shall either repair in person to the spot, or depute his Mohurhir or Jemadar, accompanied by one or more Burkendazes of the Hindoo religion, and it shall be the duty of the Police Officers to announce to the persons assembled for the performance of the ceremony, that it is illegal, and endeavour to prevail on them to disperse, explaining to them that, in the event of their persisting in it, they will involve themselves in a crime, and become subject to punishment by the Criminal Courts. Should the parties assembled proceed in defiance of these remonstrances to carry the ceremony into effect, it shall be the duty of the police officers to use all lawful means in their power to prevent the sacrifice from taking place, and to apprehend the principal persons from aiding and abetting in the performance of it.

Third – Should any intelligence of a sacrifice declared illegal by this regulation not reach the police officers until after it shall actually have taken place, or should the sacrifice have been carried into effect before their arrival at the spot, they will, nevertheless, institute a full enquiry into the circumstances of the case, in like manner as on all other occasions of unnatural death, and report them for the information and orders of the Magistrate to whom they may be subordinate.

Both the *Jamaica Paper* and the *New Lloyds Evening Post* recorded the following trial on 8 February 1815:

A special Slave Court was held at the Alley, in Vere, Jamaica, on the 6th of December, for the trial of the following slaves, viz – Aberdeen, Adam, and Preston, belonging to Salt Savannah Estate, charged with the murder of another slave, named Thomas, the property of J. Holmes Esq. by burying him alive. It appeared from the evidence that the parties were all Congees, and had made a play, according to the custom of their country, when Thomas dug a grave in which he laid himself down, desiring his companions to cover him up for the space of one hour; but that if he did not rise again in another place in that time, they were to open the grave. Aberdeen and Preston were appointed to close up the grave, and Adam to play on the *gombah* (African music), all of which was punctually performed. Some other negroes belonging to the estate appeared, however, before the ceremony was completely finished, and had sense enough to open the grave; but it was too late, the unfortunate victim of his own credulity being dead. His Honour the Custos charged the jury on the crime, when they found them guilty of manslaughter; and the following sentence was passed, viz. – each to receive 39 lashes on the spot where the catastrophe took place, in the presence of all the estate's negroes, then severally burnt in the hand, and to suffer one month's solitary confinement in the county gaol.

In the mid-1860s, when the Government railway was being constructed in Mauritius, there was a great deal of trouble with one of the viaducts over a river running through a deep gorge. This was ascribed to a mermaid who dwelt in the pool below the bridge and would only be placated by an offering of two hundred babies. These were said to have been provided by the British Government who purloined them from the black camps. Until the total was fulfilled, there was great anxiety among the Hindu women, who would not allow their little toddlers out of their sight for a moment.

A report from Russia in 1879 confirmed that witchcraft was still firmly believed in by some superstitious peasants for that very year, in the village of Wratshewo, a poor old widow was buried alive as a witch.

Another case of shameful superstition was reported from Belgrade in 1888 in what narrowly escaped being a fatal case. The police found, in February of that year, the body of a man lying in the street, apparently frozen to death. Efforts to revive him failed and, his identity having been ascertained, he was handed over to his family for interment. The cemetery was a considerable distance away and as it was being reached the driver of the hearse told the priest, who had attended for the religious service, that he had heard some noise in the coffin. The clergyman and others drawing near also heard the sounds but every one of them ran away lest a vampire should issue forth from the coffin and attack them. The driver, terrified at finding himself alone, turned about and drove the hearse to the nearest police station. By this time the knocking was distinctly audible. The coffin was forced open and the man inside was found alive but in a very exhausted state. He complained pathetically of the attempt to bury him despite his condition. The man was taken to hospital and slowly recovered. Apparently, he had been spending the evening with some friendly companions and wandered off in a state of intoxication, he then fell and became insensible from the cold. It was most probably the jolting of the hearse that revived him, doctors said. It was a superstition in Serbia and among many Slavic people that, when a man died suddenly, his spirit returns as a vampire and preys on his near relatives and friends.

Referring to the custom of immuring, an American journal stated, in 1894, that there was at least one country in the world where people were still being buried alive. It claimed that the country where the practice still remained was China, and the people who were interred alive were usually those who, either on account of their own misconduct or uncurable maladies, had come to be regarded as burdens to their relatives and as constituting not only a nuisance, but also a danger to the community to which they belonged. These interments of living men and women were generally the result of a decree of a sort of family council composed of all the principal relatives of the victim and were regarded as so legitimate that local authorities didn't hesitate to attend the obsequies. Sometimes, the decree was pronounced by a vigilance committee, or 'Vehmgericht', an institution that flourished as extensively in China in the late 1800s as it did in Germany two or three centuries before.

Ordinarily the funerals of living persons in China were attended with pomp and ceremony, especially when it was not misconduct, but merely disease or old age, which caused the family and fellow citizens of the candidate for funeral honours to desire his departure for another world. Everything possible was done to smooth the way for his or her last moments. Relatives and neighbours combined their funds to purchase the most expensive coffin they could afford. At the funeral repast that preceded the interment, the person to be buried alive was the guest of honour, and as soon as the feasting was over the procession to the grave could begin. It was led by the empty coffin, immediately followed by the 'moribund', generally wearing the superbly embroidered garments of a Mandarin, bearing a fan in one hand and a prayer paper in the other. Then followed members of the family, the village or town authorities, and neighbours. On reaching the grave, the 'undead' would arrange his garments in the most comfortable position, take a last big swallow of opium, and assume his place inside the coffin. A piece of silver having been placed on his chin, the lid was placed on the casket and nailed down by his sons or nearest relatives. The coffin was then lowered into the ground and earth battened down all over it. These statements may seem to be mere traveller's tales, but the writer claimed to have heard this matter frequently discussed during his travels within China, by people who had witnessed ceremonies of this kind. Further confirmation was afforded by duly authenticated instances described in the Austrian *Oriental Review*.

The object of burying people alive in this manner was to get rid of them in a way calculated to free those who took part from all responsibility in this world, and at the same time to save the victim from the odium of suicide in the next world. Theoretically, the person interred was a consenting party, with his relatives merely executing his last wishes in nailing down his coffin and burying him. Strictly speaking, from a Chinese point of view, there was no murder, no execution, and no suicide. It was merely a mutual arrangement, satisfactory to all parties, the occupant of the coffin complying with the desire of his family for his departure to a better place. At one point, the biggest fear of the Chinese was leprosy, whose victims were once burned or buried alive. It is noteworthy that the disease is still rife, with 3,200 leprosy cases being reported in mainland China in 2007, with hundreds of isolated leper colonies being set up by the government to keep them out of sight. Pockets of infection remain in impoverished parts of Sichuan, Guizhou and Tibet.

In 1894, a panic broke out in Sarawak, northwest Borneo, among the Chinese, the Malays, the Sea Dyaks, and even the tribes of the interior owing to a rumour that the Rajah was anxious to obtain a number of human heads to lay in the foundation of the new high-level reservoir, at the water works in Kuching. Men were said to be sent out at night to procure these heads and until the rumour was quashed there was no sleep in the native quarters. The same sort of concern spread during the building of the cathedral in Singapore, while, as the Trans-Siberian railway approached the northern boundaries of the Chinese Empire and surveys were being made for its extension through Manchuria to Vladivostock, great excitement was caused in Peking (now Beijing) by the report that the Russian Minister had applied to the Empress of China for two thousand children to be buried in the road-bed in order to strengthen the line. Shortly after the great Russian railway was opened, on rebuilding a large bridge that had been swept away several times in the Yarkand, near the Silk Road routes, it was said that eight children purchased from poor parents were immured alive in the foundations. That is the reason, the Chinese were said to have believed, why there was no more trouble with that particular bridge.

This custom used to be practised in many European countries, with the medieval practice of immuration, or the walling up of a victim. There was actually a distinguished priest in France who placed on record a midnight visit that he paid to one unfortunate man. In the mid-1800s he was called to administer the last sacrament to a man of evident education, who was being bricked up inside the wall of a dining-hall of an old mansion in Paris. He had been taken there in a carriage blindfolded. The priest could give no indication as to where the property was, except that it was located on the left bank of the Seine, a fact which he ascertained from the carriage driving across a bridge. Of course, the secret of the confessional debarred the priest from telling the sins which the man had on his conscience, but he did infer that the man had been guilty of some terrible offence against society, which could not have been punished by the tribunals without bringing disgrace upon an illustrious and time-honoured name.

Writing from Tiraspol in June 1897, the special correspondent of the *Daily News* gave interesting particulars of a living burial horror and of the Raskolniki, a group of dissenters who resisted the changes of the Russian Orthodox Church, the sect to which the victims belonged. Some of the details were almost too harrowing for reading. He wrote:

One most striking and extraordinary aspect of these tragedies is that furnished by the marvellous moral resoluteness and physical hardihood of the fanatic zealots. In my last letter I referred to the self-starvation of

Above left: Cover Image – (iStock – Caval)

Above right: Emperor Qin Shi Huang. (Public domain)

Anna Utenhoven. Jan Luyken, 1649–1712. (Rijksmuseum, public domain)

Above left: Rev. Canon K. Hink & Captain Larnder. (*The Day Book*, Chicago, 23 April, 1912)

Above right: Robert E. Lee by Edward Caledon Bruce 91825, 1901. (Smithsonian National Portrait Gallery, public domain)

Infectious Disease, Ivan Alexeievitch Wladimiroff. (Wellcome Collection)

Right: Horses
In Cologne.
(*The Sketch*, 21 June
1911)

Below: Royal
Humane Society
Receiving House.
F. Piercy, 1850.
(Wellcome
Collection)

Above left: Dr Walter Hadwen. (Public domain)

Above right: Chowchilla Kidnappers, *Los Angeles Times*, 20 October 1976. (Joe Kennedy, *Los Angeles Times*, CC BY 4.0, via Wikimedia Commons)

John Kaft. (*New York Post*, 27 October 2022)

BURIED ALIVE

MAJLECH ELENCWAJG
Jewish Medical Student

Above left: Alexei Nikolayevich Kuropatkin. (Public domain)

Above right: Majlech Elencwajg. (*The Southern Jewish Monthly*, 3 May 1946)

Below: London Stone. (*The Illustrated London News*, 13 March 1937)

Suttee –
B. Picart
Engraving,
1729. (Wellcome
Collection)

Above left: Miss Big Heart Indian. (*Daily Camera*, Boulder, Colorado, 23 March 1899)

Above middle: Miss Big Heart Civilised. (*Daily Camera*, Boulder, Colorado, 23 March 1899)

Above right: Reuben Norkin. (*Birmingham Age-Herald*, 25 December, 1922)

Left: Richard H. Davis. (*The Sketch*, 11 October 1893)

Once this street was dominated by the menace of the coaltips. Now the houses look up to grass hills.

were extreme, particularly as two of the tips were still smouldering. The NCB is determined that such a disaster shall never happen again and since 1966 has greatly improved its methods of tip control.

The scene recalls the horror of that October morning in 1966 when the mountain moved and Aberfan lost a whole generation of its children.

10,000 people attended Aberfan's mass funeral which took place six days after the disaster. These graves serve as a constant reminder.

Aberfan. (*Illustrated London News*, 1 November 1971)

Above left: Rachel Von Varnhagen. (Public domain)

Above right: Anna Held – Seattle Theatre History. (Public domain)

Above: A Burial
Vault built c. 1890
with internal escape
hatches. (*Popular
Mechanics Magazine*,
July 1921)

Left: Harry Houdini.
(State Library
Victoria, Australia)

958

those Beguni prisoners who were arrested as vagabonds for refusing to satisfy the inquiries of the census enumerators. The prison governor is absolutely convinced that they would have literally perished of hunger and thirst had not he released them at the last moment, and when they were prostrate from exhaustion. But now comes a little more convincing proof of the marvellous force of misdirected will and unflinching determination of the victims.

All the living interments took place at night, in one or two cases in the presence of two of Kovaleff's companions, and on another occasion in the presence of several passive co-religionist witnesses. All this is duly attested in the evidence carefully elicited by the examining magistrates. In each case the victims, previous to the sacrificial rite, endued themselves in their best garments, and over these enveloped themselves in funereal shrouds. They then prostrated themselves silently and resignedly in their living graves, lying in close array, and always on the right side, and without uttering an involuntary moan or cry, without so much as moving a hand or limb, they permitted themselves to be slowly buried alive by the covering earth deliberately shovelled over them by the single spade wielded by Fedor Kovaleff.

One stands aghast and dumbfounded at the bare thought, not only of the access of religious fanaticism which impelled these wretched people to a voluntary auto-da-fe, but of the astonishing physical control displayed in the manner of their self-submission to a horribly cruel death. There is something inhuman in such martyr will and martyr courage as here manifested. Any one of the victims weakly relenting their resolution at the last moment, or unable to suppress the human and physical instinct which causes a dying person to wrestle with the death agony, might have stepped out of the grave while the clods from Kovaleff's spade were still falling over him or her; but they made not a resisting movement, as is conclusively shown by the various photographic pictures showing the positions of the bodies when recently uncovered. No less strong of nerve and of fanatic fortitude must have been Kovaleff, who performed the sexton-like, or rather ghoulish, office of walling up and interring alive the whole of the victims. There were five women among the Ternofka victims, and four children. The latter consisted of Kovaleff's two children, aged respectively four months and four years, both boys; and two other male children, aged ten and seventeen years.

Further excavations were made at Ternofka in October 1897, according to Reuters, where Fedor Kovaleff was arrested in connection with the ghastly discovery of religious fanaticism in the shape of interment of numbers of his followers with their own consent, while they were alive. On opening up the ground, six fresh cases of living burials were discovered. Kovaleff, who was interred in a religious monastery for life, refused to indicate where the bodies were buried of thirty other persons who remained missing.

A few years later, cable despatches from St. Petersburg reported the discovery of the bodies of 28 more at Tiraspol who had been buried alive in April 1901. Writings found with the remains indicated that they belonged to the self-immolating sect known as the Bjeguni, which first attracted attention regarding its connections to Kovaleff. It must be impressed that the Bjeguni were not only Europeans, but Christians, who formed an ultra-fanatic division of the sect of dissenters called 'The Old Believers.' The leaders were men and women of rank and education, one of its most influential chiefs being a woman of noble birth, the daughter of wealthy parents. Developing a sudden religious fervour, she disappeared from the orthodox convent in which she held the office of Superior, under the name of Mother Vera Makaveya. When next heard of she had become high priestess of the Bjeguni in the district of Tiraspol on the gently sloping banks of the Dniester.

She was known among 'The Old Believers' as Vitalia and, at the time when the first census of the entire Russian Empire was taken, a few years previously, gave no end of trouble to the authorities by warning her disciples and followers against answering any of the questions asked by the census enumerators. She told them that the Government intended to use the information to force the Bjeguni into the orthodox church in which event they would be irrevocably doomed to everlasting perdition. To escape this dreaded fate, and in the hope of saving their souls at the expense of their lives, quite a number of the Bjeguni, Mother Vitalia amongst them, resorted to self-immolation by means of a living burial. In each case the victims, previous to the sacrificial rite, arrayed themselves in their best clothes, and over these donned funeral shrouds. They then prostrated themselves silently and resignedly in their graves, men, women and children, lying close to one another and always on the right side. It was believed that the latest victims were all buried in earth by the hand of Kovaleff.

In December 1898, Miss Slessor, of the United Presbyterian Mission at Old Calabar, was a passenger on the Elder-Dempster liner *Oron*, which left the port of Liverpool, and had with her four black children whose cases revealed a painful part in West African history. Miss Slessor had worked in Old Calabar for twenty-two years. The children were aged two, three, five and sixteen years, and each one of twins at one time appointed to die in accordance with superstitious custom prevailing in the Niger Coast protectorate.

In the course of an interview with Reuter's Liverpool correspondent, Miss Slessor said all twins born were, according to native laws, put immediately to death, and it was only those who had been rescued by missionaries and placed beyond the reach of native power who were able to escape. The children in the *Oron* were four of these. Altogether Miss Slessor had herself saved the lives of fifty-one twins. When the twins were born, they were at once taken from the mother, and if no one interceded they were taken by the feet and head, and had their backs broken across a native woman's knee in the same way one would break a stick. The bodies were then placed in an earthenware receptacle and taken to the bush, where they were devoured by flies, insects or animals. Sometimes the little victims were put in these receptacles alive, and then eaten in the same way. The mother became an outcast if she did not take her own life at once, having to flee into the bush. If she ventured near a town or village, she had to be sure not to remain on the path if any other native were passing along the same way. Her presence, according to Nigerian superstition, would defile the place for others. She was not allowed to drink from the same spring and could not touch anything even belonging to her own relations, so it was little wonder that she would try to take her own life which had literally become a living death.

Miss Slessor was accompanied on the *Oron* by Miss McIntosh, and together they intended to establish a home for the native twins. Superstition dictated that the birth of twins was a result of witchcraft and devilry. Formerly, the mother, as well as the children, were put to death. The intervention of white missionaries and traders had saved some women's life, but being despised outcasts, whom none of the natives dared speak to, their existence was simply prolonged agony. On the Reuter's representative pointing out that the country of Nigeria was a British protectorate, Miss Slessor said it was really impossible to put an end to horrible native customs. She said:

'There could not be better governors than we have at present. Sir Ralph Moor and Sir Claude MacDonald have helped all they can. The missionaries don't want them to kill the natives, but to make them abolish the shocking practice.' The women hoped that by saving the children and bringing them up like other children, to show the Nigerian tribes that they were wrong in their belief, although the natives came by stealth to get children from the missionaries. The girl being taken by boat was sixteen years old. Miss Slessor saved her and her brother, but whilst she was away from the house for a sort time, the relatives came and got possession of the boy by false pretences and killed him.

In further conversation with Miss Slessor, it was found that in Old Calabar only isolated cases of this twin slaughter took place, but some forty miles inland many children were sacrificed. Another terrible custom, she said, was the burying of living children along with their mothers when the latter died during childbirth. This was done because they had no milk in the country to sustain the little creatures after the mother's death. Miss Slessor, in the cases of the rescued twin children, had utilised condensed milk, and missionaries began to spread the knowledge of this treatment through the country in order to save the lives of other little ones bereft of their mothers.

On 18 February 1902, the steamer *Dirigo* arrived in Seattle with news that Chilkot Indians near Hains Mission, Alaska, had buried alive one of their own tribe two weeks earlier. The victim, a boy aged fifteen, had been converted to Christianity by a Methodist missionary and in a burst of religious zeal denounced the tribal 'Icht', or medicine man. This act aroused the anger of the superstitious old men of the tribe. A short time before, fourteen residents of the village of Kluckwan died of consumption and the Icht spread the belief that the boy, in league with the evil one through his knowledge of the white man's religion, had caused the deaths. The disappearance of the boy from school caused the missionary to become suspicious and he began a search. At the outskirts of the village, he found tracks leading to a fresh grave and digging down he found the boy still alive, his bloodshot eyes rolling in insane agony, hair torn in handfuls from his head. The boy's fingernails were torn off in his efforts to escape from the underground grave. The boy was lifted from the earth and carried to the village, where he lived several hours, howling and crying out like a maniac, then dying from the effects of the suffering and fright. The Icht, who was responsible for the crime, was Shun Doo, an old offender, who had previously spent a term in San Quentin penitentiary for causing an old woman to be starved to death in 1894.

Another case of superstition emerged from the Hoonah Indian village near Yuncan, Alaska, in November 1902, when the native Indians took an epileptic man, who was believed to be possessed of a devil, and made him the victim of frightful atrocities. His ears were cut off, and his body hacked in an effort to drive out the demon. The fits continued under the treatment and the poor man was finally buried alive in the earth with his scalp cut off, inch by inch. Officers were dispatched from Juneau on a special steamer. Though a very quiet and peaceful tribe, the Hoonah Indians were very superstitious and nearly every year one of the members suffered a violent death.

The story of a man having been crucified at a Nigerian festival in 1905 was terrible, but unfortunately not an isolated case. Lieutenant Colonel Augustus Mockler-Ferryman (1896 -1978) wrote a book on the country's customs and claimed that places within a day's march of the British courthouse, on the death of a chief, scores of men and women were cast alive into the dead man's grave. There were other places where the victims were killed and solemnly eaten by the mourners. The wives of the defunct chief were invariably immured alive in his tomb, but lest they should not fall in with this method of honouring the dead, their legs were broken to prevent escape!

From Preanger, a district in East Java, came a remarkable story in 1907. It shows how deeply rooted among the natives was superstition to ensure the safety of prominent buildings, with the belief that living human beings must be buried under the foundation or bricked into the walls. A mill was under construction there and the builder received a visit from a local with a mysterious look about him. The fellow offered to supply a child to be buried alive to bring luck upon the building. He would see to everything being done in the proper way, and to the child being buried in the best way to gain the end result, at a reasonable price. The builder asked whether he had done such a thing before. Yes, was the ready reply, three times already. Needless to say, the police were called in to investigate at once.

In October 1907, American news reporter Bruno Novarra submitted the following story on the peculiar methods used in China for burying natives alive by consent:

That the awful custom of burying people alive still prevails in Southern China is an old story with the foreign colony here, but the other day your correspondent and a handful of Europeans had the terrible truth brought home to them – saw the victim with their own eyes and rescued him, of course. We bought this human life for $100, paid to his parents, while the authorities agreed to see to it that the promises given were faithfully carried out. The person whose life we bought for the paltry sum is the son of a poor artisan in a Shanghai suburb, not more than twenty miles from the foreigners' quarters. He is only fifteen years old, and for ten years has been a 'terror', stealing, robbing and generally misbehaving himself. The parents came near limbering the life out of the youngster; the village elders gave him the bastonade (sic) time and again. He was placed in the pillory, was excluded from visiting his ancestors' temple; he wouldn't be good; it wasn't in him. Finally, the father called a meeting and gravely announced that he had decided to bury his wayward son. All agreed that that seemed the only way to stop his badness.

Next day the father and twenty able-bodied neighbours started out with the village elder at their head, all armed with spades and ramming blocks. In their midst walked the victim, arms and legs shackled. His three elder brothers held the ropes to prevent any attempt at flight. When the sorry procession arrived at the execution place they found it thronged with spectators. The whole village had turned out to witness the show – men, women and children. A branch of a tree was secured and the culprit's height, from the soles of his feet to his neck, was measured. At the same time the neighbours began to shovel the grave, a hole only deep and broad enough to take the body upright. When finished the lad was disrobed. The victim offered no resistance, nor did he ask for mercy. He jumped down into the hole. His father and brothers each threw a few shovels of dirt after him; the neighbours did the rest, while the whole village helped trample down the earth and ram it with sticks and clubs. The ceremony lasted but five or six minutes; after that all that was visible of the bad boy were about six inches of neck and his head.

The same evening a pale Englishman named Graham burst into the British-American Club. 'Boys, I nearly decapitated a Chinaman – must be one of those buried alive parties. The thing nearly frightened me to death, but having no tools to unbury the rogue, I drove here at breakneck speed for help. Come with me at once. My chauffeur is buying spades, axes and the like.'

The buried alive opened his eyes wide when we set to work to rescue him. He had been quite resigned to his fate – to starve to death or being eaten by dogs or hogs. Besides, he told our interpreter, it was of little use. As his parents were determined to get rid of him, they would repeat the operation as soon as he was found. Hence we had to add bribery to our Samaritan act. One hundred dollars bought the boy a berth in a reformatory, whose president agreed to see to it that his parents and the village were no more bothered with the lad. When we related our adventure at the club, a Catholic missionary, visiting there, reported a number of similar cases that came under his own observation in the course of the last ten years or so.

He said: 'China punishes murder like most other countries - with death – death by quartering or crucifixion. But, at that, according to the current interpretation of the law, burying alive is not murder as long as the head of the victim protrudes from the grave or in case the victim consented to the act. Most of the persons whom I know to have been buried alive were passionate gamblers, professional thieves, opium fiends or lepers – persons constituting a moral or physical detriment to their relatives and to the community.

'The missionary told of the strange case of an opium fiend, the head of a family. Owing to his devotion to the drug this man refused to work and in order to get money to buy opium sold first his land, then his wife, then his sons. When but one child, a promising boy, was left the family council was called, and the relatives forbade the father to dispose of that child on pain of being buried alive. The opium eater promised, but next day went and sold the boy into slavery. The proceeds of this atrocity kept him in opium for a month. Then he got more by robbing his relatives and finally sank so low as to sell the copper roof from his ancestors' temple. That settled it, a man so depraved as to interfere with the family altars was unfit to live. The opium eater was so informed, and he quite agreed with his dear relatives. Next morning four of his uncles and nephews invited him to go with them to a nearby forest, where a grave had been prepared. 'Very well,' he said, 'give me two coppers' worth of opium.' He took the drug just before he jumped into the grave, which was quickly filled with earth and stones. Before the relatives departed, they asked the doomed man if he had any further wishes. 'Yes,' he replied, 'cover my head and face with tall grass so the insects won't bother, and the dogs won't disfigure me while alive.'

In the same district, continued the narrator, lived a leper of seventy, who steadfastly refused to die. Though his children and grandchildren were tired of supporting him in the forest hut nwhere he lived by himself, he could neither be persuaded to commit suicide nor submit to burial. Finally, the relatives appealed to the vanity of the old man. They went to town and bought the most up-to-date casket to be had – one highly lacquered and decorated with tinsel trimmings. They brought it to the old man's hut, promising him the beautiful 'last coat' if he would wear it at once. The leper agreed with his children and grandchildren that the casket was a beauty, but though his life was miserable enough, he was not yet ready to shake it off. 'I might consent,' he said, 'if you set up a fine funeral dinner.'

The council of relatives called the old man a blackmailer. 'Why,' they argued, 'you are going to die in a few weeks anyhow, and if you wait that long the lacquer on the casket may wear off, or it may be destroyed by fire or stolen. Of course, we would be very sorry to bury you right away, but since it must be done, sooner or later, excuse us for wishing to make an end of the matter.' Arguments or no arguments, the living corpse insisted on his funeral dinner and got it. On the day following the agreement his relatives and friends assembled with a band of music, bags of rice, baskets of chickens etc. At noon a grand diner was spread and at its conclusion the leper laid down in his beautiful casket amid weeping and roar of cannon. The casket was lowered into the grave and covered with earth before the leper had time to rap to be let out again. The authorities knew about the arrangement but said nothing. In similar manner, another leper was disposed of, only that in his case a fine mandarin's suit constituted the bait. The sick man said he would be delighted to be buried in such noble garments. But when they came to fetch him, he had changed his mind and absolutely refused to lie down in the casket.

'What,' cried the gravediggers and other burial attendants, 'have we had all this trouble for nothing?' And the relatives swore they would not pay them a second time, and upbraided the old man as a fool who didn't know his own mind. 'Unless you consent to be buried tomorrow morning, we shall take the mandarin's clothes away, also the casket, and warn you that no incense will be burned on your grave,' said the eldest son and prospective head of the family.

'Well,' said the old leper, 'if you promise to let me have the mandarin's suit and burn incense on my grave on the anniversary of my death as long as you live, and if, in addition, you will get me up a good meal tomorrow morning, plenty of chicken, rice and pork, then I will be buried.'

The last breakfast was a big affair: not only the relatives, but the neighbours contributed to the feast. When all had their fill, the funeral procession started. Behind the empty coffin the occupant-to-be hobbled on crutches. At a little distance, to prevent contamination, walked the son with the mandarin's clothes on his arm. At the open grave the doomed man donned the fine clothes, regarded himself long and earnestly in a mirror, drank a quantity of poison guaranteed to kill within half an hour, and hiccoughing and smiling, laid down in the coffin. The son nailed on the lid and the village elder attested 'that all the formalities had been observed.'

An unusual criminal case was tried at Victoria, Rhodesia (now Zimbabwe), in August 1913, concerning a native custom of burying alive members of a tribe who had contracted infectious disease. A trooper of the BSA Police accompanied by a native constable found a cave grave under a rock, from which sounds of groaning came. They removed the piled-up stones from the mouth of the cave, and inside found an elderly man lying in a cramped position, covered with sores and apparently in a dying, delirious condition. The cave was about six feet long and eighteen inches high, the sloping roof and sides being formed of a huge rock perched on the side of a granite kopje.

A district surgeon stated that the man, whose name was Muzingwa, who was about sixty years old, had suffered very extensive injuries to all his limbs, making it impossible for him to stand or walk, and he had very limited use of his arms. These injuries were the result of old burns which had never healed and had caused great contraction and distortion of the limbs. Poor Muzingwa had very few fingers or toes left. When first seen, these old wounds were covered with maggots and bluebottle flies and were so offensive that the surgeon had difficulty examining them.

Another medical man said that from long residence in Rhodesia and a thorough knowledge of the natives and their language, he knew that it was an ancient custom to bury alive people suffering from certain diseases, namely phthisis, epilepsy and leprosy, in order to avoid contagion. It was a native belief that the spirits of these three diseases on the death of their host would pass into the first person who touched the dead body, and thus secure a new host, who would become afflicted by the disease. In order to avoid this, the natives would bury the sick person just before death, so that there was no necessity to handle the body afterwards, thus the spirit would forever be confined in the corpse in the grave and the disease could not spread. This was the reason he gave for such premature burials.

Remarkable evidence was given by Muzingwa himself. He stated that he had been a helpless invalid for two years, due to severe burns from repeatedly falling into a fire during epileptic fits and on the whole had been well cared for by his relations, though his sores had never been attended to until he fell into the hands of the white men. The day before he was buried a deputation from his kraal, including his son, waited on him, and told Muzingwa that he was such a bind to them that they had decided to bury him at once, as it was evident that he could not live much longer. The old man protested against such treatment but, being one man against many, could do nothing. The next day he was carried by his tribe in a procession to the native cemetery on an adjoining hill, put in the cave grave with a little water and food in a calabash, and walled in. He could remember nothing more until he was rescued by the policeman. Muzingwa denied that he had agreed to being buried alive, although he knew the custom in such cases, but had asked them to postpone the burial for a few days until he was really quite dead. He did admit that he once asked his relations for a knife and another time for a piece of cloth, with which to commit suicide, as he was tired of living in such a condition, but they refused.

A charge of burying Muzingwa alive was made against nine natives. Their defence was that for two years the old man had been a burden to them on account of his foul condition, but they had always treated him well. They had built a separate hut for him a little way out of the kraal and fed him regularly. On a day early in December they went to look at him, and from his quietness, overpowering smell, and swarms of flies on him, thought Muzingwa was dead. They therefore buried him according to the usual customs, which included the placing of a little food and water in the grave. That night they killed and ate a bullock, to appease the spirit of the dead man. The jury found all the accused guilty as charged but recommended them to mercy on the ground that they had only carried out an ancient native custom and bore no ill-will to the old man. The court sentenced each prisoner to twelve months' hard labour.

In September 1955, thousands of leaflets had to be distributed in Pyinmana and surrounding villages of Central Burma in an attempt to deny rumours that the Burmese Government intended to revive the ancient custom of burying people alive at the four corners of the State-owned sugar factory being built at Pyinmana to ensure the success of the project. The old Burmese kings frequently buried people alive in the foundations of state buildings in the belief that the spirits of the dead persons would remain forever to ward off evil influences. At a Press conference, the Government committee managing the sugar factory project said that the rumours had been started by political enemies of the Government.

Whilst many of these cases are steeped in ritual and superstition, in certain parts of the globe the burial alive of victims is still prevalent. One indigenous tribe, the Kamayura, who have 600 members and live on the southern edge of the Brazilian Amazon are one such group amongst a handful that engage in selective killings. Target victims are the disabled, children of single mothers, trans-gender persons and twins, whom they see as bad omens. The actual extent of this practice is hard to determine, as these tribes live in complete isolation from the outside world, and despite the intervention of missionaries, practices often go undetected, and no official data is collected. One organisation, in 2018, estimated that twenty groups out of over 300 indigenous tribes engaged in burying victims alive.

Chapter Eight

Murderous Intentions

As might be expected in a world where murder is prevalent, not all cases of people being buried alive in history are unintentional. Due to unfortunate circumstances, lack of means and sometimes the shame that society would bring upon an unmarried pregnant woman, records show that cases of babies being put to their graves whilst still breathing were brought before magistrates as early as the eighteenth century, one example being that of Mary Morgan, of the Parish of Islington, London, who was indicted for the murder of her child.

Morgan was a servant at the Red Lion inn at Holloway. She was with child but denied it, even though she did have a husband, and delivered it without anyone else's knowledge. Afterwards she said that she had miscarried but, after being constrained, admitted that she had buried the baby in the garden. When dug up, the child had two stab wounds to its stomach. A midwife at Mary Morgan's trial deposed that the baby was full term, despite Morgan testifying that it had been premature and stillborn. Later Mary admitted that the child had been alive but gave no explanation for the injuries, one cut of which had caused the bowels to spill out. The jury found Morgan guilty, and she was sentenced to death.

A headline in the *Ipswich Journal* on 10 June 1727, announced the committal of Elizabeth Archer to Newgate Gaol, for the murder of her bastard child. The judge, Sir Thomas Clarges Bart, stated that the woman had buried the baby alive in a garden at Gourton, in the Parish of Banbury, near Burton in Staffordshire. After committing the crime, Archer made her way to London and concealed herself at a house near Tyburn Road, where she was later discovered and apprehended. The following day she signed her confession before Sir Thomas and was then removed back to Stafford to stand trial at ensuing Assizes there. The woman's mother was also a prisoner in Stafford Jail, on suspicion of being an accomplice in the murder. Both were convicted of infanticide.

In such cases as that of Elizabeth Archer, one might afford sympathy as the conditions under which she lived and gave birth are unknown. Nor can we ascertain the part that the child's father played in her grief, perhaps the poor woman was abandoned in her plight, the nature of her condition both unexpected and unwanted. However, one story that beggar's belief occurred in

Strasburg (formerly known as Strasburgh) in Germany, at the beginning of the nineteenth century, where religious fanaticism spelled the end for one believer, who met her maker at the hands of her zealous son-in-law.

In 1804, there was a shoemaker named Schneider who managed to convince his many followers that he was in communication with the Divine God, supposedly predicting the end of the world and giving out prophecies in accordance with his extraordinary dreams. Living in the city of Strasburgh, as it was formerly known, on the French-German border, Schneider was so convincing that he even managed to persuade his shoemaker brother-in-law, Herr Westerman, to relinquish his trade and worldly possessions in order to await the Day of Judgement. As time passed, and the world continued on with no signs of ending, Schneider decided to quit Strasburgh and moved to the village of Hoenhelm with his mother-in-law, brother-in-law and their respective families.

Not long afterwards, on waking one morning, Schneider claimed that he had been visited in the night by the Holy Ghost, who had declared that the shoemaker's mother-in-law only had twenty-four hours to live. The old woman in question was over eighty years old and told her son-in-law that she was more than ready to submit to what she termed as the 'Will of Heaven' on whom her destiny depended, and that she would die without grief. As night fell, Schneider and Westerman set about digging a grave down in the cellar of the property in which they all lived. In the morning, they laid the old woman in the hole and buried her alive, singing psalms over her body as they shovelled in the earth, and then returned to their daily occupations. News of the burial soon spread like wildfire and an Officer of Justice was deployed to investigate. On arrival at the house, rooms were searched, and the corpse was found. Ultimately, this led to the arrest of the culprits who were admitted to Strasburgh Gaol to await trial.

An inquisition was taken before the coroner, Thomas Whitestone Esq., and a jury of very respectable gentlemen at Broadford, Ireland, on New Year's Day in 1836. It involved the case of the skeleton of a man named Patrick Barry, who was buried alive thirteen months earlier. The deceased had been a millwright in the employment of David Burns and was an old man in a very delicate state of health. Being no longer able to work at his trade, Burns sent him to some friends residing in the County of Tipperary accompanied by one of his sons and another former employee, John Connellan. On arriving at the house, they were refused admittance and were obliged to turn back. On returning, they communicated the circumstances to Burns, who asked them why they hadn't put Patrick 'into a hole and throw a ditch on him'. He immediately ordered another son to go and dig a grave in a small burial place close to the house, which he did, and then the first son and a former employee took Patrick Barry to the spot, having previously taken off some of his clothing. They then thrust the poor man into the hole and, when covering him with earth, Patrick groaned twice and raised an arm. The ex-employee called out and said that they would all be hanged, that the man was alive. This, however, did not prevent the sons from pursuing their work and the unfortunate Mr Barry was covered in. Previous to the discovery of the body, Connellan described the place where it was interred, and most accurately the position in which the body was found; the head raised, the body inclining to the right side, and one leg also raised as if indicating an effort to rescue himself, or of great suffering when they were throwing the earth upon him. It was a remarkable circumstance that over Patrick Barry's body a child's coffin was found, of which Connellan denied all knowledge. The Jury came to the decision that Barry was buried alive by James Burns, Michael Burns and John Connellan, and with the concurrence and knowledge of David Burns, the father. They were all committed for sentencing.

Cases of persons being buried alive by foul deeds were, thankfully, few and far between, but when they did reach the ears of journalists back in the nineteenth century, each was afforded a prime spot in the newspapers. One murder, in Ireland, shocked the small community of Meath as, with no apparent reason for the crime, a local was found guilty of a most heinous crime. Local papers, in 1807, reported the following:

A woman by the name of Roddy was committed to the county gaol in Meath on charge of having murdered her niece. Suspicion had arisen after the child went missing and a search was made in the local area. It wasn't long before the girl's body was found in a hole in a garden upon the commons of Gaskintown, near Duleek. The child was seven years of age and, shockingly, had been buried alive. A verdict of wilful murder was pronounced by the inquest on Roddy, but no motive was forthcoming.

Lynching was by no means uncommon in Russia in the late nineteenth century, especially amongst the peasants, who frequently took the law into their own hands. One of the most terrible incidents of this kind was reported from a village called Lepsheke, belonging to the Government of Wilna, where a number of the locals lynched a robber named Mangalas under unusually horrible circumstances. The robber was returning home with some horses he had stolen from the peasants, when he was overtaken and captured after a desperate resistance. His captors tied the unfortunate man to a tree and proceeded to beat him with sticks until he was covered with blood. On the advice of an old soldier, the peasants then determined to bury their victim alive. A deep hole was dug, and in this they placed the robber in an erect position. Despite Mangalas' tears and entreaties, he was then slowly buried alive. News of the deed soon reached the police, but when the robber's body was extricated from the earth it was found that he was dead. The guilty persons were then arrested for murder.

At the Kerry Assizes in Ireland, Catherine Harrington was indicted for the murder of her child, by burying her alive in the graveyard of Kilflyn, on Easter Tuesday, 21st April 1835. George Benson, a very intelligent boy of twelve, was sworn, and deposed that he saw the prisoner first on the road leading to the church of Kilflyn. She came into the churchyard and spoke to Benson's father over the wall, requesting that he lend her a spade for the purpose of digging a hole to bury an infant. The spade was laid on the wall accordingly for Harrington's use, and a few minutes after John Benson, still seeing the spade on the wall, said to his son, "Perhaps the poor woman is not able to dig the grave, go and dig it for her." George went over the wall into the churchyard and saw a child wrapped in a bundle of rags lying twenty yards away, close to a wall. He dug the grave accordingly about the depth of the spade's handle deep. Up to this time he did not hear the child make any noise, but when the grave was ready the woman took up the child and as she brought it close to the hole, George heard it give a weak cry. The lad said to Harrington, 'Are you going to bury the child alive!' to which she replied, 'Oh, it is a weak child, and won't be long alive.' She then laid the child in the grave and while doing so, it again uttered a feeble cry. Harrington then commenced filling the hole with earth and stones. On seeing this, George fled in terror to look for his father, whom he found half an hour later and told him the terrible tale. John Benson said, 'It is too late to save the child's life now,' and it was left in the grave until the following day, when it was disinterred for the coroner's inquest. The jury brought in a verdict of Guilty. Catherine Harrington was sentenced to execution and her remains to be interred within the precincts of the county gaol.

In October 1842, the little town of Saxe in Germany witnessed a singular act of monomania. An individual entered the parlour of an inn, where he was in the habit of passing his evenings, and without speaking a word, fired a pistol at the first person he met, wounding him dangerously. He was instantly seized but did not offer the least resistance and was taken to the town prison. When brought before the judge he acknowledged that it was the fear of being buried alive that had induced him to commit this wicked act, adding that he would rather be hanged a thousand times, or to be beheaded, than run the risk of finding himself alive inside a coffin. Witnesses proved that this idea had so firmly taken possession of his mind that it amounted to madness. They also told the judge that it was the subject of the man's conversation every evening, telling people that half the people who seemed to die were buried alive and wished everybody to agree with him. That it may prevent the recurrence of such a horrible event, carried away by this fear, and not feeling sufficient courage to commit suicide, he had recourse to assassination. The judge, convinced of his derangement, and the wounded man being out of danger, sentenced the obsessive man to be confined for life in a lunatic asylum.

At the Stafford Assizes in August 1843, Charles Higginson, aged twenty-six, was indicted for the wilful murder of his son, William, at Eccleshall on 2 April. The prisoner, who was a widower, worked as a farm labourer and received around 7 shillings a week, out of which he paid 1s 6d for the keep of his five-year-old child to a woman named Mrs Brees. At the end of March, Mrs Brees told Higginson that she could no longer look after the child for that sum. Charles Higginson was lodging with Mrs Brees at that time, and on the morning of 2 April, he told her that he was going to take William to his father's house. Once the child was dressed by Mrs Brees, he was taken away by his father and nothing more was heard of him. Some time afterwards, Charles Higginson told people that the child was dead but gave such contradictory accounts of what had happened that suspicion was aroused and Bishop's Wood, where he had been seen with William on the Sunday, was searched. The body of the boy was discovered about ten inches from the surface. Higginson had stated to his sister-in-law that William had died, and he had buried him. On being asked what William's complaint was, Charles told her his son had a bad eye. She replied that she never knew anyone die from a bad eye and he answered that mortification had ensued. During the examination of the surgeon, as to the probable causes of death, Charles Higginson exhibited the most extraordinary and sullen insensibility. When the surgeon stated that he thought the child might have received blows from a spade, have been put in the grave, and died from suffocation, Higginson said, 'I put him in alive – that's all I did.'

This declaration produced a great sensation in the courtroom, a shudder of horror running through the crowd. The constable who apprehended the prisoner stated that, when he went to take him, he said, 'Your name is Higginson.'

The prisoner replied, 'Yes, it is, you want me about my poor little child.'

Without hesitation, the jury found Charles Higginson guilty, and the sentence of death was passed upon the wretched man in the usual form, the judge wearing a black cap to announce the verdict. Higginson was executed a few weeks later.

A man and his wife were tried in Cologne, Germany, in January 1845 on a charge of having murdered a young girl. The girl had been sent to them as a housemaid by her parents to work out a debt, which they had contracted to the couple in question. However, the poor girl somehow offended her employers and they attempted to bury her alive. They did not succeed but continued to beat the poor child to death. The man was condemned to imprisonment with hard labour for life, the woman receiving a lesser sentence of two years in prison.

On Saturday, 27 March 1847, a little boy of around eight years old was found buried alive in a drain a quarter of a mile from the village of Cockburnspath in Berwickshire. A large stone had been rolled into the mouth of the drain, so as to prevent the child from escaping. His head had been put into a bag and six inches of earth laid on him. On being taken out, he was recognised as a member of an Irish family which had stopped at the village the night before, begging from house to house, apparently in the last stages of misery and destitution. During the night the mother had severely ill-treated the boy, a mere skeleton, who was crying for food, and threw him out of bed onto the stone floor. As soon as the boy was taken to the village, medical assistance was sent for, but the child died before the doctor arrived. The woman was then followed and arrested. After a post-mortem examination, a doctor declared that the child's death was caused by impeded respiration. The mother and her family, except for a five-year-old child, were committed to gaol for murder. The mother stated that they were from Roscommon in Ireland, that they were in a very distressed state, and weak for want of food, yet on being searched about five shillings in silver was found concealed on her person!

A brother and sister attempted to bury another sister, of eleven years old, alive near Cahirciveen, Ireland, in May 1847. It was supposed that their being in extreme want, and the sister sick for some time, they made up their minds to get rid of her without waiting until she had died. No other motive could be conceived for so unnatural and extraordinary a crime. After the girl had been sick for some days, the brother said she was dead, and two days afterwards he and the other sister took her body to the graveyard. The attempt was discovered by a man employed on the public works, near the burial ground, from whom they asked to borrow a spade in order to dig the grave. The girl lay on the ground without a coffin and the man swore that he could see her still breathing. Under the care of local medic, Dr Barry, the girl recovered very well. The sister was placed in custody soon afterwards, but the brother had already made his escape.

A medieval sentence of death by breaking alive on the wheel 'from beneath upwards' was pronounced on a woman named Lempeck, from Marienwerder in Germany, for the murder of her five-year-old stepdaughter, in April 1850. Lempeck deliberately buried the child alive, although, as she said in her confession, 'she resisted and shrieked dreadfully.' The woman tied the child's hands behind her, forced her into a hole and covered her with earth, even after she heard the stifled cries of the victim. She told neighbours that the girl had been sent to stay with some relations. Neither at the trial nor in her confession did the woman exhibit any signs of derangement or remorse. The sentence, in the form pronounced, had never before been carried into execution.

On 9 March 1852, medical student John Phelan was placed at the bar charged with having incited and solicited Alice Minehan to murder an infant named John Phelan. Appearing at Clonmel Court in Tipperary, Ireland, Phelan was also charged with inciting and procuring the same woman to murder another infant child named Mary Phelan. The prisoner, who was thirty years of age and the son of a respectable man resident in Cashel, was well connected. The evidence against Phelan depended solely on the evidence of Alice Minehan, who it was said was a person of the worst character. She swore she had killed both the children by burying them alive. There were no witnesses called for the defence. The jury, after about twenty minutes deliberation, acquitted Phelan.

In April 1899, some workmen were excavating ground in Knoxville, Tennessee, United States, when they broke into a cave. They entered and found the skeletons of a woman and child. A scrap of paper was discovered next to the woman's remains, and on it some writing telling how she and her child had been buried alive in the cave and left to perish by her husband. The woman had given her own father's name as Philip Gibreath, and his address as Greenville, South Carolina. The paper, which was signed 'Ada Holmes' was dated 1862. Gibreath was located and verified the disappearance of his daughter. Efforts were subsequently made to trace Mr. Holmes.

The following month, a special Court of Petty Sessions was held at Ballynahinch, County Down, Ireland, where Ellen Magennis was charged with having unlawfully and wilfully abandoned her four-month-old female child on 22 May 1899, in a manner likely to endanger its life.

Witness William Armstrong said that he was on his way to Ballynahinch and when coming opposite James Coubrey's land he heard a noise and looked into the field but could see no one. He then heard the cry of a child and looked towards a lump of clay and weeds. Removing the clay, he found a child, which was covered completely to a depth of six inches. He then called a woman he knew, a Mrs. Hamilton, who took the child from him, and Armstrong then reported the matter to the Head Constable.

Mrs Bridget McMullan testified that Ellen Magennis had left the child in her care since its birth, but on the night of 22 May, Magellan collected her, saying that she would leave the girl with a Mrs. Dornan and then go into service. Another witness had seen the woman with a bundle in her arms on the road near where it was found buried and heard the infant cry. The magistrates returned the defendant to trial at Downpatrick Quarter Sessions.

In 1839, a horrible atrocity was stated to have occurred in Constantinople, now modern-day Istanbul, Turkey. A woman from the island of Tina, resident in the Turkish sector, impaled her own son, a child of five or six years old, because he had dirty habits which she was unable to correct. Another woman, a widow wishing to marry again, found that her intended husband was unable, or unwilling, to maintain her two children by her deceased husband and dug a grave, burying them both alive. As these wretches were both Greek subjects, they were sent to Athens to await trial.

A twenty-year-old woman, named Maria Clarke, from Wingfield, Suffolk, was arrested in March 1851 on a charge of having murdered her 6-week-old baby, Arthur, by burying it alive in a meadow. She made a confession to the following effect:

> I was fearful that the young man who promised to marry me would not do so if he knew that I had a child, and I, in consequence, was anxious to get rid of it. I had not entertained the slightest notion of murdering my child until I came out of one of our neighbour's cottages, where I saw a spade standing outside the cottage. I took up the spade, went into the meadow, dug a hole, and laid my child in it. I then covered the child over with earth, and to stifle the screams I stamped upon the sod. When the child was covered up with the earth I heard it cry. I then sat down upon the place where I had buried it, and in a short time after I went home.

It appeared that around Christmas time, Clarke was confined in Depwode Union Workhouse where she was expecting an illegitimate child, being discharged with her baby on 17 March. In court Mr Dasent, appearing for the prisoner, contended that Maria Clarke had committed the deed when she was devoid of her reasoning powers. The Chief Justice, however, could see no ground for such a conclusion. He considered the crime deliberate and premeditated. The jury found Clarke guilty, and a sentence of death was passed upon her. A short time later, a petition requesting a reprieve and numerously signed by inhabitants of Ipswich was sent to Sir George Grey. Evidence of insanity was not produced at the trial, from want of money, and many persons who had known the girl as 'Maria Shulver' testified to the unsoundness of her mind. The sentence was subsequently commuted to transportation for life. Sadly, Maria was in ill health when she entered the Millbank prison pending her deportation, and continued in a low and despondent state, dying before sentence could be carried out. The jury at the inquest considered that the discipline of the prison was too severe but ultimately returned a verdict of natural death.

Salah Ben Ali, an inhabitant of the French colony of Algeria, was tried at Constantine in March 1874, for having beaten his wife Fathma so severely that she almost died from the injuries received, and having further buried her alive. At the request of his children, Salah Ben Ali did take the trouble to disinter the unfortunate Fathma, but she was then in a dying state and expired some days afterwards from the combined effects of the beating and the premature interment. Salah Ben Ali, being called upon for his defence, complained that his wife was always ill, and was altogether so useless to him that he thought it best to get rid of her by putting her to death. The murderer was sentenced to hard labour for life.

On 11 August 1883, news was received from Rule Valley, Salt Lake, Utah, of a terrible affair among the Shoshone Indians. A native tribesman murdered his wife, breaking her legs and arms and then burying her alive. The tribe took the matter into their own hands, taking the murderer, tying his hands, throwing him on his back and then tying his feet to a tree. A rope was then coiled around the man's neck and stout young men pulled at each end until the culprit was choked to death.

The Pioche Record related that in riding through Eagle Valley, Lincoln County, in June 1890, a rancher was attracted by a peculiar moaning sound. On finding the spot from where it proceeded, he removed some sage bushes and soil and found that an aged Piute Indian, known as Teekaboo, had been buried alive. He summoned some neighbouring ranchers who resurrected the Indian from the grave, and it was ascertained that he had been buried alive by his squaw, or wife, who had been left to take care of him while the young bucks and squaws were enjoying themselves at a fandango in Panaca. The old squaw left on charge of the old Indian, who was an invalid, concluded that he had but a few days to linger anyway and that if she remained with him, she would miss the fun and the possibility of losing a chance to get another husband. She therefore decided to bury Teekaboo at once, which she did, and reached Panaca in time to participate in the fandango festivities!

John Rech, who strangled his wife and buried her body in the woods near their home at Estelville, New Jersey, in March 1895, made a confession to ex-sheriff Smith Johnson shortly after being convicted and sentenced to twenty years in prison. Rech explained how he came to tie knotted handkerchiefs found around the strangled woman's neck. He said that after a quarrel in the house, which ended in him putting his muscular hands around his wife's neck, he at once made preparations to hide the evidence of the crime by burying her body. He had dug the grave and was carrying his victim towards it when he felt the quivering signs of returning life. Apparently, the open air had started the woman's respiration once more. Fearing his wife regaining consciousness and its consequences, Rech laid the woman on the ground, knotted first one handkerchief around the neck and, to make sure of his work, used a second one. They were drawn so tightly that possibility of breathing was limited. He then placed the body in the grave and covered it with a few inches of dirt before cutting down a tree and dragging it over the freshly turned earth. From his statement it appeared that Mrs Rech was alive at the time of her burial. Had the jury become aware of this at the time of his trial, there is no doubt that John Rech would have forfeited his life on the scaffold.

In May 1896, a Native American woman of the Piute tribe died of consumption in Smith Valley, Nevada. She had been doctored for some weeks by a Piute medicine man named Doctor Joe, a well-known character in that part of the country. On the same day of the death of the squaw she was buried, and according to the custom of the tribe, her wickiup, or wigwam, was burned. Furthermore, a three-month-old baby of the woman was buried alive in the grave with its mother. The day after the burial of the mother and child, it was alleged that the squaw's husband, Jim Davis, went to Dr Joe's wickiup, shot him twice with a rifle and smashed in his skull with a club. It seemed that if a medicine man of the Piute tribe lost three cases of sickness the decree was that they should be killed, with Dr. Joe meeting the fate of many tribal doctors before him. Although the murder was carried out within the tribe, authorities still got involved and Davis was taken to court along with two other native Indians from the Piute tribe.

Three years later, in March 1899, seven men were arrested and charged with burying a member of the Kaw tribe alive near Homing Post, Osage Nation, Oklahoma. The story goes as thus:

Many years before, Black Horse, the Kaw, met Thula Big Heart, the daughter of Chief Big Heart of the Osage nation. They loved each other fondly and became engaged. However, soon afterwards, Thula went away to school in Washington and forgot about her Indian lover. When Thula returned home in the fall of 1888, Black Horse was waiting for her and although the young woman showed no affection towards him, she stood by her promise and preparations were begun for the couple's wedding. The ceremony was to be held at the home of Frank Johnson, a relative of Miss Big Heart who was married to an Indian squaw. Black Horse knew that Thula didn't hold him in the same affection as she had before but said nothing. On the day of the wedding, one hundred guests assembled at Johnson's home and looked on as a very pale Miss Big Heart stood waiting in her white satin gown. It was the native Indian custom for the groom to arrive later than the bride, but Black Horse did not show up and Thula eventually invited the guests to be seated and enjoy the feast that had been prepared. When everyone had gone, expressing their surprise and regrets, Thula called together her three brothers, the three Johnson boys and her foster uncle, Frank.

'Now see here,' she said, so the account runs, 'I want revenge on that trifling Indian. He knew I did not want to marry him in the first place, and he has done this for revenge. Now I want to show him who will have the best revenge. I want you to catch him and bury him alive.'

Chief Johnson bowed low, and then they all left. At daylight they returned and said, 'We found Black Horse lying drunk beside the road, not far from his house. We woke him and asked him why he had not come before to the wedding, and he replied, as you said, that he sought revenge. So we bound him hand and foot, took him to the bank of the river, dug a hole in the sand and buried him there alive.'

The girl smiled as though well pleased. The next day she went away. As the neighbours lived far apart, neither did they know that Black Horse had not arrived at the wedding ceremony later, supposing that he had been delayed. A week later a party of Kansas hunters camped on the banks of the Arkansas River, near Homing Post. While searching along the banks for kindling wood, they noticed the sand being turned up and one man, Harry Chase, decided to investigate. The result was the finding of Black Horse's body. His mouth was open and filled with sand. His features were drawn and the body showed evidence of having been covered while still alive. Chase reported the find to Deputy Marshal McGuire, who investigated and arrested the Johnson and Big Heart boys. They ignorantly confessed, and actually believed they had done nothing wrong.

Thula Big Heart was captured at the home of an uncle near Pawhuska. She denied that she intended to escape and also said that she did not tell the men to bury Black Horse alive, saying, 'I deny any connection with this crime. My friends were angry when they discovered I and Black Horse did not marry, and they made the suggestion themselves that he should be buried alive. Perhaps I did assent, but I am sure I never told them to do it.' She was taken to the house of jailer Henderson and kept under guard.

In a talk with Doctor Hill, who called at the jail to see him, Johnson, aged sixty-five, said:

We took that young Indian down and buried him because he deserved it and had no business to spoil our girl's prospects that way. She told me she did not want to marry him, anyway, because she had a sweetheart in the East and he (Black Horse) was too common for her. We asked her what we should do with him that night if he could be found, and she said 'to bury him alive.' That's what we done, and the son-of-a-gun won't fool anybody else, I guess.

In a preliminary trial, the seven men pleaded guilty in front of Justice of the Peace McCloud and were bound over to the Indian Court in Pawhuska (see middle left and centre images on page 6 of the plate section).

A case worthy of mention is one that occurred in Italy and, although not a murder, it demonstrates how evil can prevail for years before discovery. In November 1900, a Rome correspondent for the *Morning Leader* newspaper reported a shocking case of cruelty perpetrated by Giuseppe Toia and his wife on their own daughter. The dreadful circumstances came to light at Salgareda, a little village near Venice. For some time, strange noises had been heard coming from a subterranean pigsty and the local gendarme was called to investigate. On entering, the officer found a state of indescribable filth and discovered a creature huddled in one corner bearing only a slight resemblance to a human. The body was completely nude, frightfully emaciated and uttering inarticulate sounds. When a light was shined into its eyes, dazzling the pupils, it let out a piteous scream. Investigation revealed a shocking truth. The unfortunate creature was the Toias' daughter, named Toda, and she was eighteen years of age. The poor girl was so misshapen, having been buried alive in her underground prison for fifteen years, that she had grown to just three feet in height and was unable to stand. The child had disappeared when she was three years old, her parents telling villagers that she had been drowned. Guiseppe Toia and his wife narrowly escaped lynching by the locals and were taken away to prison. Toda was put into a medical facility where doctors felt hopeful of saving her, although the poor girl's intellect was considered to be lower than that of most animals.

The discovery of the chained skeleton of a young woman revealed a tragedy that had been kept secret for seventy years. In April 1901, workmen were engaged in pulling down an old, dilapidated building in Poultney, Vermont, United States, close to Carver's Falls. The house was older than the Civil War and was originally occupied by the agent of a British nobleman who owned vast tracts of land in Vermont. The house had lain deserted for many years and when workmen pulled up a big flat stone near the wall of the cellar, one of them almost fell into a great hole beneath. It was a pit about eight feet deep and seven feet wide with a brick wall constructed on all four sides to stop the earth from falling in. In the centre was a strong three feet high iron post and to this was attached a heavy chain which led to a human skeleton. Iron handcuffs still fastened the hands of the skeleton to the chain. It was completely without flesh, time and vermin having cleaned the bones. The body was slight and doctors declared them to be those of a woman. From looking at old documents and speaking to the older inhabitants of the town, it was concluded that it could be none other than the skeleton of Pierre Bourdon's bride.

Seventy-one years before, Pierre Bourdon, a French-Canadian, moved to Vermont from Quebec. He was employed as a farm hand to a Mr Hamilton, the most prosperous farmer in the vicinity. Bourdon was very industrious, received a good wage and was highly esteemed by his employer, with his name being generally Anglicised to 'Perry Bordon.' He spoke occasionally of a girl in Canada to whom he was engaged to be married and within two years he brought a young woman named Susette to his home. She was apparently very pretty, with black sparkling eyes and ruddy cheeks, an even match for plain and plodding Bourdon. Within a month, Susette had become the object of social attention, with the local young men showing their admiration. Inevitably, the young bride became intoxicated with admiration. The old stone house in which the Bourdons' lived was remote and Pierre ordered his wife not to leave it, but Susette had other ideas and repeatedly disobeyed him. Day by day her husband's jealousy became more intense and he would hardly speak to anyone.

One stormy night in November 1831, Pierre had been kept unusually late at the farm and arrived home to find his wife out. Hastening to an inn where he thought he might find her, Bourdon found Susette dancing and flirting with a group of young men and women. Pierre sternly ordered his wife to follow him home, which she did, but it was the last time that anyone was to see the young woman again. Naturally people were still asking about Susette's whereabouts a week later, but Pierre told them simply that they had had a disagreement and that she had gone to her relatives in Canada. The answer seemed reasonable, and nobody suspected foul play.

For a year, Bourdon lived a quiet life, confiding in no one and not allowing anyone into his home. Police investigating the skeletal remains found at the house believed that Pierre spent that year torturing his wife to death. It was thought that he at first locked Susette in a room, before digging the pit in the cellar and dragging her down into her tomb. The house was far from help, and nobody would have heard the woman scream. It is thought that Bourdon then bound his wife to the post, and bricked up the sides of the pit whilst she was still living. Perhaps he gave her insufficient food so as to prolong her living death. The rats must have crawled over her and gnawed Susette as she lay helpless. When he went to work every morning, the heavy stone slab must have been placed over the top of his spouse's place of interment. A year later Pierre also disappeared.

However, that's not the end of the tale. In 1882 Bourdon returned to the town an old grey-headed man. It had been fifty years since he had last been seen and had spent the whole time at sea, being familiar with nearly every port in the world. Bourdon's mind was weak and often wandered but he never spoke about his wife or what had happened to her. Pierre returned to the house by the river and remained there for two years, neighbours taking enough food to appease the old man's hunger, but he finally became sick, and the town took charge of him. He died on 20 September 1887, and was buried in the Potter's field.

A fifteen-month-old baby, the son of a machinist named Edward Hughes, was found buried in a dismantled ironworks in Stockton-on-Tees, England, on 30 May 1903. The child's pinafore was rolled over its head and iron refuse and stones had been piled over the top of the body. There were no marks of violence on the boy, but the child was believed to have been buried alive and thus suffocated. He disappeared while playing in the street and according to a four-year-old brother was taken away by a man in order to buy sweets. The following week, an eight-year-old street match seller named Patrick Knowles, whose head just reached the broad rails in court, appeared before magistrates charged with wilful murder. According to reports, the boy was arrested in the act of taking another baby, aged nineteen months, to the banks of a stream with the intention of drowning her. Knowles confessed that he buried the child alive in some loose sand and then covered it with mud, bricks and large stones. He was immediately remanded in custody but was certified as unfit to stand trial as 'being of unsound and unformed mind in consequence of his childhood and immaturity of development, which rendered him incapable of knowing the nature and the gravity of the act of murder.' A few days later the Home Secretary ordered the removal of Knowles to Broadmoor Lunatic Asylum. Patrick Knowles was trained as a tailor and in 1911 was removed under discharge to St Thomas Home, Preston, in Lancashire. Aged seventeen, Knowles claimed not to know of any family or friends and was put under the supervision of, as his records show, a person 'who will do everything in his power to secure for Knowles a good start in life.'

A gruesome story of barbarity was related by the *North China Daily News* as having occurred in Peking, now Beijing, in December 1905. A mandarin's wife had incurred the hatred of her husband's head steward because she had refused to help procure a coveted government appointment for the man's son. However, it wasn't long before an opportunity for revenge presented itself to the steward. The mandarin was leaving on a short journey and was overheard to say to his wife, in jest, that he had fully made up his mind to have her buried alive. After his master's departure, the steward called in upon the wife and, after making the customary low obeisance, told her that he had come to carry out the mandarin's orders. The terrified wife protested that it had been a joke but the steward, aided by other servants, seized and gagged the woman and buried her alive in the garden of her own home. The mandarin duly returned and was furious. He had the steward arrested and subjected to terrible torture before he was finally beheaded. Those who had aided the man in his crime were rounded up and put to death by strangulation.

On 19 December 1906, Robert Gordon, aged fifteen, pleaded guilty to the charge of murdering Joseph Reed, aged ight, in Chicago. Gordon pulled Reed under a sidewalk, pounded him on the head with a brick until he was unconscious, then dug a hole in the earth in which he placed the younger boy. Gordon then heaped soil over Reed and allowed him to suffocate. Robert Gordon showed no emotion when he entered his plea of guilty nor when he was sentenced to the reformatory for life.

An extraordinary case of intentional live burial occurred in the Betul District of India in 1907, when a man named Dama was tried for the murder of his wife. The woman had been suffering from chronic dysentery, and the husband took her and the family to another village. He returned home with the children, saying that his wife had died on the way, and he had buried her. Six days later a villager saw something move in the jungle. A search was made by the authorities, and they found a grave with the leg of a woman clearly visible. They heard her say, 'I am not dead,' and she also told them that her husband had buried her. After being lifted out of the grave and given food the woman was sent to hospital and lived some twelve days longer. The accused man was found guilty and sentenced to transportation for life.

A gruesome confession was reported from Brussels, Belgium, in May 1908, when the bodies of two infants were discovered at Vaudignies, near Mons. Elise Mertens, aged thirty, residing in the locality was immediately arrested. Submitted to an interrogatory interview, Mertens admitted that she was the mother of the children and then confessed that she attempted to strangle them, afterwards resolving to bury them alive. She wrapped the children in linen and dug a hole, in which she interred the little ones alive, stifling their cries by covering them with earth, which she trod down upon them.

A month before, a similar but more horrific case was reported in April 1908, when Francesca Herrera was arrested in Seville, charged with secretly burying eighteen of her twenty-two children. For twenty-nine years, Herrera had lived with the anarchist Molina, who also admitted burying the children after their deaths. However, it was stated that some of the children were buried alive.

In October 1908, a grim story of the cholera visitation came from the Central Asian city of Tashkent, where the disease had hit two months before. It appeared that the first case coincided with the arrival of a lady from Russia, who was on a visit to a Sart family. Unfortunately, the mistress of the Sart household died from cholera on the very day that her visitor left. The townsfolk were greatly impressed by these facts and became convinced that the disease was circulating the area in the shape of the Russian woman. Determined upon its extermination, they waylaid the foreigner in the great square one evening and hurried her away, after which they waited upon town authorities.

'There is no danger of cholera now,' they declared.

'Why so?' they were asked.

'Because we have buried the Russian lady.'

A frantic search was made for the victim, but no traces of her could be found. However, no room for doubt was left that the superstitious mob had buried her alive. It is a remarkable fact that no further cases of cholera occurred amongst the Sarts, the only cases reported in Tashkent being in the European quarter.

Pigs rooting in a graveyard in Calabria, southern Italy, brought to light a remarkable story of love and tragedy which cost four lives in 1909. A farmer, whose swine had been in the cemetery, was driving them out when he observed that they had been digging around a newly made grave and he was shocked to see the two arms of a man protruding from the earth. In this grave a short time before had been buried the body of Giovanni Avellone, a rich landowner. His death was caused by the story told him by his beautiful daughter, Lucy. She had related to him, only when the birth of a baby made further concealment impossible, that Andrew Campanile, whom she had loved, had promised to marry her and then betrayed her. The shock caused her aged father's death from heart failure.

When the authorities came to dig up the body, which they believed had been uncovered by the pigs, they assumed that it was that of Avellone. To their surprise it proved to be the corpse of young Andrew Campanile. Furthermore, there was unmistakable proof that he had been buried alive. It seemed that when under the ground the man had awoken from a drugged stupor and had fought violently to free himself, pushing his arms up through the earth. However, Campanile could not do enough and was soon smothered to death by the mound of dirt pressing upon his face. His body showed evidence of terrible suffering. This explained the strange disappearance of Andrew Campanile a week before, but nobody could say what had become of Avellone's body. Then a young man came forward who said he had been Campanile's rival for Lucy Avellone's hand. His confession bore a most remarkable story of tragic revenge.

After the burial of her father, Lucy Avellone had called this young man and together they lured Andrew Campanile to the young woman's home. There his wine was heavily drugged, and after midnight, while he lay in a stupor, the pair carried him to the cemetery. Her father's casket was dug up and buried again under the doorstep of his home. Into the trench of the grave the living body of Campanile was dumped, which the couple then covered with earth. Lucy Avellone told the young man to go home and return in ten days when, if she was alive, she would marry him. Ten days had passed when a further tragedy was discovered.

There followed a search for Lucy and her baby. They had not been seen on the handsome Avellone estate for two days. Had they left the province it would have been noted by the authorities. A search party eventually came upon the dead bodies of the young mother and her baby in a well in the estate garden. A note under a stone in the wall of the well told the story. Lucy related how she had drugged Campanile, not to kill him by such an easy and merciful manner, but to render him temporarily senseless so that she could place him alive into the grave to which she believed he had sent her father. She wrote that before Campanile's body was wholly covered with earth, he became conscious, and she had the joy of seeing him struggle against the death that was overtaking him. Then she and the young man hurried to fill the grave so that he could not escape. She watched there until he was dead. Her revenge then being complete, Lucy prepared for her own death and that of the child. When all had been arranged, she held the baby in her arms and leapt into the well.

Twelve-year-old Cecil Hopkins, of Modesto, California, self-confessed slayer of his six-year-old brother, Theodore, made a statement in July 1909 that strengthened the official's belief that the victim was buried alive on the hill where his body was found. As he told of the shooting and subsequent burial of his brother, Cecil ate candy and apparently failed to realise the gravity of his crime. According to his story, he killed Theodore while their parents were absent from home. The brothers quarrelled over their lunch and Cecil drove his brother from the house and shot him. Fearing the consequence of his deed when his parents returned, he dug a grave in the sand. While the grave was being dug Cecil said that Theodore moaned and stretched his arms. The cramped position of the arms and the fact that the victim's mouth was filled with sand strengthened the theory that the child was buried alive. Cecil Hopkins was present at his brother's inquest but was not put upon the stand to repeat the story of his crime. His mother and father testified that Cecil had been subject to melancholy and fits of anger ever since he had been bitten by a rabid dog at the age of three. Both expressed the opinion that he killed his little brother in a fit of uncontrollable anger. Neighbours gave corroborative testimony and cited instances during that summer's hot weather when the boy suddenly showed insane fury.

From a shallow grave sunk in the sand of her front yard in Lancaster, California, a pet dog dug up the body of Frieda Schultz Castine, a wealthy ranch owner, on 14 August 1910. Every indication pointed to murder, with robbery as the motive, and telegrams were sent to all seaports and border cities between Galveston and San Francisco to arrest the woman's brother-in-law, Otto Schultz, who left the area after telling a Southern Pacific station agent that he was bound for Germany. Mrs Castine was last seen on the Friday before her body was discovered when she took a trip to receive a remittance of $6,000 from relatives in San Francisco. Investigations of deputies from the sheriff's office showed that the woman was wounded as she drove into her yard and that she was thrown into the shallow grave while still alive. An examination by a coroner disclosed the presence of sand in the lungs and bronchial tubes, drawn there by the victim's dying gasps. Frieda Castine's son found his mother's body, half uncovered and mutilated by the dog, when he returned from a trip that morning. A wide wound in the back of the head, evidently inflicted by an axe, showed that it was the work of a murderer, and the young man knew that his mother had gone to town to receive the money but could find no trace of it.

Some Berlin picnickers, passing a sandpit outside the village of Wendisch Rietz, near Lake Scharmutzel, in June 1913, noticed the legs of a child protruding from the sand. Calling a local farmer, they proceeded to scrape away the sand and discovered the body of a four-year-old girl buried head downwards. A police inquiry showed that the child had been murdered by her lunatic grandmother, who was afterwards arrested. The woman had buried her victim alive. News of the crime spread rapidly, and the villagers attempted to storm the police van, intending to lynch the woman, and officers were obliged to drive them back with drawn swords.

The body of Anna Wilkinson, aged twenty-eight, buried alive in a hastily dug grave on Clyde Wilkinson's farm near Kokomo, Indiana, United States, was unearthed on 27 September 1913. Her head had been battered in. Clyde Wilkinson, who had disappeared several days before the discovery, was arrested in Logansport and confessed that he killed his wife and believed she still lived when he crowded the body into a hole he had dug, which was too short and forced him to bend her knees to get her in. Domestic trouble had caused Anna Wilkinson to leave her home, and Clyde lured her back on the pretence that the youngest of their two boys was sick. The woman was suspicious and appealed for police protection, but as the farm was out in the country, an officer was not sent to her. When she found the child was not sick, Anna refused Wilkinson's appeal to live with him, according to his confession, and he knocked her down and kicked her several times in the head. Fearing he had killed her, Clyde resolved to bury his wife and hide all evidence of the crime. Then he sold his possessions at auction, told the children that their mother had gone away for good, and disappeared.

Moses Reynolds, who killed Nathan Hill on the Trulock plantation, Pine Bluff, Arkansas, United States, in March 1916, was convicted of voluntary manslaughter and sentenced to five years in prison. The testimony of a man who admitted he had aided in burying Hill indicated that the victim was buried alive. He said that when they were dragging him to the field, he groaned.

However, the murder of Hill was not discovered until several weeks after the crime. Nathan Hill's disappearance caused some comment among the coloured people of his workplace, but nothing was suspected until Reynolds was quietly taken into custody, together with his wife. Under questioning, Reynolds broke down and told of the killing, while his wife also made several disclosures. Visiting the Trulock estate, officers unearthed Hill's body near a house formerly occupied by Reynolds. Mrs Reynolds said that her husband and Nathan Hill quarrelled over a small sum of money and engaged in a fight. Later Reynolds hit Hill with a Winchester rifle, and when this broke he used an iron poker. With the aid of the third man, Moses dragged the body to a field and buried it just under the surface. He pleaded self-defence.

Thomas Fitzgerald, alleged degenerate and confessed murderer of six-year-old Janet Wilkinson was hanged at the Cook County jail, Chicago on 17 October 1919. Fitzgerald, janitor of an apartment building, seized the little girl as she walked along the street on 22 July. He choked Janet into insensibility to keep her from screaming and then buried her alive under a coal pile. On the eve of his death, Fitzgerald had given up all hope of a commutation of his sentence and gave out a statement saying, 'I am not afraid to die. My peace is made with God.' Fitzgerald's wife failed in a final attempt to save his life when Judge Landis denied her petition for a writ of habeas corpus in federal court. The convicted man was visited on his last night by his wife and two sisters. Permission to witness the hanging was denied to Janet's father, J.S. Wilkinson. Fitzgerald said he killed the girl because she screamed when he took her into his room to give her candy.

An attempt to bury a child alive on the seashore was described at the Dublin Police Court on 1 October 1921, when Sarah Daly and Elsie O'Keefe were remanded on a charge of attempted murder of the latter's child. It was alleged that the child had been placed in an old bucket, covered with seaweed, and put in a hole dug in the sand at Kingstown the previous night. A workman named Dixon said that his suspicions were aroused by the women's movements as he watched them from Kingstown Pier and saw one of them place a parcel under some bushes and then heard a child scream. He said that the accused, Daly, dug a hole in the sand with her hands, while O'Keefe stripped the child. He was too far away to see the bucket, but he caught sight of Daly putting the naked child in the sand hole. Dixon ran over and seized hold of Sarah Daly, calling her an 'old murderer.' She replied, 'For the love of God let me go. I would give you twenty pounds if I had it.' The child was still alive when picked up.

In September 1922, the body of an eight-year-old boy, the son of a landowner in Palermo, was found beneath a heap of stones in a ditch which was formerly used as a cistern. Medical evidence showed that the child was buried alive and must have survived beneath the ground for at least two days. The boy's father had previously received a blackmailing letter demanding 4,000 lire, which he did not answer.

On 17 April 1924, Reuben Norkin (see middle right image on page 6 of the plate section) was electrocuted in Sing Sing Prison for assisting Abraham Becker in the murder of Becker's wife, whose body was found near Norkin's Bronx welding shop on 29 November 1922. Becker was put to death on 13 December 1922. Norkin was convicted after police obtained a signed statement from him that he had acted as a lookout for Becker while the latter knocked his wife unconscious and then buried her alive in a lime pit on 7 April 1922. Later Becker had placed his four children in an orphan asylum and told neighbours and friends that his wife had deserted him. Norkin insisted that he was innocent of the crime right up until the moment of his death. He walked to the electric chair quietly and as the guards were about to strap him in said:

I'd like to announce that you all are witnessing an innocent man being put to death. My only crime was in keeping a secret.

In September 1924, officers of the Royal Canadian Mounted Police left Alaska for Vancouver, with five Indians accused of murdering a seventeen-year-old Indian boy by torture. The boy was accused of sorcery and was buried alive with his hands tied behind his back after being tied to a tree for several days. The men declared that the boy worked magic to make hunting poor for a tribe in Telegraph Creek country in British Colombia, 200 miles inland.

Marie Billings found herself in a serious condition in a Los Angeles hospital in May 1928, after having been beaten and buried alive in a semi-conscious condition. Mrs Billings, aged thirty-six, said that a man went to her home and was trying to sell her some real estate when he suddenly struck her on the head with a club. 'I remember struggling,' she said. 'I was almost completely unconscious. He then tried to choke me to death. He wrapped one of my silk stockings around my throat and twisted it until I was senseless.'

Investigators said that it appeared the woman's assailant had taken her by car into the Puente Hills, laid her in a shallow grave and covered her with dirt, in the belief that she was dead. Mrs Billings' hands and feet had been bound. She claimed to have been semi-conscious when placed in the grave but unable to cry out. Later the woman was able to free herself and struggled out of the makeshift grave. A taxi driver found her wandering on the road a mile east of Whittier, still wearing the blanket that had been wrapped around her by the assailant.

In the same year, in Monessen, Pennsylvania, 'chickens' buried in the yard of Don Hlatky proved to be twin girl babies when health department agents, investigating on the strength of anonymous letters they received, dug them up. As a result, Hlatky was held in Westmoreland County Jail at Greensburg, and his wife was put under guard in the Monongahela Hospital. The coroner's jury recommended that the parents be held for the next grand jury, which was to meet in the following autumn. The jury's verdict stated that the twins came to death through suffocation. Investigators said it was probable that they were buried alive. Neither parent attended the inquest, but four of the couple's five children were required to be present. They appeared not to understand the intricate machinery of the law. Milton, eight, remembered the twins only vaguely, and Agnes, eleven, had but a faint recollection of them. But Elizabeth, fifteen, and Margaret, fourteen, were detained by police with the intention of calling them before the grand jury with their parents. The fifth child, John, was placed in a school for correction several months before on charges of robbery.

More recently, a man was arrested on a double murder charge after a most gruesome discovery. Charles William Conlin, aged twenty-two, appeared before Stockton-on-Tees magistrates on 31 October 1928, charged with the murder of his grandmother, Emily Frances Kirby (sixty-four) and her second husband, Thomas Kirby (sixty-two). Conlin lured the couple from their bungalow in Thornaby-on-Tees to Norton, where his mother was lying ill. Once there the young man attacked them with a blunt object in order to take a large sum of money that the couple usually carried with them, and then buried them together in a shallow grave while they were still unconscious. Doctor S. McBean, the police surgeon, testified that when he arrived at the scene, the bodies were still warm. Two of the wounds on Mr. Kirby's head, he said, might have been caused by a poker. There was dirt in the man's mouth and throat, and from the condition of the lungs it was clear that death had occurred from asphyxia. On the back of Emily Kirby's head was a large swelling, probably caused by blows with a flat instrument, such as a spade. There were marks on her throat and a small bruise below the jaw. The causes of death in her case were recorded as strangulation, blows to the head and burial before life was extinct. Evidence was given that Charles Conlin had drawn only £3, 7 s. wages from his position at the Synthetic Ammonia and Nitrates Company in Billingham during the four weeks preceding the murder, and that on the day the bodies were discovered he bought a motorcycle for £21, 10s. in Darlington. The court heard that Conlin had also purchased new clothes using money in a grey wallet that was identified as Thomas Kirby's property. At his trial, the accused claimed to have no memory of the crime, but the jury subsequently found Conlin guilty, and he was hanged on 4 January 1929, at Durham Gaol.

Two-and-a-half years after Conlin's death sentence, a trial took place on the other side of the world. On 15 August 1931, medical men stepped into the witness box in Wellington, New Zealand, to give evidence in the murder trial of twenty-nine-year-old George Errol Coats. According to the coroner, a beautiful young woman named Phyllis Simons, just seventeen, had been buried alive. The girl, he told the court, bore severe marks on her body, and had died from asphyxia. Phyllis's body was found buried in a hunched position in a huge soil dump, her face pressed down into the earth. In the medic's opinion, it seemed that the girl had made a desperate effort to rise. The mysterious disappearance of Miss Simons, who had left her parents' home to live with Coats in an Adelaide Road rooming house, some time before aroused public apprehension, especially after a suicide note supposedly written by Phyllis was discovered. George Coats, who was a relief worker employed on the Mount Victoria Tunnel excavations, had been seen digging around the area on the night of his lover's disappearance. One hundred unemployed men were engaged to dig up two thousand tons of soil and, without stopping for four days, they finally found the body. The pathologist deduced that Phyllis was pregnant and had knelt beside the landfill site with a scarf tied around her head before being struck several times. Coats was found guilty of wilful murder and was executed on 17 December 1931.

Eight suspected members of a Filipino secret cult in Martinez, California, were arrested on 3 April 1933, accused of decreeing the death of a young woman compatriot in a weird midnight ritual which ended when the struggling victim was buried alive. Both men and women were taken into custody when the body of Celine Novarro, aged twenty-six, was uncovered from a shallow grave on Jersey Island in the San Joaquin River. It had lain there since the previous November. Officers accused Leon Kantinello, aged forty, of passing sentence on the young woman after she had been accused of infidelity to her sick husband. The group said that Mrs Novarro admitted the charge. Kantinello was named head of the esoteric organisation which authorities believed exercised a wide influence over Filipinos throughout northern California. As police reconstructed the alleged murder, it became apparent that Celine Novarro was ordered to appear before a meeting of the Stockton group of the cult. Previously she had admitted indiscreet conduct to her husband who forgave her. At the November confrontation she confessed again. Blindfolded, the woman was driven to a lonely spot on the island, flogged, and then pushed screaming by a woman member of the sect into a hastily dug grave. Her purse, containing $130, was flung in after her. The grave was hurriedly closed, and a fire ignited to cover traces of the newly turned soil. Authorities stated that the woman's husband died a month later of grief. The slaying was not disclosed until the following April when a Stockton Filipino woman told police the story after arguing with a fellow countryman.

Frederick Rushworth, aged twenty-nine, a farm labourer from Gellpool, near Middleham, Yorkshire was sentenced to death at York Assizes for murdering his three-week-old baby by burying it alive in a basket. He was hanged at Leeds by famous executioner Thomas Pierrepoint on 1 January 1935. The mother, Mrs Lydia Binks, a married woman living apart from her husband, was also sentenced to death at the same time but was later reprieved. The couple had been courting and had the child while Lydia Binks was working at The Dales Holiday Camp in Carperby. In her case the jury made 'the strongest possible recommendation to mercy,' and when appeals by her and Rushworth were dismissed by the Court of Criminal Appeal, Lord Hewart said the recommendation in the case of the woman would 'doubtless receive the fullest consideration from a discerning and humane Home Secretary.' Throughout the hearing in the higher court Rushworth maintained an attitude of indifference to the proceedings. Nor was he noticeably concerned when the judgment of the Lord Chief Justice, who described the crime as a 'terrible one', finally sealed his fate.

At the trial it was related how Mrs Binks had given birth to the child alone and had brought the child in a basket on her bicycle when she met up with Frederick on that fateful night. She was persuaded to hand the baby over to Rushworth, who dug a hole and buried it. Lydia said that she then put her hands over her face and ran away, sitting on a tree stump and crying. She said that while she was sitting there, she could hear her baby crying which made her feel worse. She testified that on the way back Frederick said, 'Cheer up. It will be dead now, and nobody will know.' Rushworth maintained that he thought the baby was already dead when he placed it in the hole, although an autopsy proved that it had been buried alive.

Lydia Binks' parents lived in West Hartlepool, and no fewer than 7,350 people in the town signed a petition for clemency in her case, resulting the reprieve. Lydia's age was given as twenty-four but at the trial Dr Derry, medical officer at Durham Prison, said her mental age was approximately thirteen. She was childish and credulous. The murder took place on 25 March 1934, and the scene of the crime was a lonely plantation near Carperby, Yorkshire.

In March 1941 headlines in Brassow, Romania screamed, 'Pretty Young Widow Buried Alive,' and were accompanied by pictures of a good-looking girl and a clean-cut young man. The newspaper story explained that the young man, a hard-working plumber, had hanged himself because the girl, his bride of just a few weeks, had double-crossed him.

Not long after his marriage the plumber, Julius Geyer, returned to his apartment to find his new bride drinking and carrying on with a man she had known when she was a waitress in the local train station. There was a scene. Mrs Geyer tried to explain to her husband that no real harm had been done, and that in the interest of domestic peace she would give up drinking and the men she had known before marriage. For a week or two the Geyer household ran more or less smoothly. The bride seemed properly contrite and the husband tried to forget the episode. Julius Geyer's family, however, had objected to the marriage from the start. They had looked into the background of the waitress and found her to be 'very much on the flighty side.' A family row had begun when the son married this young woman over the strenuous objections of his father, mother and elder brother. Geyer finally convinced his folk that they were wrong about the girl and, after a long discussion, his mother finally agreed to call on the new bride and assure her that her in-laws were ready to do anything they could to make the marriage successful.

The elder Mrs Geyer thought that she would pleasantly surprise her daughter-in-law by making an unannounced visit. She arrived at the apartment in the middle of the afternoon, two or three hours before her son was expected home from work. She found her daughter-in-law enjoying herself in the arms of another man and the younger woman was so drunk that she invited the older woman to join the party! That night there was a long conference at the home of the elder Geyers and when Julius left he promised his parents that he would 'do the right thing.' That night Julius Geyer hanged himself.

The pretty young widow put on a good show. She bought herself an outfit of widow's weeds and insisted on making the arrangements for a proper funeral. She invited all her late husband's friends to their home and managed to convince them that she was broken-hearted. The relatives of the dead man did not arrive until the hour of the funeral. They ignored the weeping widow and when the funeral service was over they moved away from the grave to allow the widow to have her customary few moments alone. Suddenly, like a battalion of avenging angels, the Geyers closed in steadily on the young woman and laid firm hands upon her. Not a word was spoken as they pushed her into the grave. She screamed and tried to scramble out but her heel was caught in the top of the coffin. On every side there was a Geyer hand, pushing her back in. Two of the dead man's relatives then grabbed the gravedigger's shovels and started filling in the hole with earth. The other mourners, who were in the process of leaving the cemetery, heard the commotion and sprinted for the police.

Officers reached the scene just as the relatives were tossing the last few sods of earth onto the body of the young widow. While some officers arrested the Geyers, others began to dig. They uncovered the unconscious but still warm body of the young woman and rushed her to a waiting car. At the hospital there was some doubt for several hours whether young Mrs Geyer could be revived, but she was finally brought around and filled the hospital with screaming objections at having been buried alive.

Under careful treatment by doctors and nerve specialists, she recovered and lost no time in getting away from Brassow. Not until the police were sure that the young widow had got over her almost fatal experience at the grave of her husband were members of the Geyer family released from custody. Under the circumstances the authorities believed that it was best not to hold the assailants for attempted murder!

Allegations that a newly born child was buried alive by its grandfather were made at a court in Warrington, in April 1944, when Richard Lloyd, aged seventy-five, of Church Street, Golborne, was charged with attempted murder. The police said a midwife was called to Lloyd's house, where Mrs Hampson, his daughter, eventually admitted having given birth to a stillborn child. When Lloyd said he had buried the baby in the garden the midwife began digging and heard a faint cry. The baby was still alive when removed from the ground. Lloyd was subsequently remanded in custody.

A similar case occurred when police in Italy arrested a woman on 7 May 1956, whom they accused of having buried her ten-month-old baby boy alive in a lonely wood near Rome. The woman, Angela Gasperina, aged thirty-seven, was charged with attempted murder. Police said that the baby managed to poke his head out of the shallow grave and was still alive when found, some thirty-six hours after he was buried.

Nineteen people were arrested in the Durg district of Nagpur, Central India, in September 1958, on charges of having buried alive two women suspected of being witches. Those taken into custody were all villagers from Deonra who, according to a police report, believed that the two women had used black magic to cause an outbreak of cholera. The vast majority of those accused were from lower castes with family members also being accused or used as scapegoats. A frightening statistic from the National Crime Records Bureau of India shows that since 2000 over 2,500 women have been killed after being branded as practising witchcraft. They also often face public humiliation before being put to death. In 2009 five women from a remote village in the Deoghar district were paraded naked, beaten, and forced to eat human faeces.

On 22 December 1958 California police fitted together the pieces of a plot they said led to the brutal killing of attractive Olga Duncan, whose bruised body was found in a shallow grave beside a lonely road. A labourer with a local police record told the tale of what he said was a hired slaying and led officers to a hand-scooped grave. Augustine Baldonado, aged twenty-five, said in a statement that the dead woman's mother-in-law, fifty-four-year-old Mrs Elizabeth Duncan, hired him and Luis Moya, aged twenty-two, to kill five months pregnant Olga for $6,000. Investigators said that the victim, aged thirty, may have been buried alive. Olga Duncan, a surgical nurse, had been missing since 18 November. She was the estranged wife of Santa Barbara lawyer Frank Duncan, from whom she had separated only two weeks after their marriage the previous June. District Attorney Roy Gustafson said jealousy of the older woman toward her daughter-in-law was the major motive.

Luis Moya, who denied knowledge of the murder, was described by Santa Barbara Sheriff John Ross as badly shaken upon learning of Baldonado's statement. Mrs Duncan also insisted that she knew nothing of Olga's disappearance. Police said that Mrs Duncan had been married five times in eight years. She was charged with posing in court as her son's wife, along with a paid confederate, to obtain a fraudulent annulment of her son's marriage the previous August. It was the discovery of the annulment that caused authorities to begin an intensive search for the missing woman. Mrs Duncan, Baldonado and Moya were all charged with conspiring to kidnap and murder Olga Duncan.

A court in central Shaanxi Province, China, sentenced a kidnapper to death in January 2000, for killing his 7-year-old victim by burying him alive. Sentenced by Weinan City Intermediate People's Court, it was reported that in July 1999 Pu Xiaogang kidnapped the son of a local shop owner on his way home from school. Having drugged the boy with sleeping pills, Pu telephoned the family and demanded a 500,000 Yuan (US $60,500) but panicked when the child's grandmother, who reportedly took the ransom call, recognised his voice. Pu then took the unconscious child to a cave and buried him alive.

A heroin addict who bludgeoned his father with a hammer and then buried him alive on a waste tip was jailed for life at Birmingham Crown Court in June 2001. Kenny Wilkins murdered his 47-year-old father, Kenneth, and then used money taken from his body to buy drugs and pay off a £200 debt. The court heard how Mr. Wilkins had received seven hammer blows to his body and had fractures on his arms and hands where he had desperately tried to fend off his attacker. The body was found ten days later when police searched a skip hire site in Saltley, Birmingham, where both father and son had worked. Justice Rafferty told twenty-two-year-old Wilkins, of Hernefield Road, Shard End, that he had 'demeaned his father in life and in death and had shown inexcusable callousness in murdering him'. Kenny Wilkins pleaded guilty to murder and was duly sentenced.

A man was buried alive in a shallow grave next to his murdered son in Alabama, United States, in February 2002, but he survived the ordeal and then led police to the attackers. According to the Russell County Sheriff, two men had shot twelve-year-old William Brett Bowyer three times during a robbery before slitting fifty-four-year-old Forrest Bowyer's throat and throwing him into the grave on top of his dead son. Bowyer played dead and then managed to kick free from the grave after the robbers had left, made his way to the highway and flagged down a motorist. Michael David Carruth and Jimmy Lee Brooks were arrested twelve hours later after Bowyer was able to identify them. The two suspects had pretended to be police officers but then kidnapped the father and son before demanding money and drugs. After returning to the Bowyer home to steal cash, they took the father and son to a construction site where they dug an eighteen-inch grave. The men cut Forrest's throat and then shot his son in the head, threw him into the grave and then shot him twice more. Carruth and Brooks were both sentenced to execution and remain on Death Row.

A final more recent case was in June 2002, when a farmer was arrested after he admitted burying his unmarried sister alive after she became pregnant. Moustafa Mohammed, aged thirty-five, confessed to killing nineteen-year-old Yosra near Sohag, 240 miles south of Cairo, after she told him that she had a relationship with a man and was expecting a baby.

Chapter Nine

Accidents & Natural Disasters

Throughout history there have been thousands of accidents involving miners being buried alive, as well as other risk-taking professions and pursuits. The earliest of which was reported in *Stow's Survey of London*, which gave a melancholy account of an accident which happened in London with dozens of people being buried alive under the rubble from a blast:

January 4, 1647, some people barrelling up gunpowder, at a ship chandler's opposite Barking Church in Tower Street, by some accident the powder took fire and blew up that house and demolished fifty or sixty others, and among the rest the Rose Tavern, which at that time was very full of company, it being the parish feast. It's uncertain how many people lost their lives by this blow, for when they came to dig in the rubbish, they found heads, arms, legs, half-bodies, and some whole bodies, not so much as singed. The mistress of the Rose Tavern was found sitting upright in the bar, one of the drawers standing by her, leaning on the bar with a pot in his hand, both dead. The upper timbers falling cross one another prevented them from being buried alive.

But the most remarkable thing of all was a young child found the next day, blown upon the uppermost leads of Barking Church in a cradle, alive and well, and not the least damage done to it. The parents of the child were never known, being killed, as supposed, by the fatal blast. A gentleman in the parish took the child home and brought it up as his own. Mr. Stow says he saw the same girl when she was about eighteen years of age.

In December 1822, the sexton of one of the burial grounds at Anderston, Glasgow, was literally buried alive while digging a grave rather deeper than the common depth, for the purpose of disappointing the resurrection men, or grave robbers. He had got to almost the depth he wanted when, the soil being sandy, the grave suddenly shot in on both sides and completely covered the poor gravedigger. Some weavers nearby raised the alarm and, together with two labourers, dug down until they reached the struggling man. They fastened ropes around his armpits and drew him out in a state of near suffocation, laying him on a gravestone and finally helped the sexton home as he began to recover. He declared he had buried thousands of people in his time but did not dream he was to be the victim of entombing himself!

A similar case occurred in April 1827, when assistant gravedigger Daniel Dell, of Watford, Hertfordshire, was literally buried alive. While digging a hole the earth fell in and he was soon afterwards found dead, with two feet of soil over his head. The cause of death was concluded as suffocation.

A vault was erected at Albany graveyard in 1829, its purpose being for the deposit of the dead, for a certain period, to guard against resurrection men or grave robbers, before finally being put into a more permanent grave after decomposition. One Sunday afternoon in December, the first body was deposited in the vault and the tomb closed up. A few hours afterwards, the caretaker returned to pick up something which he had forgotten earlier. While he was opening the outer door, he heard a noise inside and presumed that it was being made by the person who had recently been interred there, fearing a case of premature burial. Although his hair stood on end in fright, the man's humanity prompted him to save the unfortunate person inside and he proceeded carefully, unlocking the inner door, which was made of iron. He then positioned himself behind the outer door for his own safety and called to the supposed ghost within, telling it to push open the door and liberate himself. The confined person did so, and on making his appearance proved to be not the dead man who had been buried, but a living man who, from some cause, had remained in the vault when it had been closed up. Had it not been for the fortunate circumstance of the sexton returning, he would very likely have perished in that gloomy tomb.

Whilst employed underground in a mine in the parish of Newelyn, Ireland, in July 1830, Stephen Karkett, aged twenty-five, was buried alive by the falling in of the sides of the shaft he was in, at the depth of five fathoms from the surface. The first person who arrived at the spot was a man named George Trevarrow, who called to see if any living man was beneath. Karkett answered in a firm voice, 'I know all earthly power can avail me nothing, I feel the cold hand of death upon me; if there is any hope of my being extricated from this untimely grave tell me, and if not tell me.'

Trevarrow at once informed him that there was not a shadow of hope left for him, as upwards of four tons of rubbish had fallen around him, and that suffocation must inevitably take place before any human aid could afford him relief. On hearing this, Karkett exclaimed, 'All's well, it is the Lord, let him do what seemeth to him good. Tell my dear father and mother not to be sorry as those without hope for me, 'tis now only that I am happy, 'tis now I feel the advantage of a religious life, now I feel the Lord is my stronghold, and now I feel I am going to Heaven.' Here his voice failed him, he never spoke again.

The *Journal de l'Indre* stated that the labours for the relief of a man named Monsieur Billard, who was accidentally buried at the bottom of a well at Flere la Riviere, central France, were carried out with the utmost expedition, skill and caution, until ten o'clock at night on 29 March 1837, when the top of a vaulted mass which covered him was reached. On coming to this point, all the judgment of the engineers was required, for on inspecting the position in which the stones lay, the utmost apprehension was entertained that any attempt to remove them would cause the whole covering to fall in upon the wretched man below. His voice was heard more distinctly through the interstices, and the precise spot occupied by him was ascertained. Circumstances rendered a prompt decision indispensable. At that point Billard had been buried alive for sixty hours, without food, without being able to move, and scarcely able to breathe. His reason began to give way and delirium was induced. He was heard to bemoan his fate, then to utter loud cries demanding food, and afterwards to breakout into wild paroxysms of gaiety. A physician present declared that no time should be lost, and that every effort must be made for his release at all risks. The stones were gradually removed with care and at quarter to eleven the next morning, Billard was taken out of the well, still alive but in the last stages of exhaustion. He was wrapped in blankets, his head being covered with a light cloth, and carried into the nearest house. The poor man was put to bed in a dark room where, after taking a few spoonfuls of weak soup and a small quantity of wine, he fell asleep. Gradually his senses returned but the man's pulse was feeble, skin cold and he suffered from severe thirst. After some time, his stiff and paralysed limbs regained their powers and his body its warmth, although painful and sore. According to Billard's own account, he was standing when the fall took place and stones enclosed him up to the neck but, by some strange circumstance, the fragments formed a vault over his head. He contrived to eat a part of the leather peak of his cap, a piece of his smock and tried to gnaw one of the stones just within reach of his mouth.

A distressing accident occurred at the Workhouse Cemetery in Cambridge Street, Liverpool, in April 1846. Two paupers named James Kay and John Platt were engaged in opening a grave twenty-four feet deep, in which a number of bodies had been interred, when the ground, rendered loose by heavy rains, gave way and plunged Kay into the Charnel house below. He was found covered by the earth and embedded amongst the dead. When assistance was procured, it was found that the man was already deceased. Kay was originally a native of Tarbock in Cheshire and was described as quiet, harmless and industrious. The accident directed the attention of the authorities to the disgraceful state of the Workhouse Cemetery, which was labelled a public nuisance.

In September 1848, at about half past eight in the morning, a terrible accident happened on the branch line of the North Kent railway which was being formed at Plumstead. For some time, a large number of labourers had been employed in making extensive excavations for the new railway, which was intended to run to New Cross, Deptford. The workmen had been making a cutting and, while they were digging by the side of a large embankment, an immense portion of it fell upon them with a loud crash, completely burying them. An instant alarm was raised, and men set to work to extricate the missing labourers. Within a few minutes two were discovered in an insensible state, both seriously injured. They were carried to the surgeon's house in the village where their wounds were dressed, after which they were taken to their respective homes. A third man, named John Craddock, aged twenty-five, was discovered to be so terribly injured that it was deemed necessary to take him to the accident ward of St. Thomas's Hospital in London. House surgeon Mr Hartnell ascertained that Craddock had received a compound fracture of the right thigh, severe scalp wound, fracture of the right arm, and extensive injuries to the ribs. Various parts of his body were also lacerated and contused. The first two men progressed favourably but poor Craddock was described as being in a hopeless condition.

An occurrence of an extremely tragic nature took place in Belfast in June 1849. Patrick Breen, a private of the 13th Light Infantry, and his wife, Sarah, had been married at the District Registrar just a few hours before their fatal accident. Mr Jas Carson, on being examined by the coroner, stated that he was employed as a labourer in a sandpit belonging to Mr J. Millar, at Ulsterville, near the Institution of the Deaf and Dumb and the Blind. About half-past six on the Saturday morning, on arriving at work, Carson found that there had been an extensive fall of sand from one side of the bank since his last visit the previous Wednesday. He stated that no sand had been removed by carts on the Friday. On shovelling away two loads of sand, Carson was astonished to come across a woman's bonnet, and immediately afterwards her bare head. He communicated the find to another employee who went to fetch the master. Police were then informed of the accident. It was proven that the young woman had left her house at six o'clock on Friday evening and had afterwards been seen walking with her husband on the Botanic Road. It was clear that there had been a heavy shower at seven o'clock and indications showed that the couple must have taken shelter from the rain under the bank of sand. A juror observed, quite properly, that as it had been so wet on the Friday, the brow of the pit must have been saturated and heavy. When both bodies were recovered, it was seen that the young woman's arm was still around her husband's neck. A verdict of accidental death was returned, accompanied by a unanimous recommendation that more attention should be given to the condition in which the banks of the pit were preserved, and that no dangerous excavation should be permitted. Sarah Breen was from Dromore and was a domestic servant for a respectable family on the Botanic Road. Patrick was a native of Dublin and had enlisted in the army four years previously. Both were committed to one grave in Friar's Bush burial ground, at a funeral accompanied by soldiers of the 13th Regiment in which the young soldier was enrolled.

A very sad accident occurred in Glaslough, Ireland in August 1850. A poor, industrious old man named Owen Corley, who had been struggling against poverty and ill-health, was employed in breaking stones in an old quarry near the town, in order to support his family. He had been picking some stones out of a bank when a large quantity of clay gave way, burying him under the weight. Nobody was around to lend assistance and poor Corley remained there until his wife came to see what was keeping him so long from his dinner. When she found him literally buried alive, there was nothing to be seen but her husband's hand. Help was called for immediately and Corley was dug out, but sadly he was already dead.

A great sensation was created in October 1855, in consequence of a man named Thomas Carter being buried alive in a gravel pit. The unfortunate 40-year-old was engaged in laying down some earth pipes into a main sewer near Battersea Bridge, London, when the gravel gave way and buried Carter beneath. Men were instantly set to work to extricate him from the frightful situation, but it took a great exertion and many hours to retrieve him. Eventually they managed to ger the poor man out and removed him to Chelsea workhouse. Sadly, although every possible assistance was rendered, Thomas Carter died within a few minutes of arrival.

In July 1889, a discovery of remarkable circumstance was made at York. A boy named Henry Steward, eight years of age, from Dundas Street, was missing. The Chief Constable, G.W. Whitfield, placed the case in the hands of Police Constable Blackburn, with the result that the child was found entombed in some old buildings in Skeldergate, which were being pulled down for the purpose of making improvements. It appeared that the boy had gone there to gather old wood and the roof of the building had fallen in and buried poor Henry in the debris. When found he was naturally in a very weak state, but with care soon recovered. He had been entombed without food or water for three days, and Henry's timely discovery undoubtedly saved him from a terrible and lingering death for, at his tender age, he could not have held out much longer.

A terrible disaster occurred in St. Anthony, Newfoundland, in April 1891 when a heavy accumulation of snow, which had gathered on a high cliff, swept down and buried the dwelling of Levy Andrews. Nine people were in the house at the time, five in the loft and four in the kitchen. Mrs. Andrews was just going out of the porch to see what the terrific noise was when the avalanche crashed into the building. Six days later her lifeless body was found under fourteen feet of snow, her head smashed, her neck and arms broken. The Andrews' eldest daughter was found dead lying across the stove, which had been shattered to smithereens. One of the sons, who was rescued alive, died afterwards from a combination of his injuries, exposure and starvation. George Reed, who was in the loft, was so badly injured that he was unable to lift his arms but did go on to make a good recovery. Another rescued daughter suffered a broken leg.

A frightful accident occurred at the Vogel Ironworks in Wartberg, Austria, in August 1892. During some repairs to the furnaces, a workman named Pacher was, through some terrible oversight, immured in one of the flues. It was supposed that Pacher had fallen asleep after his work and escaped the notice of the men who were employed in bricking up the flue. Two days passed and naturally the man's relations, on becoming anxious, went to the ironworks to make inquiry. It was then remembered where Pacher had last been seen at work. The flue was pulled down, and the poor man's charred remains were found. Bricks torn out in the interior of the furnace showed how desperately the unfortunate victim had struggled for his life.

In May 1893, an account was received in St. Petersburg of a remarkable experience that befell a young woman named Alexandrina Schitkine, seventeen years of age, who was discovered lying in a state of complete exhaustion near the village of Bogorodskaya, in the province of Moscow. The girl related that she had fallen asleep in the evening on a heap of straw, and on waking some hours afterwards found herself under a mass of snow that had fallen during the night. It had enveloped her to the depth of three feet and all attempts by Alexandrina to extricate herself proved unavailing. She remained buried under the snow for fifty-one days, the only sustenance during that time being a few morsels of bread that she happened to have with her. When at length the young woman was rescued, she was found to be in a state of complete exhaustion and lack of nourishment, and it required several days of constant care and nursing to restore her strength. On recovering, Alexandrina stated that she had not experienced any excessive cold and had only occasionally been seized with shivering.

It was a terrible imprisonment that Richard Davis (see bottom image on page 6 of the plate section) suffered for forty-seven hours in the Dolcoath Mine, 412 fathoms beneath the earth's surface, in October of 1893. About a hundred men were engaged in the rescue work after the collapse of a mine tunnel and after a great deal of weary waiting they managed to reach Davis, who alone of the imprisoned men was alive. Strange to say, he was apparently little worse for his long incarceration. Davis's safety depended on the fact that a portion of a stall, a framework of board in which he was found, remained intact. As the exploration party neared the place, one of the crew crawled underneath the fallen timbers and grasped Richard by the hand, saying, 'How are you, old fellow?' to which the former cheerfully replied, 'Getting on all right, but feeling a bit grubbish!' Davis was carefully drawn out and after receiving some light refreshments, was quickly removed to the surface where further refreshments were administered. Unhappily, he could give no information respecting his comrades.

A tragic accident, by which a young married man named Peter Bradley, residing in Derrymore, near Newry, Ireland, lost his life was reported to the coroner for South Armagh on 27 August 1902. It appeared that the deceased was working alone in a sandpit, situated in the townland of Tullyhappy, owned by a woman named Eliza Gracey. At half-past five in the afternoon, Mrs Gracey had a conversation with Bradley where he was working at the pit and left him shortly afterwards to attend to some other duties. On her return at six o'clock, she was shocked to find that a portion of the bank had fallen in and buried Peter Bradley alive. On closer examination, Mrs Gracey saw the hands of the deceased protruding from under the soil. Information was at once sent to the Bessbrook police, and in a short time Sergeant Lowry and a couple of constables arrived. They removed the sand but when the body was recovered it was found that life was extinct. Bradley was a hard-working man, and much sympathy was felt in the district for his wife and other relatives. He had only been married for three months.

A shocking triple fatality took place in the vicinity of Whaley Bridge, Derbyshire on 13 October 1905, three men being buried alive in the presence of a crowd of onlookers who were powerless to save them. The names of the unfortunate victims were father and son Richard and Samuel Walker, and Harry Wooley. They were standing near a great heap of refuse which was being cleared from around the mouth of a disused colliery when, without warning, hundreds of tons fell away like an avalanche, completely burying them. Frantic efforts were made by a gang of men to disentomb the men before they were suffocated, but sadly when they were reached all three were dead standing in an upright position. Attempts at life preserving failed. All three were miners employed at a neighbouring pit.

Joseph Murray sadly lost his life in Perry's Brewery, Rathdowney, Ireland, in November 1906. The barley on No. 2 kiln, where Murray was working, was being emptied and it was assumed that he got inside to walk through the grain to push it down. Unaware of Murray doing so, another workman drew the slide at the bottom of the kiln to allow the grain to pass into another receptacle. Joseph Murray, together with some of the barley, slid into the aperture and when it was closed by the man below, sixty barrels of grain came toppling down on the unfortunate man burying him beneath it. Fellow workers were immediately apprised of the situation and had the pile of grain removed as quickly as possible but when Murray was extricated life was extinct.

Lindsay B. Hicks created nationwide attention in the United States when he was buried alive for fifteen days after an accident in near Bakersfield, California. Hicks was one of six miners who went to work in the Kern River Canyon mine on 7 December 1906. Soon after they entered the mine, there was a cave-in seventy feet below the surface and three men were killed outright. The others, including Hicks, survived in the debris, but two more died before help reached them. Hicks was pinned to the ground but fortunately underneath a tramway car. On the surface hope that the men were alive was given up.

Three days later, workmen who were excavating the tunnel preparing to recover the bodies heard queer tapping on one of the tramway rails. Some believed it was an echo, it was so faint, and others could not hear it at all. However, when the men rapped on the rail, their signals appeared to be answered. It was decided to force a half-inch pipe along the flange of one of the tramway rails. When it reached the entombed man, he thought it was a pick or drill and believed his rescuers to be nearby. Finding it to be a pipe, he called through it and told the workers that he was still alive and had subsisted by chewing tobacco. Hicks' right hand was free and with it he brought forth from his pocket a new plug of tobacco he had purchased before entering the mine.

The first pipe was withdrawn and another of the same size was inserted to transmit liquid nourishment to Hicks. A surgeon stood on the outside end of the pipe and prescribed the amount of milk and other stimulants to be sent. Hicks talked through the pipe, telling how he had battled mental tortures and insanity, and how he heard rats gnawing in the pit. A phonograph was installed, and Hicks listened by the hour to music. This was on the twelfth day, and it caused him to laugh like a child.

Meanwhile the outside world watched the progress of the rescue. Newspapers from many periodicals sent correspondents and photographers. Rescuers reached Lindsay Hicks at midnight on the fifteenth day, tied a bandage over his eyes to protect them from the outside light, placed him on a stretcher and carried him out. When the news reached Bakersfield there was a big celebration. Hicks displayed no serious ills. Cases of chewing tobacco and even marriage proposals arrived. Hicks went on the lecture circuit but interest in him soon died out. Later he was hired by a Chicago museum, lecturing on how it felt to be buried alive.

Forty workmen were buried on the evening of 4 January 1907 in the cutting of a new railway line between Lamscheid and Leining, near Bingen, Germany. The dead bodies of thirteen men, and fifteen injured workmen, were recovered. An embankment had collapsed, burying two men. To rescue them, large parties of other labourers employed along the line were immediately set to work, and a wide pit was dug in which were about fifty men, when the overhanging hillside fell, burying forty of the labourers under masses of earth. The rescue work, which was continued throughout the night, was dangerous, owing to the possibility of fresh masses of earth falling on the workers.

In March 1908 a Reuter's message from Brigue, a favourite Swiss resort on the Rhone, near the entrance to the Simplon tunnel, stated that considerable damage and loss of life was caused at the village of Goppenstein, situated at Loetschberg tunnel, by the collapse of an hotel built at the southern entrance to the tunnel, and of the offices of the Loetschberg works. Between twenty and thirty persons were buried under the ruins. According to the initial news reports twelve people were killed, with ten of the bodies being recovered. Doctors and engineers attached to the Leotschberg Works were advised of the catastrophe in the course of the night and at once set out with a rescue party, the disaster being attributed to an avalanche.

The destroyed buildings did not lie in the path of the avalanche but were literally hurled down by the displacement of air, caused by the fall of an enormous mass of snow. The disaster occurred just as engineering and clerical staff were sitting down to dinner. Suddenly a loud noise was heard and two children rushed into the room crying out, 'An avalanche! An avalanche!' At the same moment a violent rush of air, caused by the fall of the enormous mass, wrecked the buildings, burying about thirty people in the ruins. The post office, which was also occupied by the local police, keeled over to an angle of forty-five degrees. A profound sensation was caused amongst the inhabitants of Goppenstein and the tunnel workmen, and many of the latter left the area soon afterwards. The tunnel works were not damaged, but work was suspended for some days.

Heroic deeds were performed by two doctors, a Catholic priest, and others, at the little mining village of Oulton, near Leeds in May 1910. Several new pits were being dug there and a party of pit sinkers were engaged about a hundred yards down one of the shafts when, owing to a support having given way, a huge slice of the side of the pit gave way. Four of the men, William Senior, Patrick Gill, William Harrison and John O'Brien, were buried and it was surmised that the were killed immediately.

A far more horrible fate, however, was reserved for Patrick McCarthy who was also one of the party. The men were working on a wooden platform and when the landslide occurred this tilted slightly, with McCarthy's leg slipping in between the platform and the side of the shaft. The earth then continued to fall, and as the platform righted itself McCarthy was trapped fast. His shouts for help quickly attracted the attention of his workmates at the mouth of the shaft, who realised that something untoward had happened. The shower of earth and huge stones continued to fall down the pit and any attempt at rescue was considered impossible. Pinned helplessly against the side of the pit, poor Patrick McCarthy was unable to dodge any of the missiles which were pelting down upon him, some of them from a great height. His agonised shrieks became unbearable to the listeners at the shaft head and eventually a volunteer, knowing it was long odds against his returning alive, decided to go down and see if anything could be done. He was lowered down into the pit but found he could do nothing and was pulled up again, being cut and injured by falling stone.

Ultimately two local doctors went down the shaft, it having been suggested that if McCarthy's leg were amputated his body might be drawn out. The idea, however, proved impracticable and the plucky doctors had risked their lives in vain. Suddenly a new horror dawned when water started rising from the bottom of the shaft. Slowly, as the hours passed, from eight in the morning when the initial collapse occurred, to eleven, the water rose until it reached the poor man's feet. Inch by inch it crept up while onlookers at the pit-head watched helplessly, until towards three o'clock it reached his chin.

Realising that all hope of saving Patrick McCarthy was gone, Father White, who had been fetched from Leeds, decided to take his life in his hands and go down to administer the last sacred rites to the unfortunate man, who was of the Catholic faith. The priest made the descent, but his heroism was in vain for McCarthy breathed his last breath before Father White got down to him, the water by that time being up to his lips and still steadily rising. The two doctors and the priest escaped injury, as did Mr Odgers the mine manager and mining inspector Mr Pickering, of Doncaster, who also ventured down the shaft.

A negro woman was buried alive near Ponce de Leon Avenue, in Atlanta, in June 1910, and the discovery of her head protruding from the ground, with just enough of the mouth and chin left above the surface for her to breathe, created wild excitement in the neighbourhood. Police investigation proved that she had been buried some half hour before she was discovered by half a dozen negro men, and it was at first believed that some horrible cruelty had been inflicted upon her. However, when she was dug up the woman indignantly protested that nobody had treated her wrongfully, and that she had been buried at her own request as a cure for rheumatism. She told police that when she wanted to be dug up her son-in-law would come and do the job. The officers reburied her and charged nothing for the task!

An earthquake that struck Mexico City in November 1912, placed the number of dead at over 1,000. Every building in the city of Acambay was demolished. Over 100 people were worshipping in a church when the structure crashed down upon the congregation, and all were buried alive in the wreckage. Half of the bodies were unable to be recovered until weeks later. Other towns in the northern part of the state were reported to have been destroyed with hundreds more killed or injured. A great hill in the centre of the stricken district was said to have turned into a volcano, smoking and throwing up great masses of rock which crashed into the village at the foot of the hill. Scientists declared that it had become a new earthquake centre which would constantly menace Mexico City as it is less than 50 miles away. Slight shocks were felt at intervals after the largest quake and the district rapidly became depopulated. People left by the hundreds, abandoning all their possessions, and leaving the bodies of the dead unburied.

Two men, survivors of a mine explosion at Finleyville, Pittsburgh, United States, were rescued on Saturday, 26 April 1913, after having been buried alive since the disaster on the previous Wednesday noon, when between 90 and 115 men lost their lives. Their escape was regarded as miraculous. After the mine inspectors had left, two members of the rescue crew entered the hole to look for bodies. Two-and-a-half miles from the entrance they heard a cry for help and found Charles Crawl and Philip Legler, both thirty-six-years-old. The men were sent to the Monongahela City Hospital, four miles away. At the time of the report, 93 bodies had been recovered and 40 identified.

Jacob Marner, an old-time resident living ten miles north-west of Warden, Washington, United States, was buried alive in a cistern he was digging on his ranch in July 1913. The soil where he was working was a black sand and Mr Marner was cementing as fast as he dug down, but when about twelve feet down the walls began to cave a little, so his wife went down to help. They were both working to get the wall repaired so that it would hold, when a large quantity of sand caved in and covered Jacob up to his neck with his hands pinned down by his sides. Mrs Marner was partially covered up but managed to free herself. She was trying to help her husband out when the whole wall fell in, covering him to a depth of four feet and trapping Mrs Marner up to her armpits. She managed to free herself again and get out, running to the nearest neighbour, a quarter of a mile away, where she got help but it was too late to rescue the unfortunate man.

In May 1916, a serious accident occurred near the Belgatchia Bridge in India, where the Calcutta Improvement Trust coolies were digging out earth from a trench. It appeared that the trench had been excavated to the depth of about fifteen feet. At midday the workers adjourned for their meal, but four of them, together with a young boy, went down into the trench to protect themselves from the sun. There they lay down and were resting when a tram passed by the road about forty feet away. This caused the ground to vibrate, and one side of the trench caved in, burying them. An alarm was raised, and a rescue party began to dig the men free, but it was too late and all five were found dead.

Mr. Bompas, along with other Improvement Trust officials visited the scene and held an enquiry with a view to prevent a recurrence of such an accident.

A child on holiday at Aberdovey was buried alive while digging a tunnel in the sand dunes in August 1920. The victim was the nine-year-old son of Guy Alastair McDonald, of Tunbridge Wells and New Zealand. The boy's nurse was with him, and was only a few yards away, when the sand fell in on him, but the child was dead before he could be extricated. A verdict of accidental death was returned at the inquest. It was only three weeks since a similar fatality occurred at Aberdovey, to the ten-year-old son of novelist Ladbroke Black.

In August 1938, a Shrewsbury father helped the police and other civilians to dig out his little daughter, who had been buried by a fall of earth, but sadly the child was dead. The girl was Marjorie Brenda Waters, aged seven, daughter of Robert Waters, of 25 Harlescott Close. The tragedy occurred when the child was playing with several friends near her home. A twelve-foot trench was being dug for a sewer and Marjorie called on her companions to follow. As they were about to do so, a huge lump of clay fell from the side of the trench and buried the child. Screams from the other children brought many helpers to the scene, including Mr Waters and the police, and desperate efforts were made to lift the clay. The rescuers had to jump for safety themselves, as another huge lump fell and buried Marjorie more deeply. A small army of men dug frantically for two hours by artificial light, and the little girl's body was eventually recovered.

Fifteen Portuguese peasants, two of whom were rescued in a dying condition, were buried alive in December 1941 as they searched in an abandoned mine for wolframite. About fifty peasants sneaked by night into the long unused galleries at Lugar de Santo, near Oviedo, hoping to extract the metal, much sought after in war time for use in the manufacture of steel, when one of the galleries collapsed.

Rainstorms caused the worst recorded floods for a century on Kyushu Island, Japan, in June 1953. After days of torrential rain, riverbanks broke causing landslides, with 376 lives being lost and over 1,000 missing. Police said that several villages had simply disappeared, together with all the buildings and inhabitants. At Kumahoto an asylum collapsed, causing thirty-six elderly residents to be buried alive. US Army forces in the Far East flew to Fukuoka to help with rescue operations with bulldozers and helicopters trying to clear roads and deliver safe drinking water.

On 24 August 1953, two women were rescued after being buried alive for twelve days under the ruins of their house, which was destroyed in an earthquake at Argostoli on Kefalonia Island, Greece. The women had managed to survive by eating raw potatoes. Most of the people on the island were living in tents following several earth tremors. Another woman, aged seventy-three, was buried alive for nine days without food or water, but she was pulled free in remarkably good spirits and refused to leave the rubble of her home.

The Welsh community are no strangers to incidents relating to the coal-mining industry, but one disaster will forever be etched on the minds of the whole country. On 21 October 1966, nineteen people, mostly children, died when a sliding pit heap buried a school at Aberfan, near Merthyr Tydfil (see top image on page 7 of the plate section). Another 100 children and 30 adults were reported missing after the rain-soaked mountain of coal slurry, an estimated 2,000,000 tons, had engulfed the school, a row of houses and a farm. The landslide, caused by heavy rain, moved swiftly and without warning to crush Tantglas Infant School just as the 200 children had begun the day's first lesson. A massive rescue operation was immediately launched and rescue workers tore at the rubble to reach the trapped children. Miners at Aberfan Colliery were hurriedly recalled to the surface to join police, firemen and civil defence workers in the rescue battle. No survivors were found after 11;00am on that morning. The disaster resulted in 144 deaths, including 116 children, but sadly it was a week before all the bodies could be recovered. A tribunal's findings blamed the accident on the National Coal Board, the South-Western Divisional Board and certain individuals.

Chapter Ten

Fear & Wills

For centuries, fear-stricken individuals have made provision for the prevention of premature burial in their Last Will and Testament, occasionally imposing strict orders to be followed to ensure that life is, in fact, extinct. Although cases of people being interred whilst still alive decreased with medical advances, the possibility of such an occurrence was not altogether impossible. It is well known that owing to this slight possibility, remote as it is, many otherwise strong-minded people have lived under the shadow of a great fear and have directed payments to be made to doctors in their Last Will and Testament who would be willing to run the risk of murder to prevent someone from being buried alive. However, at the turn of the century, the *British Medical Journal* thought that the horrors of this fatality were more imaginary than real. It said in a report: 'If a person in a state of trance were to be buried while life still persisted in a latent state, it is scarcely conceivable that the victim could awake. The unconsciousness of catalepsy would simply deepen until it became fixed in the dreamless sleep of death.'

One of the earliest recorded cases of a Will being made in fear of being buried alive was left by a lady in Holborn, London, who left fifty shillings to her surgeon on condition that he cut her throat as soon as she had been dead for twelve hours.

In November 1808, a corpse was taken from Charter House Square, London, and buried in Islington Churchyard. A stone was erected with the inscription:

In Memory of
MRS ELIZABETH EMMA THOMAS,
Who died 28th October 1808
Aged 27 years.
She had no fault, save what travellers give the moon,
The light was bright, but died, alas! too soon.

Mr Hodgson, the coroner, received a letter, intimating very strong suspicions that the deceased had not died naturally, in consequence of which he applied to the Parish Officers, who ordered the grave to be opened. It was done on the morning of 8 November and the body removed to the vault under the church for the inspection of the jury, which looked upon it in the course of the day when the following appeared in evidence:

The lady died on a Friday, was buried on the Saturday, and the gentleman with whom she lived (not being married) left town on Sunday and embarked at Portsmouth on Monday for Spain. On examining the body, a silver pin, about nine inches long, was found sticking in the heart through the left side of the body. A medical gentleman, who attended the deceased, declared that the pin was inserted at the request of the gentleman, to prevent the possibility of Mrs Thomas being buried alive. The jury brought in a verdict of 'died by the visitation of God.' The corpse remained unburied in the vault until a later date.

The Last Will and Testament of veteran and eccentric artist James Northcote RA was presented to Doctor's Commons in August 1831, and what an extraordinary document it is. Born in Plymouth in 1746, Northcote directed that his body be kept uninterred as long as it was possible to prevent the possibility of being buried alive, and to be inspected by a competent surgeon. Mr Northcote desired to be buried either in the vault under the new St. Marylebone Church, near to his late friends, Mr Conway and Miss Booth, or in St. Paul's Cathedral, near his late lamented friend and master, Sir Joshua Reynolds. He directed that Francis Chantrey, RA, a sculptor, would execute a fit and proper monument to his memory, for which he ordered his executors to pay one thousand pounds; the same artist to execute a monument for the deceased's brother, Samuel Northcote, to be placed in St. Andrew's Church, Plymouth, at an expense of two hundred pounds. James Northcote died on 13 July 1831, aged eighty-four, and a monument created by Francis Chantrey was erected in Exeter Cathedral, just as the aged painter had wished.

Among the numerous suicides that took place in the nineteenth century in England, a suicide committed from a fear of being buried alive must surely be counted as a singular occurrence. Letitia Grant, aged fifty-six, killed herself for this very reason in September 1832. James Coster, her nephew, who gave evidence before the coroner, said his 'aunt was naturally a very timid woman, and always expressed her alarm at the least infection.' The previous week Miss Grant complained of a bowel problem which, despite all opinions to the contrary, she insisted was an attack of cholera. She recovered but was so fearful of the disease that every morning she fumigated the room with preventatives of various description. The following Monday Letitia, fearing another attack, asked to be removed to the Cholera Hospital and requested that if she fell victim to the illness, that she might be bled, lest the medical men should be deceived and inter her alive. James called in medical aid to convince his aunt that there were no grounds for her fears, yet still she declared that she had the disease. In the afternoon, about three o'clock, James heard a noise in his aunt's sitting-room and upon running upstairs found the woman on the floor, lying in her own blood with her throat cut in the most horrid manner. She was quite dead with the razor, with which she had committed suicide, lying by her side.

One of the most curious bequests was reported in the *Publicateur d'Arles*, in France, when in December 1844 an old lady from the town died. She had always expressed a dread of being buried alive and left a legacy of 600 Francs to the person who would, immediately on her death being declared, begin to tickle her feet! They were to continue to do so for the customary forty-eight hours which elapsed between death and burial, in order that no possible doubt could be entertained of her being really dead. The maid servant, who had been apprised of this legacy whilst her mistress was still living, began to tickle her feet the moment death was declared. However, after eighteen hours of almost incessant application, the maid was obliged to relinquish the task from exhaustion and was followed by another person, the two agreeing to share the fortune. The time having expired, and the old lady giving no sign of life, she was placed in her coffin and interred.

In September 1867, a rare instance of burial thirty years after death occurred in Berlin, East Germany. The dead woman who had lingered so long above ground after her demise was Rachel Levin, the celebrated beauty and author (see bottom left image on page 7 of the plate section), and wife of the late Herr Von Varnhagen, a well-known Prussian diplomat and writer on contemporary history. Having a mortal fear of being buried alive, Rachel Levin ordered in her last testament that the upper part of her coffin should be made with a glass window and the coffin watched constantly for a month after death. It was then to be deposited in a special hall for a period of thirty years, all of which was duly carried out as per the woman's instructions.

The fear of being buried alive has often made people do strange things. An instance was afforded by the curious interment in Manchester which was thus given in the local obituary in 1868: 'On the 22 of July were committed to the earth in the Harpurhey Cemetery, the remains of an eccentric old lady named Miss Beswick, removed from Peter Street Museum'. The explanation was that the lady, who was believed to have died more than a hundred years before, left some property to her medical attendant 'so long as she should be kept above ground.' The doctor embalmed the body with tar and, leaving the face exposed, wrapped it in a strong bandage. This homemade mummy long adorned the meeting place of the Manchester Natural History Society but, as one of the local papers drily put it, 'the Commissioners charged with the rearrangement of the Society's collections have deemed this specimen undesirable and have at last buried it.' But what was the true nature of the mummification of Miss Beswick?

Born in the year 1688, Hannah Beswick was the daughter of a wealthy landowner from Birchen Bower. She had two brothers, but when the father died she is said to have claimed and taken possession of the largest share and made the family property her residence. Hannah lived to a grand old age and had for her medical attendant a Doctor White, a physician of some standing and wealth in Manchester. In her latter days, Miss Beswick appears to have gone to reside and end her days at Dr. White's, possibly to be near a doctor whom she could trust, and in his house she died in 1758, aged seventy years. Dr. White was executor of Hannah's will and was bequeathed £400 to pay the cost of her obsequies. The bequest was coupled with the requirement that she should not be buried for some time after her death. Some say that to escape lessening the sum thus set aside for a funeral, and to keep the £400 for himself, the doctor embalmed her body and kept it in a room in the older portion of his house, Cheetwood Old Hall. However, the property seems to have been unsuitable for Dr. White to stay, and he moved to Ancoats Hall, taking the embalmed body with him, but once there it was placed on the roof. After a short stay he moved to Sale and again placed the body on the roof, where it remained for over thirty years, long after the doctor's death in 1776. During a change of tenancy, the mummy was handed over to the Natural History Society where it became an object of awe and intense observation until its subsequent burial.

Edward Bulwer-Lytton, Conservative politician and writer, seems to have had a morbid fear of being buried alive if we judge by the following directions as to the disposal of his body after his death in 1873:

> I desire that it may not be disturbed from the bed in which it may be lying, nor prepared for burial, nor, above all, be placed in a coffin, till three medical men of high standing and reputation shall have inspected it separately, and not in the presence of each other, and shall have declared in writing, to be signed by them respectively, that the signs of decomposition have unmistakably commenced. And I desire that two out of the three medical men shall be other than the medical men who have attended me in my last illness. I forbid all dissection or autopsy of my remains, unless there be a suspicion in the mind of my executor that I have not died a natural death, but earnestly request that the most approved means (short of mangling the body) may be used for restoring my life in case there be any doubt of my decease, or I appear to be in a catalepsy or trance.

In January 1876, Joseph Wild, 18 years of age and residing with his mother at No. 6 Wellington Street, Rochdale, attempted suicide by inhaling chloroform. Wild's mother frequently had to leave her son in order to go about her business and was absent from home one Friday afternoon, returning at five o'clock to find Joseph lying in an almost lifeless condition. His face was deadly pale, although she detected him snoring a little. Thinking he was dying, Mrs Wild ran to fetch Dr Bland, who was fortunately at home. On arriving at the house, the doctor found that the young man was suffering from the effects of chloroform inhalation, with an empty bottle which had contained the drug being found near him. Joseph's lungs were almost paralysed, but measures were employed to restore his breathing and ultimately the lad was brought round. But for the opportune return of the mother, death might have ensued, as the doctor was only just in time to save Joseph's life. Wild had been out of employment for several months and occasionally complained of being very low-spirited. When the young man recovered, he stated that he had sniffed at the bottle of chloroform, becoming unconscious immediately, and recollected nothing until the doctor's second visit. A pocketbook was found in which, prior to inhaling the chloroform, Wild had made certain statements as to why he had determined to commit such a foolish act. He apparently feared being buried alive and gave directions that an examination should be made to place beyond doubt that he was dead, and not in a state of coma. Dr Bland reported the matter to the police and stated that the lad required careful watching. Joseph was removed to Prestwich Asylum, as he was evidently in a very low condition. When he recovered, Wild made the almost incredible statement that he had procured no less than two ounces of chloroform from a druggist in Rochdale.

A curious will was left by Captain Hartmann in 1881. He was a retired officer from the British Army who had been living on an estate in Jamaica for many years. Many eccentricities seemed to have marked the conduct of the gallant officer, amongst them a morbid fear of being buried alive. The captain accordingly directed that his body should remain in an open coffin as long as possible and, when burial became absolutely necessary, ordered that his head be cut off. For performing this operation, two medical men were to be paid a fee of £10. Captain Hartmann's chief characteristic was an exaggerated sympathy for animals. In his will, it was stated that his hundreds of acres of grazing and breeding farms were to be kept on until the mules and horses died a natural death. The animals were not to be used for any purpose whatsoever but were to be allowed to roam about in perfect freedom. Provision was also made for his pets – dogs, cats and birds – a person being placed in charge of them and the estate not to be released until the last of them were dead. The proceeds were then to be bequeathed to the Society for the Prevention of Cruelty to Animals.

The body of Dr Charles F. Heuser, who died at 214 South Sharp Street, Baltimore, in January 1891, was cremated at Loudon Park. He was a well-known physician and apothecary. The circumstances connected with his ghastly directions for the disposal of his remains make his story and that of his family a very remarkable one. Dr Heuser left a will in which he requested that his heart be taken from his body in the presence of witnesses on the day of his death, and that his remains be afterwards cremated, the ashes to be distributed among his friends. The strange clause concerning the heart of the dead physician caused somewhat of a sensation, but his friends resolved to carry out his wishes as nearly as possible.

A number of doctors and surgeons declined to mutilate the corpse of their dead friend, but Dr Bernard Meyer, in the presence of a few colleagues, removed the heart from the body. Then replacing it, the remains were made ready for cremation. The ashes were disposed of as directed in the will. The strange request of Dr Heuser was accounted for by someone who knew him well and from the fact that he had entertained a horror of being buried alive. Heuser often talked on the subject, and his fear of premature burial was increased after a talk with a physician from Virginia who said that, in a number of cases, he had seen corpses disinterred which showed that the person had come to life after burial. Some of the bodies were drawn up in the coffins or lay on their sides dreadfully contorted.

Resolved upon escaping premature burial by having his body cremated, Heuser determined to avoid the possibility of being burned alive by the singular expedient mentioned. A circumstance that adds additional interest to the ceremony is the fact that Dr Heuser, after his wife's death some years before, drove a knife into her heart to protect her from the possibility of being immured alive. He had frequently told the story of this affair himself, and said it was the most terrible duty he ever had to perform, to thrust cold steel into the bosom of the woman he loved, as she lay on the bier before him, yet he could not think of letting her run the awful risk of coming back to life in her grave.

Another peculiar but related circumstance is that many of Dr Heuser's family had their hearts pierced or their veins and arteries cut after death. The fear of premature burial seemed to have pervaded the whole family and led to the utmost precautions being taken to ensure escape from such a fate. None of them, however, except the doctor were cremated.

George W. Fay, of Hammonton, New Jersey, who died in January 1891, was haunted by a terrible fear of being buried alive and compelled his relatives to promise that, before they consigned his remains to the grave, they would plunge a dagger into his heart. During his last illness, Fay often dreamed of having fallen into a trance and being buried prematurely. These dreams formed the motive for his dying injunction. He stipulated that his body should be kept above ground until there were distinct signs of decay and then, in order to make doubly sure, that a dagger provided for the occasion should be plunged into his heart in the presence of witnesses, and there left. This request was carried out after the body had rested in its coffin for two weeks above ground, and when

George Fay's remains were finally consigned to the cemetery the fact of his death had been proven beyond any possibility of doubt.

Actuated by a similar fear of premature interment this same practice was observed by the members of a Virginia family noted in the state's political and social history for more than a century. While the commonwealth was still a colony, occasion arose for exhuming the body of a member of the family. The indications were to the effect that the unhappy person had been buried alive, and to prevent a recurrence of the catastrophe, that and succeeding generations adopted the plan of stabbing to the heart each deceased relative, whether man, woman, or child, the knife being wielded by the head of the house. However, in the mid-nineteenth century, the custom was abandoned under circumstances of peculiar horror. A beautiful young girl had been pronounced dead by the attending physicians, and after the preparation of her body for burial her father plunged a knife into her bosom. At the touch of the steel, she sprang up, uttered a scream, and fell into true death. The father committed suicide with the same blade which he had used to cause his daughter's death and the family thereafter relinquished the time-honoured practice.

In December 1892, there was an attendant at the Odd Fellows Cemetery in San Francisco whose duty it was to enter a vault there at brief intervals and to look into the face of the dead. He continued the vigil until fifteen days had passed, performing the wishes expressed in the will of the late Augustine Perichon, a Frenchwoman who died in the city. Madame Perichon entertained a fear that it would be her lot to be buried alive and the story of her dread is an interesting one.

Augustine Perichon was born in Orleans, France, in 1826. In 1848, when she was 22, she emigrated to the United States and was married in New York City. From early childhood she loved to read tales of romance and fiction, but nothing held greater fascination for her than the story of some poor unfortunate whose fate it was to be buried while in a trance. It is said that Augustine accumulated the printed announcements of all the most horrible incidents of this kind recorded during the first half of the nineteenth century. In 1854 she crossed the continent to San Francisco. Two years after her arrival, Mme Perichon obtained a divorce from her husband but soon married again. Her second husband died in 1858.

Besides a few personal effects, Augustine left money and jewellery to the value of almost $6,000 but had no relatives either in America or France to inherit from her, although during the last few years of her life she spent a lot of time and money trying to trace descendants from either her father or mother's family. Mme Perichon directed in her will that after the doctors pronounced her dead, her body should be placed in a coffin and then in the vault of the Odd Fellow's Cemetery. The lid of the coffin was to be so arranged that her face could be seen, and someone should be paid generously to look upon it at brief intervals. This was to be kept up for fifteen days, during which time preparations were to be made to place the body in its last resting place in the same cemetery.

Some years before, Augustine Perichon had purchased a plot in the cemetery, and her will directed that a vault be built in it suitable for the reception of three bodies – her own and those of two friends. The exact dimensions of the grave were given, with an iron framework to be placed at the bottom, upon which, side by side, the three coffins were to rest. Besides this, directions were given with regard to the headstones and the epitaphs they should bear, as well as minute details of less importance. One of the two friends who was to share the grave with the remains of Augustine Perichon was still living at the time of her death. No one seemed to know why these two, of the many who formed her circle of friends, were singled out, although those closest to her said that if Augustine were alive she would have declared it to be nobody's business but her own. The two who were to share the grave were Monsieur J. Bonde, a Frenchman, who died five years previously and whose body was moved to the Odd Fellows' cemetery, and William Weissman, a German. The latter was seventy years old in 1892 and was an inmate of the Old Soldiers' Home in Santa Monica.

In one of Lord Randolph's plays, occurs the following dialogue:

Deilus: 'Death to me is terrible. I will not die.'
Aphobus: 'How can you, sir, prevent it?'
Deilus: 'Why I will kill myself.'

A poor London clerk escaped the terrors of death by the same effective means in March 1896. He seemed to have been oppressed by the fear of being buried alive, and to escape that awful possibility he committed suicide by taking a dose of poison. Among the numerous letters which he wrote before he committed the deed was one in which he said:

'I have for years had the dreadful thought and sensation that I shall be buried alive. Will you, my old neighbour, please make quite sure that I am actually dead before having me screwed down? Please do this for me; it is my dying request. Be sure you do not forget. I daresay you know the sign of true death.' Clearly in this case the poor fellow's reason had given way, but many people, Edgar Allan Poe among them, were troubled by a similar fear.

For thirty days and thirty nights, counting from 6 February 1896, the date of the funeral, the lid of the casket in which lay the body of John G. Rose was not allowed to be screwed on. Mr Rose was a wealthy brick manufacturer who died at his home at Roseton, New York, four miles north of Newburg. The casket was held in a receiving vault in Cedar Hill Cemetery, half a mile from the late residence of the dead man. John Rose had, in his later years, been haunted by an acute fear that he might be buried alive, and it was in accordance with his often repeated wishes that the precaution of keeping the coffin lid unscrewed was taken. The door of the vault remained unlocked so that in case Mr Rose awakened from a trance, he could raise the alarm if unable to make his way out of his resting place. Two guards were positioned at the entrance of the vault, one at night and the other in the day, until the body gave positive evidence of decomposition, or the specified time had elapsed. One of the guards employed was a local from Roseton, the other a long-trusted employee of the deceased man. One theory offered by a relative was that Mr Rose was apprehensive that body snatchers might seize his corpse and hold it to ransom. The spot in the cemetery where the body was interred was at the centre of three vaults. One was built by Henry Ball, of the jeweller's Ball & Black of New York, the other belonged to that of gentleman George Gordon.

The coroner for Central London held an inquest in June 1900 concerning the death of Ella Decroix Bannister, aged thirty-three years, a single woman of independent means, who had been living at the Great Western Hotel in Paddington, London. Miss Bannister committed suicide by shooting herself. Mr Charles Potter, an Indian merchant, told the coroner that the deceased was his sister-in-law. It was stated that Ella Bannister had written a letter to her sister, in which she said, 'Immediately on hearing of my death communicate with Mr George Broadbent, my solicitor, who has my will and full instruction. I feel sure that you will carry out my last wishes. I have always had a great horror of being buried alive, so I make sure of death. I have injected morphia and have shot myself, so if the shot does not take effect, I hope that the morphia will.' The jury returned a verdict 'That the deceased committed suicide while of unsound mind.'

There was a great deal of discussion about the singular provision contained in the will of the late Duke of Saxony, which was to the effect that before his coffin was closed, a cut or incision should be made in his body, to make absolutely certain that he was dead. A similar clause was contained in the Last Will and Testament of the Reverend Dr Kerrick, President of Magdalen College, Cambridge, in 1904. He left ten guineas to his doctor on condition that he should cut off his head as he lay in his coffin, and he also desired that his eldest son should witness the deed. This wish was duly carried out, but it had a severe effect upon Kerrick's son, who was, unsurprisingly, ever afterwards a distinctly nervous man.

James Green Wellington of Corning, New York, died suddenly of heart disease in July 1907 at the age of seventy-six. Wellington had a horror of being buried alive and, several years earlier, made his brother promise to use every known test upon his body before giving up consent for burial. The doctor promised, if he survived, to carry out his brother's wishes. So, at the time of death, the body was carried in and placed beside Dr Wellington, who was bed-ridden, having been an invalid for fourteen years. The examination of the body was painstaking. Not until Dr Wellington was absolutely assured of death after half an hour expended in the closest scrutiny did he give consent to turn the body over to the undertaker. For many years James Wellington had been engaged in the banking business at Corning and he had also served as mayor and treasurer of the town.

The Pittsburgh police had to be called on 16 January 1910, to keep an inquisitive public from tearing down the house in which the body of Laura White, a rich recluse, was found partly gnawed by rats. The death of Miss White precipitated serious trouble between the Fidelity Trust Company of Pittsburgh and Doctor Robert White, the only living relative of the deceased. Dr White insisted that the proposition of the will made by his aunt, which said that she should be stabbed three times through the heart after she had been dead ten days in order that she would not be buried alive, be dispensed with. However, President Gray of the Fidelity Trust insisted that the requirements of the will be carried out in full. Dr White considered taking the company to court to prevent what he termed 'an unholy desecration' on the body of a woman. The corpse was removed to the undertakers who was given orders to cremate Miss White's body as soon as the stabbing was finished.

From those who had known Laura White for a long time, it was learned that for forty-five years she had been haunted with the fear that she would be buried alive. Apparently, in her youth Laura White had been engaged to marry a young man who died suddenly. Months later it was necessary for the family to disinter the body and move it to another graveyard. The coffin was opened, and the corpse was found to have turned over on its side, showing evidence that the young man had been buried alive. For weeks after that discovery, Miss White lay with brain fever and she never fully recovered from the horror of the discovery, hence she made arrangements to prevent herself from the same fate as her beau.

Elaborate precautions against premature interment were ordered in the will of Thomas Douglas Murray, of Iver Place, Iver, in Buckinghamshire, who died in November 1911. He was instrumental in establishing the first permanent bandstand in London's Hyde Park and was interested in the breeding of Pekinese dogs in England. Murray left an estate valued at £28,288. The testator directed that,

> on his apparent death, his body should be kept in a well-warmed bed for thirty-six hours thereafter. The body should then be placed in a coffin in a

warm room with the windows partially opened and watched for four days and nights. During this period the tests given in a pamphlet by Sir Benjamin Ward Richardson, *The Signs and Proofs of Death* were to be applied, and also during this period a bell attached to his wrist which could be easily audible both within and without the room. When decomposition has set in, a surgeon shall completely sever the spinal cord high up in his body, and his coffin may then be lightly fastened, but shall not be screwed down until the twelfth day after his death. His remains shall then be cremated either on the Downs near Stonehenge or the Downs near Battlesbury Hill, Wiltshire, or if impracticable, then at Woking, the ashes to be scattered to the four winds of heaven.

Murray also desired that no hatbands or mourning of any kind should be worn at his funeral, and that there should be no procession or parade when his remains were taken to the place of cremation. One hundred pounds was left to each of the executors of his will on condition that the above directions were carried out. He also left £200 to University College, London, for a travelling scholarship in the Egyptology department of the said college on condition that Mr. Flinders Petrie was connected therewith at his (the testator's) death and carrying on his excavations in Egypt.

Strict directions concerning his funeral were given in the will of John Clarence Hudson, of Plymouth Grove, Chorlton-upon-Medlock, Manchester, a retired solicitor whose estate was valued at £13,512, when he died in 1914. Hudson had left to each of his executors £50, to be increased to £150 if his directions as to embalming or burial should be carried out. He asked that his remains should be embalmed in the best and most efficient manner known to science, regardless of cost. He further stated that, having given considerable time and attention to the subject, having collected evidence that the premature interment of human remains instead of being of rare occurrence, was on the contrary a calamity of such appalling frequency as even to call for legislative interference. 'I hereby direct that if for any reason the imperative directions for embalmment herein contained shall not be carried out, my interment shall on no account take place until after the lapse of seven clear days from my death or supposed death.'

Fearful of being buried alive, a fate his dreams had pictured as having befallen a brother, Andrew J. Turner of Spruce Street, Philadelphia, a widely known cotton broker, exacted from his wife and daughter a promise, the fulfilment of which deferred his burial. Mr Turner died suddenly. Mindful of the solemn promise she had made to him that his body would not be buried until there was not the slightest chance a spark of life still remained, Mrs Turner refused to make arrangements for the funeral. A week following his death a service was held at the home, with Father Kieran of St. Patrick's Catholic Church officiating. Daily visits of an undertaker to the Turner home aroused the interest of neighbours in the fashionable Spruce Street area. There was much conjecture and finally one of the neighbours telephoned the bureau of health. An inspector was sent to the house and the strange request of Mr. Turner became known to the public.

It was explained that years previously a younger brother of Andrew Turner died suddenly of heart disease. He was buried after three days. On the night following the funeral Andrew had a disquieting dream. He saw his brother stirring in the coffin, gasping for breath and tearing at the cover of his living tomb. Often the dream recurred to him in all its horror. Fear of burial alive became almost an obsession with Andrew Turner and he made his wife and daughter promise over and over again that under no circumstances would his body be buried until death was absolutely certain.

Mr. Turner suffered from kidney trouble from time to time and his death was attributed to that illness. Doctor Fairies, of Twentieth and Walnut streets, who had been his physician for years, was summoned when Mr. Turner was found lifeless in bed. He said there was no doubt about the man being dead, and as Mrs. Turner was away, the body was embalmed. The undertaker who embalmed Andrew Turner said there was no possibility of him living in a trance with the poisonous fluid in his body. Yet Mrs. Turner would not consent to burial after the customary period. She had promised her husband to keep his body, and nothing could cause her to break it, she said.

Andrew Turner was forty-nine-years old. He was the son of the late William J. Turner, a cotton and wool importer. During the summer he went with his family and Mr. Hawes, his father-in-law, to their cottage at Newport. Early in September he and Mr. Hawes returned to the city, leaving Mrs. Turner and their daughter at Newport. The Spruce Street house was opened up and the two men were living there alone when Andrew was stricken. He complained of not feeling very well and went to his room. Several hours later Mr. Hawes went up to inquire how he felt and found his son-in-law dead in bed.

Still another who had a fear of being buried alive was Mrs Joanna Mitchell Thompson, who died on 14 April 1916 at East Orange, United States, and who in her will directed that a friend, Stephen Baldwin, inspect her body daily for forty days after her supposed death, to make sure that no signs of life returned. The health authorities and the management of Rosedale Cemetery objected, but the body, after unusual precautions to make sure that death really had ensued, was hermetically sealed in a casket and buried in a concrete grave. Each day for forty days Baldwin sat beside the grave, with his ear close to the ground listening for a sound from within. For this task, under the terms of the will filed for probate, Baldwin was to receive $200, if it was decided that by doing so he had carried out the instructions of the testatrix.

That some people have a mortal fear of being buried alive is evidenced by the strange request in the will of the late Mrs Maria L. Thompson, who died in Florence, Italy, and whose will was filed in Georgia, United States, on 27 October 1917. Mrs Thompson provided in her last legal testament that:

> As I die a member of the Roman Catholic church, if the permission of the church can be obtained, I wish my body to be cremated. If this cannot be done, I request that it be opened in such a way as to prevent my being buried alive and that quicklime be thrown on it so as to consume it quickly, and that my ashes be placed near the graves of my children.

In November 1918, George Philip Hitch, nearing ninety years of age although remarkably active, was at Laurel, Delaware, superintending the digging and arranging of his own grave. Hitch had spent most of his life in the town, but since the death of his wife a few years before, he had made his home with his children in Port Norfolk. Hitch had an obsessive fear of being buried alive. In preparation for his death, George Hitch had a coffin made up at his Virginia home, in the old style with a hinged door and glass over the top. This, he said, could be easily broken and by unfastening the door he could crawl out in the event of his 'being laid out' alive. He requested that no earth be put over the grave.

When Mrs Lucia Rosher, of Glanhonddu, Lanvihangel, in Monmouthshire, died in 1929 she left £5,642. She directed that she should be buried in the family vault at Oldcastle and also 'that an antique-shaped chest be made by Lewis Parry of British heart of oak, and the shell, made of elm, enclosed in lead. And that I be clothed in an ordinary black dress, without anything on my head and no shroud; that there shall be strong rings screwed on the inside opposite the ankles and waist for a scarf to be fastened through and across on account of the steepness of the road; that the vehicle (not hearse) be covered with free tree branches from Glanhonddu and flowers, which are not to be made into any symbolical design.' Mrs Rosher also stated: 'To avoid the danger of premature burial, from which several of my family have narrowly escaped, I desire that the lid of the shell or chest shall not be closed until the first signs of dissolution appear, and that the burial do not take place until at least seven days after the certificate of death is issued and the body has been seen by two qualified doctors.'

A Washington woman, who died in August 1948, asked in her will that her body not be embalmed for at least two weeks after her 'supposed death' in case she might only be in a trance or state of catalepsy. The will, filed for probate on 24 August in District Court, was that of Emma Von Toerne, aged fifty-three, of Kenyon Street, whose body was found at her home. Two days of newspapers accumulated at her door led to the belief that death had occurred on 1 August. Miss Von Toerne's will disposed of, among other property, 'my occult books covering astrology, numerology, mental magnetism and psychology.' A codicil dated 9 April 1943 to the 1934 will stated: 'If possible I would prefer that my body not be embalmed until at least two weeks after so-called death, as the spirit does not leave the body until decomposition sets in; and as long as the body is stiff the spirit still resides in the body and is merely paralysed so that movement cannot be made.' The codicil went on to say it might happen that her body would come back to life. It added there might be some danger connected with 'my spiritual investigations' since she might be in a trance or state of catalepsy for a few days or more and seemingly dead. Emma Von Toerne, for thirty years an employee of the Maritime Commission, left most of her estate to her mother, Augusta.

Finally, the true story of a man who erred on the side of caution.

A watch repairer in Istanbul, Turkey, was so afraid of being buried alive by mistake that he had a special grave built in 1964. Inside, the 72-year-old installed a push-button electric alarm, so that if or when he was prematurely buried, he could press the button to alert the guardroom in the cemetery!

Chapter Eleven

Science & Progress

The fear of being buried alive has tormented the human race from the very earliest times, and now and then the opening of tombs and coffins in graveyards has revealed most distressing evidence that those who were dear to us have come to life and become conscious in their graves. Indeed, many have left specific instructions in their Last Will and Testament to drain their arteries to make sure that they will not awake in the grave, and many wills are on file which provide that means be taken for keeping the supposed dead body under observation to give immediate relief at the first sign of reappearing life.

With the popularity and demand for embalming bodies growing steadily in the nineteenth century, the likelihood of a person being buried alive naturally decreased. There were various reasons for the necessity of removing organs and preparing bodies for their grave, not least to halt the emission of noxious gasses and natural putrefaction. Renowned Scottish surgeon William Hunter wrote extensively on the subject of embalming in order to preserve bodies and his brother, John, applied these methods in his funereal services from the mid 1700s. Embalming gradually became accepted for practicality, such as when a person died overseas or at a distance from their home and the family wished to ship the remains for burial, one prime example being during the American Civil War when servicemen died on the battlefield. It was also recognised that embalming would help to control the emittance of contagious and transmittable diseases. Also, as was the custom of viewing the dead before a funeral, it made the body of the deceased more presentable to mourners if it had been prepared in a sympathetic manner with the natural process of decomposition being somewhat delayed. Lord Nelson, for example, was killed at the Battle of Trafalgar and his body preserved in brandy and wine mixed with camphor and myrrh for over two months. By the time he was interred at a state funeral in 1805, his body was still in a remarkably lifelike condition.

Until the early 1900s embalming fluids often contained arsenic until it was discovered that less toxic chemicals would suffice, amid concerns that arsenic might contaminate the ground and water supplies. It also meant that if a person had actually died from arsenic poisoning and was later exhumed for post-mortem, their murderer might get away with the crime if the body had been embalmed, the medical examiner being unable to determine whether foul play was the real cause of death due to the formula in the embalming fluids. However, the views taken on embalming vary according to different religions, such as Jewish law which forbids embalming, requiring instead that the body be buried as soon at the earliest possible convenience. In Islam too, embalming is not practiced by Muslims unless the law requires it for specific reasons, such as when the deceased needs to be transported overseas. Followers of Islam bury their dead within twenty-four hours, believing that the soul should makes its journey to the afterlife as quickly as possible.

Whilst the usage and application of the chemicals used in the embalming process were strictly regulated and controlled, the deadly combination of formulas led to the death by embalming alive of one poor woman in 1929. However, a special grand jury investigating the death of Mrs. Garrett of Elizabeth City, North Carolina, failed to find sufficient evidence to bring charges against those involved. The woman died at St. Vincent's Hospital in Norfolk after an operation, following an injection of formalin from a bottle labelled nitrate of silver. Sadly, there were many factors lacking at the hearing. Sister Evelyn Fittsimmons was in charge of the hospital pharmacy where the bottle labelled 'Nitrate of Silver' was filled with a solution of formalin. Rather conveniently, a few days after the death of Mrs. Garrett, Sister Fittsimmons became ill, and had to be sent to St. Joseph's Hospital in Philadelphia. Thus, she was not available at the grand jury investigation. Another nurse involved in the case, Miss Eggleson, was recovering from an operation and was also unable to be present in court. Had these two important witnesses been able to attend the investigation and shed what light they could on the terrible death of a woman who was essentially embalmed alive, the report from the grand jury may have been altogether different. As it was, the jury were unable to wait for the two nurses to recover.

The whole incident, as terrible as it was, was hushed up by both the hospital officials and Norfolk coroner. However, here are the facts. Doctor Payne, the surgeon who treated Mrs. Garrett, knew that something was wrong when he gave her the injection on 23 April 1929. She suffered such pain that it was necessary to give her both morphine and chloroform to quiet her. Dr Payne knew that injections of a one per cent solution of silver nitrate didn't have that effect on patients. Two days after the horrible injection was given it was discovered by St. Vincent's staff that formalin had been injected into Mrs. Garrett's kidney. Nothing was done about it, the patient being sent home, kept in ignorance of the mistake, and permitted to suffer torturous pain for two weeks.

Norfolk coroner, Dr McDonald, delayed rendering a verdict on the case and found various excuses to postpone the inquest until 20 June, almost six weeks after Mrs. Garrett's death. Cecil Garrett, husband of the young woman who was literally embalmed alive, was much grieved over the fact that he was not notified of the inquest date and given no opportunity to be present. Mr. Garrett duly employed a law firm to handle his case against Dr Payne and the hospital.

In his court testimony, Dr Payne relayed how he had examined Mrs. Garrett and found a slight inflammation of the kidneys and proceeded to give an injection from a bottle labelled silver nitrate from one of the nurses, the fluid being given through a catheter. On realising the pain and distress that the patient was in, Dr Payne administered drugs to relieve the discomfort and recommended a further night in hospital for observation. The following day Mrs. Garrett had recovered sufficiently to be allowed home. It was fourteen days later that Dr Payne saw the woman again and on attempting to give a second injection he countered an alarming obstruction. The region of the left kidney was rigid and sensitive, and Payne decided upon an operation. On opening up the patient, the surgeon discovered that the ureter had turned black, and the left kidney black and gangrenous, he therefore removed both organs. Profoundly disturbed, Dr Payne took the organs to the pathological laboratory for analysis, where an immediate strong odour of formaldehyde gas was detected. It was then that the surgeon began to fear the truth. Mrs. Garrett died two days later, on 12 May. The hospital issued a certificate stating the cause of death as 'acute nephritis and heart failure.'

Among the inventions that commended themselves to public notice during the latter part of the nineteenth century were those relating to coffins, graves and burials. One of those was intended to furnish the tenant of a grave who had been buried prematurely with a means of escape or arousing the neighbourhood. This invention was a simple affair, being merely an open tube provided with a rope ladder and a bell and cord. Should the occupant of the coffin awake from a trance, he could climb the ladder and make his way back to the world or pull the bell and alert the townsfolk. For those whose only fear was that they may not be allowed to rest undisturbed, being the victim of grave robbers, one considerate inventor provided a 'torpedo grave' which, if disturbed, exploded at once and scattered the vandals to the four winds!

Cremation, as a means of disposing of the bodies of the dead in the United States, when first tried in New York state, on 4 December 1885, attracted a great deal of attention and there was also considerable discussion as to the relative merits of the new method as compared to the usual custom of underground burial. Many people were superstitious regarding incineration. People were at first loath to give consent to this disposition of the bodies of their friends and relatives. Those who favoured the new method urged its adoption, giving as their reason for the change that it was cleaner, cheaper, and did away with the necessity for elaborate funerals. It was also urged that the incineration of corpses of persons who had died of contagious diseases would lessen the dangers of contagion and would be the safest way in which to dispose of such bodies. On the other hand, the fear of being buried alive caused some to strongly advocate cremation. As an aid to the adoption of the new method, endorsements were secured from ministers and others, in which they said there was nothing unscriptural in disposing of the dead by means of fire and advocating the method as cleaner than burial.

The first cremation in New York state was at the Fresh Pond Crematorium, on Long Island, facing the Lutheran cemetery. This was on 4 December 1885. Since that time, cremations grew in popularity and gradually increased by fifty each year. The number of cremations at Fresh Pond up to the beginning of 1897 was given as 1,881. Of this number, 1,213 bodies were those of men, 98 of boys, 496 of women and 73 were the bodies of girls. There was a charge of $35 for the incineration of each body. This charge was only for the consuming of the body by means of heat, the body being placed in an airtight compartment of an immense furnace. Enough ashes were left to fill a small urn. It took several hours to dispose of a body, after which the ashes were collected and placed in the urn which had previously been purchased. Often the ashes were taken away by relatives, or at other times they were deposited in alcoves in the walls of the columbarium where the body had been cremated. By the requests of relatives endeavouring to carry out the various peculiar wishes of the departed, the ashes were also sometimes taken and scattered elsewhere.

There was a charge for the door which was placed in front of the niche. Urns could be bought from $9.50 up to $45, while the cost of the niche in the wall was between $15 and $25, according to its location. The cost of the cremation, $35 in 1897, was added to the cost of the urn for the ashes and the niche for the reception of the urn if required. When the body was borne to the crematorium, or columbarium as it was known at the time, there were extra charges according to the number of carriages brought into service. With cremation there was no necessity for the purchase of a burial plot, although many people did opt to bury the ashes of their loved ones.

On 11 June 1897, the sanitary committee of the New York Health Board approved plans of a new mausoleum company for the establishment of a sanitary mausoleum near High Bridge, with a capacity of between ten and twelve thousand bodies, and in which it was proposed to entomb the dead in cement receptacles. The bodies were to be exposed for several months to a current of air made chemically dry by passing it over sulphuric acid, the air to be purified afterward by fire. When the bodies were thoroughly desiccated the receptacle was to be made airtight. The mausoleum was to resemble a well-appointed library, with a main corridor and diverging halls leading to different sections.

The sepulchres were to be made of solid concrete, four inches thick and a little larger than an ordinary coffin.

One advantage claimed for the new system was security against grave robbers and a novel feature was protection against premature entombments. Electrical apparatus was to be provided and so adjusted to reach the body that the slightest movement would sound an alarm that could not fail to be heard by a watchman. There was also an indicator connected with the electrical apparatus showing exactly which sepulchre the alarm came from. According to the plans filed, a body was to remain in its sepulchre for three months before the tomb was hermetically sealed. Each sepulchre was to be constructed with a conduit of fresh air and with another to permit the egress of air after it had absorbed the gases and fluids of the body. The egress conduit was to terminate in a separate building, where the vitiated air would be purified by passage through a furnace, and thus, the company claimed, all noxious vapours would be destroyed.

On 24 February 1910, the annual meeting of the Association for the Prevention of Premature Burial was held in London. Dr Stenson Hooker, the vice-president, who occupied the chair, said that of all the associations in London he could not imagine one which had such deplorable details of real tragedy brought to its notice. There was a constantly increasing list of dangers from premature burial, to say nothing of the cases of actual burial. Hooker spoke of the increasing number of cases of trance and stated that only a few months before it had been his duty to be called in to see a little child who had collapsed, and for all the parents knew to the contrary, had passed away. He inquired what the child had been eating and discovered that it had been living on cheap sponge cakes which had poisoned it. The doctor stated that if the parents had been uneducated people there was a serious danger that they may have buried their child alive. Dr Hooker said that there was an increasing number of people who were actually giving orders that they be mutilated in some way to make sure that they would actually be dead before being buried. They constantly heard of well-known public men and women leaving instructions that a finger should be cut off or that a knife should be plunged into their neck to ensure that they were dead. He claimed that the whole question of burial reform was in a very relaxed and uncertain condition and required as much attention as the House of Lords, which caused much laughter among those present.

Dr. Walter R. Hadwen, of Gloucester, moved the following resolution:

That the meeting earnestly call upon the Government to seriously consider the necessity of speedily remedying the present unsatisfactory and dangerous state of the Burial Laws, and pledge itself to strenuously support the Bill of the association, entitled 'Death Registration and Burials Bill', which provided for the compulsory examination of bodies by qualified medical men before death be certified.

Dr Hadwen stated that it was the fashion among the medical profession to ridicule the thought of a person being buried alive and added that he knew of a woman who carried her death certificate in her pocket, after having been declared dead, and of another person, a collector of curios, who had his own death certificate framed and hanging in his drawing-room. A case was investigated in Lancashire in which a woman had obtained three death certificates in order to get insurance money upon the alleged death of her child.

There was considerable confidence placed in the opinion of medical men, but there were cases where the doctor had not even seen the patient, and in nine cases out of ten he never saw the corpse. There were, in round numbers, in the early twentieth century, 10,000 deaths registered every year in which the causes of death were never stated. It was recommended by the society that there should be a strong protest against hasty burials, especially in cases of judicial hanging. Dr Hadwen said the Government should make it compulsory that every corpse should be carefully examined by a qualified medical man before he signed a death certificate. He also advocated the establishment of waiting mortuaries, so that no body would be buried until the first appearance of putrefaction had set in – that, in his opinion, being the only sure and certain sign of death. Dr Brindley James, in seconding the resolution, stated that some years before in Bermondsey, London, he was requested to examine a man who had hanged himself. Two medical practitioners had stated that the man was dead, but he (Dr James) did not think so and after an hour's artificial respiration, the man began to breathe, was sent to Guy's Hospital and recovered. The resolution was carried.

The annual report for 1910 stated that the movement had made steady progress during 1909. During the five years, 1902–1906, the number of uncertified deaths in England and Wales was 43,817, or an average of 8,763 per annum, thus illustrating the necessity for reform. It was hoped that the Deaths Registration and Burial Bill would receive adequate attention and support by the new Parliament, and thus provide a much-needed safeguard against the serious perils of premature burial.

It is a very strange fact that up until the 1920s, science with all its research had been unable to suggest any certain and practicable method for determining positively that death had really come. Many tests, such as applying a lighted candle to the fingers to see whether a blister formed or not, injection of fluorescein into the veins, which would give a yellow cast to the face if there was the least flow of blood, and various other means, but none were satisfactory or positive.

In 1922 scientists conducted extremely interesting experiments starting at the very bottom of the ladder and examining into the well-known phenomena of suspended animation in the animal world with the hope of finding out more definite facts about death. It had been long known that germs, and indeed fish and reptiles, may be frozen stiff in a block of ice and yet thaw out into life and full activity. As everyone knows, bears and other animals curl up in the autumn and 'sleep' through the long, hard winter months until they wake up with renewed vigour, in what we call hibernation.

Professor Carrel of the Rockefeller Research Institute made many advancing steps in his studies by demonstrating in his laboratories that he could keep alive certain tissues and bones of the human body long after the corpse had been thoroughly dead and dissected. Physicians knew that certain persons had been buried alive in the sense that while the heart's action was still at a minimum they have been placed in a coffin. Stories of persons 'laid out' for the undertaker, and revived on his arrival, were not unknown. Some people revived on the bier, but the number of persons buried while the body as a whole lived was, in reality, very small. Moribund persons were buried at times of great confusion during plagues and epidemics. This happened when the people were in a state of narcolepsy or suspended animation.

In the first few years of the twentieth century, science pried into the mysterious secrets of suspended animation and began to understand how Hindu fakirs buried for months and sealed up in their tombs came to life again. The most recent case in which a person ran the risk of being buried alive in that era was that of Anna Held, the famous French actress (see bottom right image on page 7 of the plate section). The exact nature of Anna Held's illness proved an enigma to more than a score of physicians. After several guesses had been made and abandoned it was accepted for several months that she was suffering from multiple myeloma, a very rare condition affecting the bone marrow, of which in 1918, when she died, only fifty-two cases had been recorded. Then, in the last few weeks before her death, it was seriously questioned whether the diagnosis was correct. In addition to all the uncertainty about the nature of her illness, Anna Held presented a case of 'suspended animation' in her last hours, a mysterious condition which proved an inexplicable puzzle to doctors and scientists and caused terror to countless people who feared being buried alive while in an apparently lifeless state.

Reports tell us that Anna Held had been in a semi-conscious condition for about a week. At five minutes to four in the afternoon, the dying actress's watching daughter saw that her mother's breath had suddenly stopped. She called the attention of the attending physician, Dr E.M. Overton, who declared that

Anna Held was dead. The news was sent out to the press and Anna's friends. For nearly two hours, Anna Held looked and seemed, to all accounts, dead. Those mourning by her bedside were, therefore, naturally amazed to suddenly see her breathing again, her eyes open wide and the colour flushing into her cheeks. The doctor pronounced Anna Held alive and a correction was sent out to the newspapers who had received the earlier announcement. Then, within a few minutes, breathing stopped again and all the signs of death returned. Those in the room with Anna watched her for hours, hoping once again for signs of life, but this time the physician decided that death had indeed come.

That 'suspended animation' really occurred, there can be little question, but scientists differed as to the nature of the condition. Some believed that there may have been a suspension of the vital functions, while others asserted that these functions – breathing, heart action, circulation – were in a state of extremely low activity and were difficult to perceive.

So many reputable witnesses declared that Hindu fakirs had the power of voluntarily putting themselves in a state of suspended animation that the fact can hardly be questioned. The fakir, wishing to pass into this condition of suspended animation, composed himself into a very calm and impassive state of mind. Assistants would then turn the tongue back into his throat, stop his ears and nose with wax and cover him with sackcloth. After this the fakir could exist without food, water, or air, and remain apparently lifeless for many months, and could even be buried below the earth. At the end of a certain time, he is revived and returns his breathing, circulation, and heart rate to normal. This strange system of 'mock death' has been made the subject of many stories. In Robert Louis Stevenson's *Master of Ballantrae*, the villain, finding escape from his mortal enemies impossible, resorts to the fakir's method of burying himself alive. However, a mistake is made in the resuscitation method and the Master dies a horrible death.

Doctor J. Brindley James of London discussed many cases of suspended animation and wrote:

In the *Medical Times* a distinguished British General reported that he had seen a fakir disinterred from a grave wherein he had been placed forty-two days before, over which, during these six weeks' interval, corn had grown, and within which it was manifestly impossible for any sustenance or atmospheric air to reach him. The limbs of this apparent corpse were stiff and shrivelled, though the face was normal, but no pulsation was perceptible anywhere. Yet this man speedily revived, and to such good purpose that he voluntarily offered to be buried again in the general's own garden throughout another six weeks.

Dr Franz Hartmann, a noted authority said:

Apparent death is a state that resembles real death so closely that even the most expert observers believe such a person to be really dead. In many cases not even the most experienced physician, coroner or undertaker can distinguish a case of apparent death from real death., either by external examination or by means of the stethoscope, or by any of the various tests which have been proposed. It is now useless to discuss these tests at length because the medical profession has already agreed that 'there is no sign that a person is really and not apparently dead except the beginning of a certain stage of putrefaction.

Dr John B. Huber, a well-known New York physician, discussing the subject in 1918 said:

There have been cases, even where death from illness was not impending, in which a general inertia and catalepsy have very closely simulated the condition and the state of the dead. There have also been cases of a spasmodic state in which only a slight quivering of the eyelids has evidenced the continuation of the vital processes. The onset of such a lethargic or trance-like condition may be gradual, or it may come with startling abruptness. The appearance may be one of natural sleep. All sensations appear to be abolished, and yet, on returning to consciousness, the sufferer who has passed through such an experience will be able to report all that has occurred during the weird somnambulance. In such a case the pulse rate may be so diminished that there may appear to be no pulse at all. The breathing may be so shallow and infrequent that doubt may well be entertained whether there be any breathing at all. The temperature may be so subnormal that one may doubt whether any functioning (during which bodily heat is always generated) is continuing. The limbs may be rigid, as in death.

He goes on:

Such a state may last minutes or hours or, indeed, months, and then, of a sudden, it will be terminated by the utterance of a few delirious words or by a fit of gruesome and uncanny laughter, or by a flow of tears, or perhaps a convulsive seizure. There is no reason, from a careful review of the history of such cases, to believe that there is ever such a state of practical death, with a return later to living functioning. The functioning is, though remarkably attenuated, going on all the time. It is amazing, however, how such a syncope will simulate real cessation of the vital processes, while there will yet be no real death.

Dr Huber was asked how it was possible to make sure that a person was really dead and not in a state of suspended animation.

> We do not rely exclusively on any one sign, but we combine together, such as we will now consider, and then there will be no doubt in any given case, nor any occasion to fear premature burial. First, there is absolute and unmistakable cessation of the heart's action and of the flow of blood in the vessels. Of this the experienced physician can beyond peradventure assure himself by the means mentioned. Also, the radial artery at the wrist may be opened, if no blood appears the sufferer has died.

Medical science claimed, in the case of Mrs Walter Ackers of Los Angeles, literally to have raised her from the dead by manipulation of her heart after it had ceased beating for three full minutes. Mrs Ackers died while undergoing an operation to remove gallstones. The physician in charge, after he saw life had passed, thrust his hand through the surgical incision made in her side, reached upward past the visceral organs of the abdomen and grasped the heart. He manipulated it counterfeit to its pulsation while an assistant physician started artificial respiration Within ten minutes Mrs Ackers' heart began to beat, she breathed and came back to life (see top image on page 8 of the plate section).

Investigations into this phenomenon were conducted by Professor D. Fraser Harris, of Dalhousie University, Canada, who gave the results of his laboratory experiments in a 1922 edition of *Science* magazine.

He wrote:

> To the ordinary person, nothing seems easier than to be able to distinguish between life and death. A person naturally thinks of the entire organism as alive, the signs of its life being that it is warm, that it breathes, that its heart beats, and that it is aware of its surroundings, all of which is in sharp contrast with the cold, still, unconscious corpse in which the beating of the heart has ceased forever.
>
> What is known as trance, or narcolepsy, is the form which latent life takes in the human being. Every now and again, we hear of cases of persons, usually young women, going into profound and prolonged sleep from which they do not awake for weeks or months. During that time they take no

food, they scarcely breathe, their heart's action is at a minimum. That is, of course, quite different from the hypnotic or mesmeric trance.

Possibly the most famous case of narcolepsy is that of Colonel Townsend, of Dublin, which was described by the well-known Dr Cheyne as follows:

He could die or expire when he pleased, and yet... by an effort he could come to life again. He composed himself on his back and lay in a still posture for some time. I found his pulse sink gradually till at last I could not feel any by the most exact and nice touch. Dr Baynard could not feel the least motion in the breast, nor Dr Skrine perceive the least soil on the bright mirror he held to his mouth... could not discover the least symptom of life in him. We begun to concede he had carried the experiment too far, and at last we were satisfied he was actually dead. By nine in the morning, as we were going away, we observed some motion about the body, and upon examination found his pulse and the motion of his heart gradually returning, he began to breathe heavily and speak softly.

Still more extraordinary were the narratives of the Fakirs of India, who were said to allow themselves to be built up in sealed tombs for weeks without food and to be alive at the end of this time. Reports of these cases of human suspended animation were too numerous and too well authenticated by European eyewitnesses of unimpeachable integrity to be set aside as either in themselves untrue or as due to collective hallucination. The Hindu wishing to pass into this condition of suspended animation composed himself into a very calm and impassive state. He fasted for a suitable length of time and made other necessary preparation. His ears and eyes were stopped with wax and his friends then turned his tongue back into his mouth. Then the spell of narcolepsy overcame him, and he could live in this state of suspended animation and be brought to life afterward apparently without doing the slightest injury to his body.

On 7 August 1926, an international new report from Berlin announced that those who lived in fear of premature burial 'will be able to set their minds at rest.' It went on to say that these fears could be allayed by Johann Grundel, a young self-taught chemist, who had invented a test whereby burial alive 'becomes impossible.' The inventor had a small room in a private house which he used as his laboratory. 'The test is extremely simple,' Grundel explained, 'Chemically treated thread and a needle are all that will be required. Human blood is slightly alkaline, but on death it turns slightly acid. If a piece of this thread is passed through a fold of the skin and left for thirty minutes, it will show whether death has taken place or not. Death is shown by the thread turning yellow.' Surprisingly, there is no recorded medical evidence of the practice being adopted by physicians in the mainstream!

A coffin was one of the principal articles of furniture in the home of Christian Straube, a German living in New Jersey, United States, who was proud of his final habitat which he had built with his own hands and according to his own ideas. Straube occupied a small hut in the woods between Richland and Milmay and in the 1920s the shack consisted of just one room, containing a stove, a small table, a cot, a chair and the coffin. This coffin was Straube's pride and joy, not on account of its intrinsic value nor expensive material, for it was made of boards sawed from trees in the surrounding woods, but because of its completeness. The grim box contained paraphernalia to safeguard the occupant from unnecessary suffering in case he was buried without being really dead. In the cover, above where Straube's nose would be, was a hole in which a ten foot pipe extended above the surface of the earth, affording plenty of fresh air to the 'corpse.' On top of the pipe was a large bell connected to a rope that could be placed in the occupant's hand so that he could ring for rescuers if he happened to regain consciousness inside the coffin.

Straube didn't believe in embalming and from his youth thought with fear and anguish of the possibilities of being buried and then coming to life when put snugly away under six feet of earth. He made a fresh sandwich every two or three days and instructed friends that the last one be placed in his hand immediately after death. It was often talked about in the area, that at some point in the future, people might hear a bell in Mary's Landing cemetery and know that it was Straube coming to life, breathing the cool air and eating his sandwich, waiting for someone to answer the bell and bring him to the surface.

Chapter Twelve

Fakirs & Circus Men

The phenomenon of hibernation yields some sort of countenance to the idea that the animal organism is capable, under certain circumstances, of living for weeks, if not months, without food or drink. The alleged proceedings of Indian fakirs and Persian dervishes are cited in support of the possibility of human hibernation in underground cells. They certainly achieved some very extraordinary feats of endurance and self-abnegation. Tales of prolonged living were common enough in India, but they were rarely subjected to scientific observation or systematic monitoring and in some cases the grave in which the devotee has proposed to hibernate has been uncovered after a lapse of a few days and its occupant found dead.

In a Persian work, the *Dabistan*, on the religious sects of India, the statement was made that there were individuals who possessed the power to separate the soul from the body and to bring them together at will, and that such persons could exist without breathing for weeks at a time. European scientists refused for a long time to believe this but experiments actually proved the marvel. The first exhaustive information received in Europe about the Indian fakirs was from Dr Honigberger, who spent many years as a court physician at various Indian capitals. Dr Honigberger, after paying a flying visit to Germany, returned to Lahore in company with General Ventura who told him what had happened with the Fakir Haridas during his absence. An Indian prince had heard that this fakir possessed the miraculous power of allowing himself to sink into apparent death, to be buried, and to be kept in his grave for a number of months before being exhumed and again brought to life. The Maharajah summoned the celebrated fakir to his court and bade him make the experiment. The fakir did not hesitate.

He sank into a condition resembling death, and his body, in the presence of the prince and grandees, was wrapped in linen and placed in a box, on which the prince himself placed the lock. The box was then buried in the garden of one of the ministers, outside the city. Over the grave barley was sown, round about it a high wall was built, and sentinels, who were relieved every few hours, were placed on watch. Forty days afterwards, the prince, accompanied by his Ministers of State, General Ventura, an Englishman, and a physician, went to the garden. The box was exhumed, and in it lay the fakir, cold and stiff. By the application of warmth to the head, the blowing of air through the mouth, and energetic rubbing of the body, the man was quickly resuscitated. One of the ministers then said that he had known the same fakir to have been buried for four months. On the day of the burial the chin had been smoothly shaven, and on the day of exhumation it was found to be still perfectly smooth. The *Calcutta Journal of Medicine* reported that the same fakir had frequently been subjected to similar experiments by Englishmen, though, with them, he had always insisted on having the box hung up in the air instead of buried, as he feared the ravages of ants.

Doctor Honigberger said that the way the fakirs went to work to produce the peculiar condition was to have the little ligature under the tongue cut, whereby they were enabled to stretch the organ out to a great length. Then they turned it back, inserting the end into the throat, and at the same time closing up the inner nasal apertures. The external apertures of the nose and ears, he said, were closed with wax, and the eyes covered to exclude the light. Long preliminary practice was, however, needed in holding the breath, and a long course of fasting before burial.

Professor Preyer, in his work *Erforschung des Lebens*, said that a number of cases of this kind had been verified, and reported at length on the preparations which the fakir must observe. Preyer came to the conclusion, from a study of cases of suspended animation of both men and animals, that between life and death there is another condition, which he described as 'anaboise' or lifelessness. The German savant came to the belief that there is a state in which consciousness and the functions of life are brought to a standstill, but in which the capability of existence remains. Life is extinguished, but death has not begun its work. To bring on this condition at will, he said, was therefore the fakir's art and secret.

It is difficult to imagine any living soul volunteering to be buried alive, but that is exactly what was reported by a correspondent of the *East India Magazine* in February 1837. He wrote:

A man who had been buried a month on the bank of a tank near our camp, was dug out alive, in the presence of Esur Lal, one of the Ministers of the Muharwul of Jaisulmer, on whose account this singular individual was voluntarily interred a month ago. He is a youngish man, about thirty years of age, and his native village is within five miles of Kurnaul; but he generally travels about the country to Ajmeer, Kotah, Endor etc, and allows himself to be buried for weeks, or months, by any person who will pay handsomely for the same. The man is said, by long practice, to have acquired the art of holding his breath, by shutting the mouth, and stopping the interior opening of the nostrils with his tongue. He is sewn up in a bag of cloth, and the cell is lined with masonry, and floored with cloth, that the white ants and other insects may not easily be able to molest him.

The place in which he was buried at Jaisulmer, is a small building about twelve feet by eight feet, built of stone, and in the floor was a hole about three feet long, two and a half feet wide, and the same depth, in which he was placed in a sitting posture, sewed up in his shroud, with his feet turned inwards towards the stomach, and his hands also pointed inwards towards the chest. At the expiration of a full month, that is to say, this morning, the walling up of the door was broken, and the buried man dug out of the grave. He was taken out in a perfectly senseless state, his eyes closed, his hands cramped and powerless, his stomach shrunk very much, and his teeth jammed so fast together that they were forced to open his mouth with an iron instrument to pour a little water down his throat. He gradually recovered his senses and the use of his limbs, and when we went to see him, was sitting up supported by two men, and conversed with us in a low gentle tone of voice, saying 'that we might bury him again for twelve months if we pleased.' He told Major Spiers at Ajmeer of his powers and was laughed at as an imposter. But Cornet McNaughten put his abstinence to the test at Hokhur, by suspending him for thirteen days shut up in a wooden chest, which, he says, is better than being underground.

There are other stories of fakirs who existed not for months, but for years, in a comatose state. Other Indian travellers reported marvels connected to fakirs. One story was told of a fakir who wandered about and allowed himself to be subjected to interment whenever he was paid, arranging the length of time according to the amount of his reward. He was buried with the walls of a small house, the door of which was then bricked up, and a guard placed outside. Four weeks afterwards the body was removed and found in the same position as when it was buried. The fakir's teeth were so firmly pressed together, however, that an iron instrument had to be used before the mouth could be opened and water trickled into the man's throat. Consciousness returned slowly, the fakir began to speak in a low voice, and after a while grew so lively that he expressed his readiness to submit to burial for a year longer if only the prince of the region should so command him.

In another case a fakir was buried without first being placed in a box. The experiment was carried out at a military station and the officer in charge became so frightened that he ordered the disinterment after only a few days. Though the process of resuscitation occupied more than an hour, it was successful.

A native of Ohio, Andrew J. Seymour was adept at palmistry, mind-reading and powers of mesmerism, who from an early age began locating lost articles, transferring thoughts to volunteers and later assisting the police in solving murder cases. When the *Medical Journal* were told that Seymour 'the thought-reader' proposed to be buried alive at Chicago and remain underground long enough for a crop of barley to grow on his grave, their response was, 'we incline to share the general impression that, if he carries out his plan, he will probably remain underground for good.'

Planning to mimic the feat of Rungeet Singh, a fakir who was buried alive for ten months, Seymour's intended performance was thwarted by Mayor Harrison of Chicago, who refused the necessary burial permit.

On 10 March 1896, an article appeared in the *Yorkshire Evening Post* and read:

Government will have to interfere with the trance experiments. They are getting ghastly. Yesterday, in London, a man was hypnotised into complete insensibility, placed in a coffin with his nostrils and ears closed with wax, and then buried in a pit several feet deep. All the coffin is covered except for an aperture over the face, and watchers will be on the spot to note developments until Saturday next. It is a gruesome business and may someday be carried too far.

A strange case of trance, or suspended animation, puzzled medical men in Hawaii in May 1898, but it terrified the Chinese community who set large quantities of peanut oil burning in the joss houses of Kamaole in Maui. Ah Yung, a Chinese man, aged forty, was found in his bed one morning supposedly dead. There were no signs of respiration or heartbeat. The face was cadaverous in appearance, and even what seemed to be rigor mortis had set in. All the usual tests to determine whether life was extinct were applied and preparations for the funeral were begun. The authorities were notified, and the deputy sheriff and a police officer viewed the remains and certified officially that Ah Yung had joined his ancestors in the next world. However, scarcely had these formalities been completed, with Ah Yung clothed in a shroud and placed in a coffin, when he sat up, looked around in a surprised manner, knocked over all the joss sticks that were burning around his bier, and began asking what was going on.

The white garbed mourners were thrown into panic and rushed from the room, sending the local Chinese population into uproar. As soon as the authorities heard about the incident, they took Ah Yung into custody at the Makawao courthouse and sent for a physician. Police heard that the man had been acting strangely for some time before his pseudo death and it was supposed that he was insane. His condition was thoroughly examined as it presented some very unusual features, leading doctors to believe that Ah Yung's trance had been self-induced.

An extraordinary story reached London from the Reverend Ruttonji Nowroji, of the Church Missionary Society, Aurangabad, Western India, in November 1898. A Mohammedan youth in a village there was bitten by a venomous snake and died soon after. Twelve days after his burial, a Mohammedan fakir offered to raise him from the dead. The villagers dug up the body, which was in an advanced state of decomposition. There was much excitement, and the crowd taunted the Christian onlookers that the fakir was a greater wonderworker than Christ. Needless to say, the fakir's incantations were in vain. The police arrived a short time afterwards and took the fakir into custody, ordering the body to be reinterred.

An interesting article entitled 'Feats of Hindoo Fakirs' appeared in the *Detroit Free Press* in February 1899 and reads thus:

During the past five years many of the travelling hypnotists of this country have advertised as their star performance the burial of a living subject, who, placed in a cataleptic state by the hypnotist, is allowed to slumber for a given period of time, usually forty-eight hours, when he is revived and presented to the admiring audience as an illustration of the wonderful powers of the operator. This so-called 'burial' is a fake, pure and simple, and with but a minimum of danger to the subject, as one of the precautions taken at the interment is the insertion of a four-inch air shaft directly over the subject's face, in case the test should fail, and the man revive before the appointed time.

This test, as many know, is but a burlesque on the wonderful living burials of India, where it is looked upon by the native worshippers of Buddha as the supreme test of mind over matter. The fakirs and religious mendicants of India perform many feats of endurance which to the average mind are little short of incomprehensible, such as lying for days at a time on a board bearded with needle-pointed spikes, burying their heads in the earth for hours at a time, holding the arms upright above the head for weeks, and in some thoroughly authenticated cases, for ten or more years, and other similar feats which none other than the fanatical Oriental mind could devise.

The living burial differs, however, from any of the above-mentioned 'holy' exercises, for while the former require only the physical endurance and the fantastical courage and contempt of pain common to the Oriental, the latter is only to be accomplished after a score of years of the most arduous training ever devised for subjecting the physical man to the complete mastery of the mind.

The fakirs who have survived the crucial torments which must be undergone to reach the perfect stage are looked upon by the Buddhists as the holiest of holy men, and believe them to be gifted with the power to save them, to bring good or ill luck, or to grant them the means to carry out their most coveted ambitions.

The writer was fortunate enough to witness a fakir's remarkable test of endurance in the interior of India:

While spending some time in Mandalay in the fall of 1888, I made the acquaintance of some British officers stationed there and accepted an invitation of one, a Major Ralston, to accompany a party who were going to the palace of the rajah of a neighbouring province to witness the burial of a Buddhist fakir. I at once accepted, and a few days later our party, consisting of two surgeons, the major, Captain Harris and myself, were escorted with great state into the low, rambling palace of the native king. This gentleman was one of the many Indian princes who, although educated in England at the English Government's expense, still clung to his father's religion, and contributed generously to the devotees of Buddha. This invitation to visit Madipore was the outcome of an argument between the sceptical Major Ralston and himself, which he proposed to decide by an actual test.

The devotee who had undertaken the task of proving the truth of the rajah's assertion was a tall, dignified fellow, about forty years old, whose ascetic face and bony frame, wrapped in the loose, coarse garments of his sect, proclaimed the courageous fanatic in every line. The night following our arrival we were entertained in true oriental style, with feasting, dancing and music, and on the following morning we were taken to a small enclosure in the interior of the courtyard, where the tomb had been already prepared to receive its living occupant. A small hut of mud and stone had been erected, and within this a grave had been made in the round. It was about eight feet long, six feet deep and four feet wide. At the bottom was a layer of flat stones, and at one side sat a rude wooden coffin and a huge stone slab, the latter to be placed over the grave.

We announced ourselves as thoroughly satisfied that, once we saw the fakir buried, we would rest content that no trick would be played upon us, and preparations for the burial began. The fakir entered the hut, accompanied by a native bearing a basket containing a large white linen sack and several other articles necessary for the interment. The fakir then sated himself upon the floor and the attendant handed him a ball of reddish wax which he proceeded to make into small pellets and force into his ears and nostrils. This, the rajah explained, was to hermetically seal all air passages and prevent the entrance of any insect. He then drew out a wonderfully elongated tongue, which he turned backward and allowed to glide down his throat, thus effectually closing that passage. This accomplished, he bowed to us, and then salaaming with deep reverence to the rajah, he bent his gaze upon his abdomen, and in a very few minutes lost consciousness. His attendant then produced the linen sack, into which the stiffened form of the fakir was put, and one of the surgeons, after satisfying himself that the body was in a cataleptic state, tied the neck of the sack with a cord, and stamped his seal into the wax which was poured upon it. The sack was then placed in the box, and it in turn lowered into the grave, the earth shovelled in, and the stone slab placed above all. Mud was then brought and plastered around the slab, into which we set the seals of our various rings. The door to the hut was afterward closed and sealed in a similar manner and we returned to the palace. Here we arranged to meet again in six weeks, the appointed time for this modern resurrection of the dead. On our way back to Mandalay the major laughingly offering heavy odds that we would find a dead Indian, but without any takers, for we all felt very sceptical of the result.

Six weeks later the same party gathered at the palace in Madipore to witness the result of the test. The rajah welcomed us cordially, and we went at once to the tomb. The exterior was just as we left it, the marks of the seal rings being still plainly visible in the dry clay. When we had satisfied ourselves thus far, the work of exhuming was begun, and before long the box was reverently lifted from the grave by the native attendants. In the meanwhile, the Indian who had assisted at the burial had brought in a tiny stove, and now busied himself in what looked to us like the preparation of a meal. One of the surgeons remarked that he thought it would be some time before the fakir would eat, but the rajah only smiled in reply. When the box was opened the major leaned forward and grabbed the sack, intent upon seeing if the man were really there. It crumbled almost to dust in his hand, so frail was the cloth from mildew!

The fakir, or what was left of him, was then lifted from the box, and turned over to the care of his assistant, not, however, before the surgeons had made an examination of him, and declared that while life was to all intents and purposes extinct, they thought they could detect a bit of heat at the corona, the base of the brain. The assistant had made a steaming pile of pancakes, and as soon as the body was given to him, he proceeded to apply these to the back of the fakir's neck, at the same time withdrawing the plugs from the ears and nose. He then called to two of the natives to chafe the bony and almost fleshless limbs of the body, while he pried open the mouth, drew the tongue from out of the throat, and poured melted butter or grease into the mouth. These operations continued for forty-five minutes, interspersed with snapping the fakir's eyelids, and vigorously rubbing his head with heated cloths. Then slowly but surely the limbs became less rigid, his pulse revived, and at five minutes past the hour he opened his eyes, looked at us a moment, and smiled feebly. We had gathered closely about him now, and ere many minutes elapsed he opened his lips and whispered, scarcely above his breath, 'You believe?' 'You bet we do, old boy,' shouted the major, and he voiced the sentiment of the entire party. Before we left, the following day, the fakir was well on the way to recovery after his long sleep.

The *Scottish Surgical and Medical Journal* of 1900 quoted a remarkable case of Indian magic recorded by surgeon James Braid, whose observations on mesmerism were well known.

At the palace of Runjeet Singh – a square building which had in the centre a closed room – a fakir who had voluntarily put himself in a comatose condition was afterwards sewn up in a sack and walled in, the single door of the room having been sealed with the private seal of the Runjeet. To exclude all fraud Runjeet, who was not himself a believer in the wonderful powers of the fakir, had established a cordon of his bodyguard round the building, and in front of the latter four sentinels were stationed who were relieved every two hours and were continually watched.

Under these conditions the fakir remained in his grave six weeks, when the building was opened in the presence of Runjeet Singh, and the seal and all the walls were found uninjured. In the dark room, which was examined with a light, the sack containing the fakir lay in a locked box which was provided with a seal, also untouched. The sack, which presented a mildewed appearance, was opened and the crouching form of the fakir taken out. The body was perfectly stiff. A physician who was present found that nowhere on the body was a trace of pulse beat evident. In the meantime, the servant of the fakir poured some warm water over his head, removed the wax with which the ears and nostrils had been stopped, forcibly opened the teeth with a knife, drew forward the tongue, which was bent backward and repeatedly sprang back again into its position, and rubbed the closed eyes with butter. Soon the fakir began to open his eyes, the body began to twitch convulsively, the nostrils were dilated, the skin, heretofore stiff and wrinkled, assumed gradually its normal fullness, and in a few minutes the fakir opened his lips and in a feeble voice asked Runjeet Singh, 'Do you now believe me?'

While tales of Indian fakirs are calculated to excite distrust, and impostors trade on the credulous for purposes of gain, the fact remains attested by well authenticated cases that certain men can voluntarily put themselves into a state in which no vital phenomena are demonstrable by careful examination and can wake later to a normal life. It is almost akin to the hibernation of animals in which the state of sleep is so deep that the awakening process is gradual.

A very curious story was reported from Lexingham, Kentucky, in the United States in July 1900, concerning a young girl of fourteen called Maud Matthews. According to *La Patrie* newspaper the girl was hypnotised by a doctor, placed in a wooden coffin, and then taken to the Woodlawn Park Cemetery. Once there, the coffin was lowered into a grave and covered with earth. After remaining there for five days, the coffin was exhumed in the presence of a large crowd, the lid unscrewed and Maud found to be lying there is a hypnotic state, apparently as perfectly still as when she had been placed there. The doctor then bent down and whispered in the girl's ear, after which she got up, climbed out of the coffin, embraced her friends and returned home.

A strange tragedy took place at the fashionable location of Treport, France, in August 1903, when a smartly dressed woman threw herself from the cliffs and fell upon the rocks below, a distance of over 700 feet. Death was instantaneous. In a letter found on the body it was discovered that the woman's name was Aline Thierry and that under the name of Bronwonska she had appeared at county fairs as *'the woman buried alive,'* remaining in a coffin sometimes as long as twenty days without tasting food. In the letter Thierry said that she had committed suicide because she had been unsuccessful in her enterprise.

A practising physician from Hartford, Connecticut, United States, took a very peculiar means of proving his belief in hypnotism in 1906. The doctor put his wife into a hypnotic trance and then exhibited her in a shop window with the grim announcement that he would bury her alive for a week. A protest from residents caused the police to put a stop to this unpleasant exhibition, and the physician thereupon closed the window curtains intimating that he would not change his plans, but refusing to say where he would bury his spouse lest his lunatic plan should be stopped by injunction.

One man who did succeed in burying his wife alive was 'Professor' W.A. Barclay, a coloured hypnotist from Kingston, Jamaica. On 10 October 1906, he successfully hypnotised his white wife in the presence of a large gathering of the public and buried her in a coffin eight feet underground. The 'Professor' announced that he would leave his wife buried for six days, declaring that after digging her up again she would be as fit and well as before burial. The ceremony took place at Rockport Garden, with the grave already having been dug before the couple arrived, the coffin placed by its side.

As the performance began, Mrs Barclay stepped into the coffin, lay out at full length and closed her eyes. 'Professor' Barclay, after making passes over his wife's head, announced that she was hypnotised and ready for burial. The coffin lid was then fastened down and the coffin lowered into the grave. Two air shafts were attached to the specially made coffin and then earth was piled on top to a depth of the whole eight feet. Barclay assured the people present that his wife was not in the slightest degree affected by the burial and suffered no discomfort. In fact, he said she was much better off than a good many who were walking on the earth.

When the full details of the burial became known a storm of protest was raised in Kingston. Mr Forster Davis, who had control of Rockport Gardens, sent a letter to Barclay declaring that he had no idea of the performance, adding, 'In these circumstances I must ask you to be good enough to make arrangements to disinter your wife this evening.' On receiving the letter, Barclay replied that he had pledged his word to the public that he would bury his wife alive for six days, and he did not mean to break it. The matter was at a standstill, with Barclay refusing to bring his wife to the surface, and the authorities afraid to do so owing to the possible consequences of removal.

'Professor' Barclay kept his wife in her living tomb for 104 hours. The grave was surrounded by an immense crowd day and night, with the locals taking turns at peering through the air shafts to satisfy themselves that Mrs Barclay was not being fed. She remained in the same rigid position throughout, and when she was brought up it was found that she was perfectly well but had lost eight pounds in weight. Barclay claimed to have done the same thing before and offered to hypnotise any other willing person and keep them asleep in a glass case for advertising purposes in a shop window!

An interesting article on the subject of fakirs by Dr Woods Hutchinson was published in the *American Magazine* in November 1908. It reads:

Some of the trance-like conditions into which individuals fall and lie for days or weeks have been studied and have been found to be frauds. The 'subjects' are surreptitiously supplied with food and drink by their attendants or family. The same is true of the alleged power possessed by Hindu fakirs and ascetics of all ages, of going into states of trance in which they will allow themselves to be buried alive and dug up again and revived after several months have elapsed. In one instance on record an individual of this class allowed himself to be buried alive and his grave watched by a guard of English soldiers and was dug up at the end of the time, exceedingly dead. In another, the English officer in charge became alarmed on the third day, and had the fakir 'resurrected,' when he was found still alive. A reed or bamboo at one corner of the grave to supply air would explain all these cases. The whole subject is involved in such an atmosphere of mystery and 'fakery' that it is impossible to attach serious weight to the claims made.

Most of the claims, both Occidental and Oriental, to the power of existing for indefinite periods in this trance-like sleep seem to rest simply upon the well-known power possessed by many weak-minded individuals or throwing themselves by auto-suggestion into a hypnotic sleep. In this condition, or awake, life can, of course, be easily supported for many days, or even weeks, without food, as has been often illustrated by the feats of professional fasters who easily reach forty or even sixty days. It is, however, a significant fact that none of these 'sleeps' can be carried on in a hospital where the patient is under observation of competent and unsympathetic nurses. For, although food can be done without, water cannot, and these sleepers will invariably be found resorting to the water bottle and responding to the calls of nature within twenty-four hours. In their own homes, where they can help themselves surreptitiously to the water on the washstand, they may keep up the farce for weeks without detection. All 'sleepers' investigated by physicians are found to take water regularly, and often food, and are usually cases of hysteria or mild insanity.

Nailed up in an ordinary coffin and buried six feet deep, Florence Jessie Gibson, a pretty girl aged eighteen, was sleeping away in a ten-day hypnotic slumber in mid-August 1908. She was put into the trance by Bunda Kupparow, a Hindu mystic, near the grave in Cedar Point Park, a pleasure resort near Sandunsky, Ohio. It was reported that thousands of people gathered daily to take turns peering down through a glass-covered chute upon the face of the young woman.

The crowd could be roughly divided into three camps. Firstly, physicians and scientific investigators who had gathered there from all over the state, glad of a chance to study the case. Secondly, members of humane societies who made a determined effort to have the exhibition stopped on the ground that it was barbarous and cruel. The third, this being the largest group by far, the morbid and idly curious who had come from the same impulse that caused so many persons to flock to the funeral of a stranger. The box that held the girl was of an ordinary casket design, with a satin lining upon which her head rested. Apparently, the likeness to a coffined body was ghastly.

To satisfy the humanitarians that Miss Gibson was in a good physical state the Hindu had the sand which filled the hole shovelled out. At his request physicians unscrewed the coffin lid and examined the sleeping female. Her face was white and pinched looking, but she breathed regularly, and her pulse was only slightly below normal. There was a lot of excitement during the exhumation, as it had been reported that the society would make an effort by force to rescue the sleeping girl from the East Indian. The body, however, was returned to the earth after Kupparow had demonstrated that no imaginable defect could tie up the automatic pumps and valves by which fresh air was carried down into the grave. Mrs. Fannie Everett, President of the Sandusky Humane Society, had been working hard to stop the show by legal means. She asked for an injunction, but the court could find no law to cover the situation as the girl was of age and voluntarily submitted to the ordeal of burial alive.

Florence Gibson was a Pennsylvania girl, a fragile, blonde thing, and by the side of the bearded chocolate-coloured East Indian whom she worked with, she looked like a child. Florence had been travelling the United States with Kupparow for some time. Usually, he would display her in a show window after hypnotising her. After lying in a hypnotic trance in the grave for ten days, Florence Gibson showed no ill-effects of her ordeal.

However, there were cries of 'fake' as the girl was raised from the grave before a huge crowd. Reporters who jumped into the grave after the girl was taken out found that the coffin did not rest upon the ground and apparently had a false bottom. In a tent in which Kupparow lived, the reporters alleged that they had found a deep hole under the board flooring. 'Tunnel,' yelled the crowd, as it rushed into the tent pulling it half down. The special police were called in to beat back the crowd from the tent.

Florence Gibson, meanwhile, was carried from the grave into the opera house on a stretcher. Her body was cold and stiff, the clothing clammy. The Hindu mystic worked over the girl, blowing breath into her mouth, and with low sobbing and cries of pain Miss Gibson 'came to life.' Within five minutes she walked across the stage. 'I will never be buried alive again,' she said. 'It is the most terrible thing one can imagine. I felt all the time as if I were dropping, dropping, from a high building down through the earth. At last I struck the bottom and thought I was being dashed to pieces. That was when I awakened on the stage.'

Kupparow and his assistants filled up the grave as soon as Florence was taken out, throwing dirt in on the investigators. Watchers expressed the opinion that the young woman really was in a hypnotic state but were unable to discover whether she was taken from the grave by tunnel at night and given food and water. When she revived, Florence expressed no desire for food, but cried for water.

On 28 April 1926, in the presence of fifty medical men at the Scala Theatre, Tottenham Court Road in London, the Egyptian fakir Rahman Tahra Bey pledged himself to a supreme test of his powers. He was to return to Paris, where he would put himself in a cataleptic trance; his body was then to be put in an airtight coffin and taken back to London by plane the following weekend.

The journey would take about two hours and to this must be added the time required to get the coffin to either the Albert Hall or Scala Theatre. Doctors were on hand to closely examine every stage of the cataleptic burial in Paris, its journey, and the unsealing and emergence of the fakir from his temporary tomb in full view of an audience.

Rahman Bey, with a committee of the fifty doctors around him watching every movement, put himself into a state of catalepsy by auto-suggestion, and the manipulation of the carotid artery and nerves of the face and head. In this state he was placed in a coffin. Cotton wool was pressed into his nostrils and mouth, sand was heaped over his head and shoulders. The coffin was covered with a lid, a mound of sand was piled over the top and sides of the box and hammered flat with a spade. At the end of ten minutes, the period he had requested, the coffin was uncovered and raised with the lid off in full view of the doctors and the audience. The fakir was deathly pale.

Gradually he recovered and was led down to the audience, which pressed him about him scrambling for 'talismen' slips of paper on which was written an Arabic word. During the ten minutes of unconsciousness the fakir's breathing and circulation had stopped. On emerging, his pulse was found to be beating at only four beats to the minute. This was the culmination of a series of experiments, which medical men confessed baffled them.

Sir William Simpson, one of the eminent doctors present, with a long experience of India, told the *Westminster Gazette* that there could not be fake in the demonstration: there were things he could not understand, only a psychic explanation was possible. 'In India,' he said, 'I have seen these fakirs in catalepsy turning on a spit, hanging head down from the feet, over a big fire.'

While Rahman Bey was in the coffin his English announcer read extracts from his book on Eastern Mystics. He belonged to the Mohammedan Chavk of Dancing Dervishes but declared that certain Buddhists and Brahmins had practised similar control for thousands of years. A fakir, he said, is allowed to be the father of one son only, who is separated from his mother and trained to his function. But if that function has led, through one or more thousand years, only to controlled hypnosis, telepathy, insensibility to pain, and trances for long or short periods, it is an experiment that merely repeats itself without a spiritual motive. The Mohammedan fakirs were Sufis, but the Sufi philosophy would be there without their physical feats. Neither does the Buddhist tranquillity depend in essence upon almost inhuman mortification, feat of physical distortion, and manipulation of the limbs, the pulse, and the breath.

Three days after Rahman Bey's public performance, the Lord Chamberlain made an objection to the future plans for the fakir to make displays at the Little Theatre. Jose Levy, lessee of the theatre, said he believed that the Lord

Chamberlain had the wrong impression of the display and sought to put the facts before him. He also invited the Earl of Cromer to witness the demonstration, although that being of a private nature was not affected by the temporary ban. Meanwhile, Mr Levy was obtaining legal advice as to the rights of the Lord Chamberlain to interfere with an entertainment of that nature and raised the possibility of taking the matter to court.

Just a few months later, American escapologist Harry Houdini (see bottom image on page 8 of the plate section) duplicated the feat of Rahman Bey in New York. Houdini, famous for getting out of things, managed to stay inside a six-and-a-half-foot coffin submerged in a swimming pool for an hour and a half. Houdini thus at one stroke added the title of fakir to his list of appellations and removed a thorn that got stuck beneath his skin a month before when Egyptian Rahman Bey arrived in town. The previous July, Bey asserted that no ordinary man could stay alive in such a coffin more than a few moments. It took, Bey declared, a man who could put himself into a hypnotic trance. When these matters had been properly impressed upon the general public, Rahman Bey went into a trance and was placed inside a coffin that was lowered into the East River. Nineteen minutes after the submersion the telephone bell connecting the coffin with the breath-bated outside world rang. The coffin was hauled up and Rahman Bey was still in a trance, or so it appeared. On a subsequent attempt he remained in the coffin for an hour. It was said that Harry Houdini snorted on both occasions.

So, on the morning of 5 August 1926, Houdini went to the swimming pool of the Hotel Shelton, on Lexington Avenue and 49th Street, closely followed by his personal representative, James Collins, and several reporters. There a galvanized coffin was pronounced airtight by those who examined it. Houdini, clad in a white shirt and dark trunks, stepped inside, and the lid was soldered. It was lowered to the bottom of the pool and six bathers volunteered to sit on it. Mr. Collins stood at the edge of the pool holding a telephone connected to another telephone and a signal bell inside the coffin. Every five minutes, Collins would ask, 'How are you?' Conserving his breath, Houdini would push the button and ring the bell to answer. Half an hour passed.

The six bathers began to get bored. One poked a finger in the ribs of a second. Both rolled off and the others laughed. They rolled off too and the coffin bobbed up. The bell rang and Mr. Collins answered.

'What,' came a most indignant voice over the wire from the casket, 'is the big idea?'

Mr. Collins explained the tickling incident apologetically and the six bathers remounted. Another half hour passed, and Collins began inquiring about Harry Houdini's health every minute. Every minute, on the minute, the bell rang. After an hour and a quarter Houdini announced, 'It's leaking,' meaning the casket.

About three minutes before the coffin was brought to the surface, Houdini reported, 'I'm getting a little numb down here.'

At the end of an hour and thirty minutes Harry Houdini gave the word for the resurrection. A moment later the lid was ripped off and they helped him out. He was so exhausted he could hardly speak. He refused a glass of water, saying he had 'had enough.'

Dr McConnell of the Philadelphia Health Council, who had examined Houdini before the submersion, reported the pulse before going down as 84, afterward 142. When he had somewhat revived Houdini said:

There is nothing supernatural about it at all. We are all human. I am an ordinary man. The casket is not airless, but it is airtight. You don't have to go into any 'trance' to do it. The trick is to take short even breaths of the air already in there. In that way you conserve it. This ought to be a good thing for miners and such people who work underground you know.

Dr McConnell said that after two or three minutes of ordinary breathing in the casket all the oxygen would have been used up.

The following year at a circus show in Riechenberg, Germany, the 'star' turn was the performance of an artiste named Ruzicka, who posed as a fakir. The man allowed himself to be buried alive in a grave dug in the circus ring, a cord tied to his hand serving as a signal of distress should anything go wrong. Sadly, at the end of an agreed half hour, the grave was opened and Ruzicka was found dead. An inquest found that he had suffocated.

A gruesome struggle for life after being buried alive was revealed in Buenos Aires on 5 September 1929, when the body of an Indian fakir, a performer attached to an itinerant circus, was dug up from six feet under the ground. The man was placed in a sealed coffin equipped with a glass window on top and lowered into a grave. After a long period, while hundreds of spectators thronged to the spot to watch him emerge, the soil was thrown back and the coffin revealed. Sadly, a horrible sight met the crowd. The fakir had been dead for hours, and the glass shattered and blood-stained. It told of a terrible underground struggle for life as the performer was being slowly suffocated while his cries were deafened by the solid mass of earth above him.

On being dug up after performing a 'buried alive' trick in a circus at Cordoba, Spain, 'Blackman' a well-known Indian fakir was found dead in October 1929. The broken window of the coffin and bleeding hands and face were evidence of his struggle for life. In the performance the fakir allowed himself to be placed in a hermetically sealed coffin with a small glass window, and buried six feet underground, remaining in this state for roughly three hours. The secret to the trick was that the coffin contained just sufficient air for the person inside to breathe for that length of time. It was assumed that the fakir lost his presence of mind, and as soon as he felt the earth falling on the coffin, he broke the glass in a frantic effort to get out, thereby releasing the small supply of air that was supposed to keep him alive. The circus proprietor was arrested.

Unbelievably, there have been, at various intervals in time, those who have volunteered to be buried alive underground as part of an experiment, entertainment, bet or test of endurance. Sometimes they end with tragic results whilst at others not the merest change is observed in the subject interred.

On Thursday, 11 December 1930, an *Irish News* reporter, who was accompanied by a representative of another Belfast morning newspaper, had the pleasure of shaking hands with Bertini, the hypnotist, who was becoming quite famous in the British Isles on account of his remarkable powers. The secret of hypnotism was such an elusive thing at the time that it was something quite out of the ordinary to meet a man who claimed to have solved the mystery of the mind. Therefore, the news reporter admittedly gazed on Bertini longer, and with more curiosity, than was in keeping with good manners but no doubt Bertini was used to it as he did not seem to mind in the least. The representative was impressed by the presence of a man whose power inspired such confidence in a girl that she was willing to face the awful ordeal of being buried in the earth for an hour and a half.

The incident had occurred some time before at Bilston, near Wolverhampton, West Midlands, and would have been carried through but for unforeseen circumstances in the way of interference by the police, who claimed that life was endangered. The young lady referred to, Miss Elsie Dyson, was present at the interview, and conversation naturally turned on this subject. Such was the confidence of Bertini and the girl that this amazing feat could be carried through successfully that they were disgusted at not being able to demonstrate it when preparations had been made. 'If arrangements can be made in time I will do it in Belfast,' Bertini remarked. The details were discussed by the four present, in the rooms of a well-known Belfast theatre. It was decided that the attempt would take place in a field near Milltown Cemetery on the following Saturday morning. Just before noon on the Saturday a small group of men assembled around a freshly opened grave with just a little anxiety. Trestles were taken along and an aluminium coffin placed on top. In a few minutes Elsie climbed into the coffin and lay down. Bertini made a few gestures with his hands, while all the time gazing at the woman intently, and gradually she fell into what appeared to be a peaceful sleep. While the anxiety of the Press men increased, the lid was screwed down firmly, the coffin lifted from the trestles and lowered into the six-foot grave. Then the gravediggers began their task. The rain was falling gently as they shovelled earth upon the coffin, and they worked with vigour until the grave was filled up. The minutes dragged by while the group watched the mound. After thirty-five minutes, the diggers began again, clearing away the soil until they could finally bring the coffin to the surface. When the lid was opened, Miss Dyson was brought around by a few passes over her face by Bertini and then she stepped out of the coffin with a cheery remark. Later Elsie said that the only sensation she felt while underground was one of coldness. Bertini told the reporters that this was the first occasion on which this kind of hypnotism had been done and added that he 'could have sensed' no danger to Miss Dyson while she lay buried in the coffin. He claimed that he could have kept her underground for three hours in safety.

Orange County police arrested the Reverend Madison Russ on 'suspicion' in New Jersey, United States, on 19 May 1931, together with a man who identified himself as Sankah Bey. Forty-one-year-old Russ was the negro pastor of the Friendly Rescue Mission. Having been informed that a man was being buried alive in the mission churchyard, police dispatched a few detectives who found that a man had indeed been buried underground. Reverend Russ had just patted down the last spadeful of earth when they arrived and told the officers that it was 'The peer of African mystery' who had been buried. Police began to dig. Four feet down they reached a crude coffin-shaped box and inside found a man wrapped in a shroud. He was unconscious but still breathing. An inhalator was brought into play and soon 'The peer of African mystery' opened his eyes. The peer, who identified himself both as 'Sankah Bey & Co' and Joseph Ross, said that he had just been practising. He had persuaded his friend, the pastor, to bury him alive, a stunt he hoped to use in a carnival that summer. Sankah Bey had taken a ruler with him into the coffin and tapped on the side of the box to indicate that he was still living. When the Reverend Russ failed to hear the taps, he became alarmed, and friends called the police.

A story of being buried alive for three days and nights so that her babies might eat was told by a twenty-two-year-old mother in September 1932. Week after week, Lorena Braum Carmichael of Oakland, Kansas, was buried alive, then 'arose' from her grave before the startled eyes of the big top circus followers. She had been forced to become the breadwinner of her little family as a result of desertion by her husband. However, the young star of mid-west travelling troupes put her experience behind her as she followed a less thrilling occupation as waitress, for the experience of being buried under six feet of earth, although air pipes led to her casket, was threatening Lorena's health. The story was discovered when Robert Murns, one-time deputy sheriff in Rollins County, visited a downtown restaurant and found Mrs Carmichael employed there.

Years later Egyptian fakir, Rahman Tahra Bey, failed in his attempt to give investigators a demonstration of his abilities. At Carshalton Beeches, Surrey, on 15 July 1938, Bey went into a trance and was buried in a grave in which he was scheduled to remain for an hour. However, three minutes after the first shovelfuls of earth had been thrown over him, he rang an electric bell and the experiment ended. The investigators had to dig for twenty minutes to get the fakir out. The experiment took place at The Halt, which was placed at the disposal of Harry Price, secretary of the University of London Council for Psychological Research. A six-foot pit was dug in the lawn. Watched by Professor C.E.M. Joad and other professionals, Rahman stood with his hands pressed hard to his forehead. For a few minutes he swayed backwards and forwards, finally falling back, with eyes closed, into the arms of an assistant. With his hands still pressed to his forehead, he was placed at the bottom of the pit with an electric bell-push on his chest. From the bell-push ran a wire to a bell above the ground with which he was to give warning if the trance was broken before the hour had expired. Heavy planks were laid along wooden supports a few inches above the fakir's body and earth was shovelled into the pit. A little over three minutes later, when the pit ad been more than half-filled, there was a sort ring on the bell and Rahman was dug out. He explained the trance was apparently broken because his hands were jerked from his forehead while he was being buried. Rahman Bey said he intended to repeat the experiment.

Elsewhere in 1938, Bertram Mills was touring England with a dazzling array of talent gathered from the 'four corners of the earth.' The most talked of act was Koringa, who claimed to be the only female fakir in the world and allowed herself to buried alive in sand for five minutes at the climax of the show. However, holding her breath under the ground was just one of Koringa's many talents. Appearing at the Empire Theatre, Sheffield, in November 1939, the woman was bitten by one of her crocodiles in the first performance! It was given to the fakir by the London Zoo and had only been with the circus for three days. During the act, Koringa, was seen to hypnotise the creature and was bitten after reviving it, receiving a wound to her right calf. Another part of the act saw her lying with her naked back on broken glass and standing on the razor edges of swords. Few could rival Koringa in fitness and bodily health and asked her secret she replied, 'Discipline is the first thing. Myself, I eat just once a day. No meat – but fruit, especially lemons. It is only by mental relaxation and particular attention to breathing that my art can be accomplished.'

Of Indian-Algerian descent, Koringa was just five feet two inches tall, with a mass of black fuzzy hair and a sallow complexion. Modern make-up and European clothing were said to accentuate her Eastern beauty. Circus owner

Cyril Mills discovered the female fakir playing one-night stands in Denmark and convinced her to sign a contract to work for him.

Huge crowds saw a forty-five-year old yogi, Swami Ramdasji, dug out alive from an airtight cement crypt where he had been buried for eighty-seven hours on a bed of nails in April 1950. To make things even tougher, the little man with the black beard had been completely submerged in water until his release after three-and-a-half days. Ramdasji climbed into the wooden coffin and lay down on a bed of nails, the sides of which also had nails that dug into his flesh. The coffin was then sealed inside an eight foot by six foot cement crypt. Ramdasji's disciples then sat by the crypt day and night, chanting Hindu vedic prayers while keeping a sacred fire burning. On top of the crypt, they placed coconuts and flowers. Then they bored a small hole into the crypt. Into the hole they pushed a hose from a nearby hydrant and immersed the air-starved Hindu in water.

Many of the thousands of people who rose before dawn to make sure of a ringside seat at the disinterment obviously believed that Swami had bitten off more than he could chew. They watched tensely as his followers hacked the cement away with picks. Then they crawled down to the coffin with blankets. They lifted Ramdasji, still in a Yogic trance and dripping wet, onto a dias where all could see him. The disciples slowly massaged his head, arms and body until the yogi opened his eyes and looked slowly around, smiling. Doctors pronounced him all right.

When a jury returned a verdict of 'death by misadventure' at the inquest of Reuben Maurice Shill of Buckingham Road, Bicester, who died during a 'buried alive' act at a local fete in Luton in June 1951, they commented that 'sensational stunts like this should not be encouraged.' Mr Shill, a former music hall artist, died in brightly coloured pantaloons and a turban after accepting a challenge to be buried under four tons of sand for twenty minutes. The stuntman was rolled up and tied in a blanket before the sand was shovelled over him, with compere Peter Smith prodding the sand with a metal rod every five minutes to check that Shill was alright. After fifteen minutes Smith thought the act had gone on long enough and asked the crowd to help remove the sand, thinking it a joke when Shill lay still with a blackened face. The police tried artificial respiration and rushed the entertainer to hospital where an oxygen tent had been prepared but Reuben Shill was dead on arrival. Shill's widow, Florence, said that she had performed the 'sand act' five or six times and her husband three or four times previously. The coroner asked whether Mrs. Shill considered it to be a dangerous act, to which she replied, 'No, definitely not. I never felt any danger.' Earlier the coroner, Mr. J.H. Hoare, said he hoped that the publicity surrounding the case would discourage such morbid and disgraceful stunts which were likely to endanger human life. Doctor Wainwright attending pronounced death as primarily due to shock, but he thought that asphyxiation also played a minor part. After the jury's verdict, the Fete Committee said that they considered that they were entitled to rely on the long professional experience of Mr. Shill. Florence Shill, whose professional name was Tanta Sheley, performed as a snake charmer. Sadly, she was found dead just a few months later in a caravan in Gloucester, with a fifteen-foot python curled up in a wooden chest beside her.

Narayan Acharya, who buried himself alive on 29 January 1953, near Mahatma Gandhi's cremation ground as a penance in the cause of world peace, was dead when taken out on 7 February. Disciples who had kept a constant vigil beside the tomb were convinced that Acharya was in a state of 'divine unconsciousness.' A crowd of two thousand onlookers gathered at the grave and had to be held back by police as the disciples walked around chanting that he was still alive. It was recalled that Acharya had buried himself twice before for up to twenty-hours and had emerged alive.

Tim Hayes, a twenty-nine-year-old dockyard worker from County Cork, Ireland, became a world-record holder in December 1966. He was buried alive in a coffin on Christmas Day and managed to stay underground for 101 hours, breaking the previous record of a Swede by one hour. Mr. Hayes said that his only concern had been for a spider and fly which had kept him company during the trial. 'The fly is missing, and the spider does not look too well,' he added! However, Tim Hayes' victory was short-lived, as less than a month later his record was beaten by Verneri Viillos from Tammerfors, central Finland. Despite Mr Viillos succeeding in his feat on 19 January 1967, he told onlookers that he intended to remain in his coffin, which lay underneath a greenhouse, until the following Sunday. At a special ceremony arranged to mark the occasion, he received twenty hot dogs and soft drinks. Viillos complained that water was seeping into his coffin and had caused him to lie at one end of it. The Finn, on completing his challenge, had managed a total of 170 hours underground.

Not to be outdone, Tim Hayes began a second attempt to beat the world record on 28 May 1970, beginning his ordeal at the Monamolin Festival in Ireland. He was buried six feet down in a standard sized coffin. The festival site was known as a 'fairy field' and therefore the identities of the gravediggers were kept secret as part of a plan to outwit the fairies, in case they might have any objection. After 239 hours and 15 minutes, Hayes was dug up and emerged waving a toy leprechaun.

Glossary

Apoplexy – medical term for a stroke
Asphyxiation – death caused by lack of oxygen
Cataleptic – in a trancelike state with a rigid body
Cholera – a dangerous intestinal infection caused by contamination
Corporeal – related to the nature of the physical body
Dead-house – an early term for mortuary
Dehydration – the result of the body being starved of water
Embalm – to treat a dead body with preservatives
Fakir – a Hindu holy man
Funeral Pyre – a pile of wood for cremating a corpse
Heretic – a person who holds unorthodox opinions
Hypothermia – abnormally low body temperature
Immured – imprisoned or shut away from society
Interment – burial
Inquest – an official inquiry, especially to determine cause of death
Laudanum – a tincture of opium
Mortuary – a building where dead bodies are kept before burial
Resuscitate – to restore to consciousness
Sacristan – a person in charge of the contents of a church
Shroud – a piece of cloth used to wrap a dead body in
Syncope – fainting or passing out for long periods
Taphophobia – the fear of being buried alive
Trance – a hypnotic state resembling sleep where the person cannot move

Bibliography

Aberdeen Press & Journal – 4 August 1885, 13 September 1991
The Alaska Daily Empire – 9 October 1922
Albuquerque Morning Journal – 20 December 1917
Alexandria Gazette – 11 December 1895
American Magazine – 20 November 1908
American Settler – 16 September 1882
The Anaconda Standard – 26 April 1891
Armagh Guardian – 18 January 1861
Baigent & Millard's History of Basingstoke 1675
Ballymena Weekly Telegraph – 16 August 1902
Bath Chronicle – 19 July 1832
Bedfordshire Mercury – 22 November 1912
Belfast Commercial Chronicle – 27th July 1825
Belfast Morning News – 20th November 1900
Belfast Newsletter – 31 January 1834, 29 April 1904, 7 May 1956
Belfast Protestant Journal – 10 April 1847
Belfast Telegraph – 28 March 1905, 8 August 1905, 24 January 1912, 13 June
    1951, 7 February 1953, 25 October 1954, 18 September 1956, 5 February 1958,
    10 September 1958, 8 June 1964, 30 December 1966
The Bemioji Daily Pioneer – 2 May 1919
Berkshire Chronicle – 8 June 1867
The Billings Gazette – 21 February 1902
Birmingham Daily Gazette – 25 February 1910
Birmingham Daily Mail – 8 March 1879, 21 January 1905
The Birmingham Post – 13 May 1998
Bournemouth Daily Echo – 14 April 1904
Bradford Daily Telegraph – 9 May 1910
Bridgeton Pioneer – 8 April 1886
Bridport News – 18 September 1896
Brighton Gazette – 18 September 1832
The British Chronicle – 24 March 1785
British Medical Journal – August 1893
British United Press – 15 August 1934
Brownsville Herald – 8 August 1926
The Burial Reformer – 1906
Burton Chronicle – 28 October 1897

The Call – 12 June 1897
The Call – 15 August 1910
The Call – 1 December 1911
Canterbury Journal – 1 July 1761
Carmarthen Journal – 1 September – 1832
Carrick-Fergus Advertiser – 21 October 1898
Catholic Standard – 24 May 1957
Catholic Telegraph – 5 December 1863
Central News – 3 December 1905
Chambers Journal – 29 August 1898
Cheltenham Examiner – 14 August 1913
Chester Courant – 15 October 1799
Civil & Military Gazette – 8 July 1891, 22 December 1907
Civil & Military Gazette (Lahore) – 27 December 1907
The Clare Journal – 7 January 1836
The Coleshill Chronicle – 6 September 1902
Cork Constitution – 24 April 1830
Cork Examiner – 28 October 1842, 1 October 1849
Courier Democrat (Langdon N.D.) – 13 May 1909
The Daily Bulletin (Honolulu) – 26 January 1891
Daily Express – 15 November 1901
Daily Gazette for Middlesborough – 25 September 1905
The Daily Graphic – 19 April 1914
Daily Herald – 16 July 1938
Daily Mail – 26 October 1855, 5 August 1903, 22 July 1915, 20 June 1925
Daily Mirror – 18 March 1904, 11 July 1930, 23 December 1981
Daily News (London) – 6 June 1913, 27 October 1924, 22 April 1944
Daily Record & Mail – 14 October 1905
The Daily Sentinel – 23 February 1906
The Dalles Daily Chronicle – 19 October 1891
The Dawson News – 26 February 1908, 8 April 1908, 8th June 1910, 18th
    November 1919
The Day Book (Chicago) – 23 April 1912, 26 April 1913, 27 September 1913
The Day Book (US) – 27 May 1916
Derby Mercury – 29 July 1768
Detroit Evening Times – 30 March 1941
Detroit Free Press – 6 February 1899
Derry Journal – 24 December 1900, 3 June 1903
Detroit Evening Times – 29 July 1945
Devon Valley Tribune – 29 July 1924
Dimensions of the Cloister by Francesca Medioli
Downpatrick Recorder – 30 June 1849
Drogheda Argus – 31 January 1891
Drogheda Conservative – 27 April 1901

Dromore Weekly Times – 27 January 1906
Dublin Advertising Gazette – 10 February 1872
Dublin Daily Express – 30 October 1863
Dublin Evening Mail – 3 February 1905, 21 June 1954
Dublin Evening Packet – 21 November 1829, 3 December 1829, 23 February 1854
Dublin Evening Post – 1 November 1827
Dublin Evening Telegraph – 5 May 1906, 26 October 1906, 25 March 1924
Dublin Morning Register – 16 December 1829
Dublin Weekly Mail – 6 April 1901
East India Magazine – 20 February 1837
Echo (London) – 7 July 1890, 25 November 1898
Edinburgh Evening News – 28 March 1874
Edinburgh Evening News – 20 April 1904
Edinburgh Evening News – 19 March 1925
Edinburgh Journal – May 1839
Ellis's Missionary Annual – 14 November 1832
The Englishman – 5 May 1916
Evening Herald (Dublin) – 29 June 2001
The Evening Post – 21 December 1881
The Evening Standard – 12 August 1887
Evening Star – 22 December 1958
Evening Star (Washington DC) – 27 January 1914, 14 March 1924, 30 September
    1924, 25 August 1948, 20 January 1950
Evening Telegraph – 11 August 1920
The Evening Times (Grand Forks ND) – 13 August 1908
The Evening Times – 17 January 1910
Evening Times – Republican – 17 May 1904
The Evening Tribune – 8 December 1896
The Exchange – 2 October 1915
The Factory Times – 20 December 1889
Falkirk Herald – 22 May 1935
The Fitzgerald Enterprise – 4 July 1908
Fort Worth Daily Gazette – 26 January 1887
Freeman's Journal – 14 August 1830, 1 November 1833, 30 April 1850, 25 March 1851
Friend of India – 4 June 1868, February 1876
Glasgow Evening Citizen – 11 September 1867
The Globe – 3 March 1894, 9 June 1897, 27 October 1908
The Globe Republican – 31 December 1890
Gloucester Citizen – 10 July 1948
Gloucester Journal – 22 August 1868
Gloucestershire Echo – 23 May 1917, 21 October 1922
Grant County Herald – 3 October 1908
The Greeley Tribune – 15 September 1910
Guernsey Evening Press & Star – 8 April 1908

Halifax Evening Courier – 6 October 1951
The Hattiesburg News – 6 February 1911
The Hawaiian Star – 16 May 1898
Hereford Times – 4 April 1846, 26 July 1862
Herts Advertiser – 3 March 1877
Herts & Cambs. Reporter – 18 June 1909
Huddersfield Daily Chronicle – 6 August 1890
Hull Daily Mail – 26 January 1906
The Illustrated Leicester Chronicle – 17 June 1922
Illustrated Police News – 8 May 1875
Imperial Valley Press – 22 September 1932
The Independent – 16 August 1929
The Independent (Honolulu) – 18 February 1899
The Indianapolis Times – 3 April 1933
Inverness Courier – 19 December 1822
Ipswich Journal – 4 January 1896
The Irish Daily Independent – 31 May 1899
Irish Independent – 24 January 2000, 28 August 2001, 21 February 2002, 26 June
   2002, 8 March 2006
Irish News – 5 November 1900, 4 February 1901, 28 April 1908
Irish Rosary – June 1906
Irish Times – 13 May 1952, 29 June 1953, 25 August 1953, 24 August 1960,
   20 January 1967
Irish Weekly – 20 December 1930
Jackson's Oxford Journal – 23 November 1901
Journal De L'Indre – 8 April 1837
Kentish Mercury – 8 August 1835
Kentish Weekly Post – 18 August – 1736, 26 July 1740
Lancashire Evening Post – 8 April 1915
Lancet – 15 September 1900
Laurel Outlook – 19 April 1950
Leeds Times – 24 September 1892
Leicester Evening Mail – 1 January 1935
The Leinster Reporter – 3 November 1906
Limerick Reporter – 10 January 1845
Lincoln County Leader – 28 January 1910
Lincolnshire Echo – 27 August 1923
Lisburn Herald – 8 October 1892
Lisburn Standard – 29 November 1902, 20 June 1903
Liverpool Chronicle – 17 April 1846
Liverpool Echo – 18 August 1938
Liverpool Evening Express – 5 May 1903
London Evening Standard – 23 March 190, 3 April 1914, 9 September 1915
London Express War Special – 6 October 1904

London Telegraph – 18 January 1889
Londonderry Sentinel – 23 June 1900, 21 February 1907, 9 February 1929, 5 October 1929
Lurgan Times – 2 April 1904
Luton Reporter – 12 April 1915
The Lynden Tribune – 10 July 1913
Manchester Courier – 13 April 1905
Manchester Evening News – 5 May 1870, 24 May 1904
Martinsburg Evening Journal – 27 November 1918
Maui News – 31 March 1906
Merthyr Express – 12 February 1898
Messager du Midi – 9 May 1874
The Middlesex Times – 3 December 1907
Milford Chronicle – 7 February 1908
Millom Gazette – 7 November 1896
The Morning Astorian – 5 July 1907
Morning Post – 20 January 1846, 6 January 1871
Mower County Transcript – 8 March 1893
Munster News – 6 August 1851
The Nebraska Advertiser – 14 November 1902
New Britain Daily Herald – 6 August 1926
New Britain Herald – 18 April 1924
Newcastle Daily Chronicle – 23 July 1894
Newcastle Evening Chronicle – 21 October 1966
The Newcastle Guardian – 12 January 1895
New York Herald – 22 April 1901
New York Tribune – 11 May 1914
Norfolk News – 17 November 1849
Northampton Mercury – 22 March 1794
Northern Standard – 27 August 1850
Northern Weekly Gazette – 14 March 1896
Northern Whig – 6 May 1847, 5 December 1898, 28 August 1902
Nottingham Guardian – 25 February 1910
Nottingham Journal – 14 November 1927
The Observer – 29 April 1898
The Ohio Daily Express – 23 March 1950
Oriental Annual – 19 November 1835
Pall Mall Gazette – 1 September 1869, 12 November 1869, 5 January 1892
Paris Siecle – 28 January 1852
The Parma Herald – 29 July 1909
Pearson's Weekly – 2 September 1898
The People – 22 April 1979
The Pilot – 17 August 1831
Pine Bluff Daily Graphic – 12 May 1916

The Prescott Daily News – 23 November 1912
Press Association – 19 May 1906
Press Association (War Special) – 30 December 1914
Publicateur D'Arles – 28 December 1844
The Republican – 14 January 1897
Reuters – 5 October 1897, 8 August 1931, 5 September 1955, 11 September 1922
The Richmond Palladium – 20 December 1906
The Right To Kill by Cleuci de Oliveira – 9 April 2018 (Foreignpolicy.com)
Rochdale Observer – 1 January 1876
Rock Island Argus – 13 August 1883
Rock Island Daily Argus – 24 January 1891
Royal Jamaica Gazette – 20 June 1840
The Saint Paul Daily Gazette – 1 July 1888
The San Juan Times – 7 February 1896
Saunders Newsletter – 11 September 1823, 17 September 1824, 3 January 1835
Scots Magazine – 10 November 1755
The Scotsman – 16 September 1901, 16 September 1991
Scottish Surgical & Medical Journal – 27 October 1900
The Seattle Star – 4 August 1904
The Semi-Weekly Interior Journal – 13 November 1885
The Semi-Weekly Leader – 3 January 1914
Sheffield Daily Telegraph – 28 November 1939
Sheffield Evening Telegraph – 2 July 1889
Sheffield Independent – 4 January 1893
Sheffield Weekly Telegraph – 17 May 1887
Shoshone Journal – 24 March 1899
South Eastern Gazette – 10 April 1827
The Southern Herald – 18 March 1921
The Southern Jewish Weekly – 3 May 1946
Southern Reporter – 24 July 1830, 25 August 1832
South Wales Daily News – 19 May 1908
The Standard – 15 May 1895
The Star – 8 November 1912
The St. Charles Herald – 2 December 1922
St. James's Gazette – 12 March 1884
The St. John's Herald – 6 November 1890
The St. Mary Banner – 19 October 1907
Stockton Herald – 6 October 1906, 11 April 1914
Stow's Survey of London – 4 January 1647
Sun (London) – 16 May 1804
The Sun & Central Press – 21 December 1872
The Sun (Wilmington) – 16 March 1901
Sunday Independent – 27 March 1988
Sunday Tribune – 16 January 2000

Taunton Courier – 30 September 1868

Telegraph – 24 January 1887

The Times & Democrat – 5 August 1886

The Times Dispatch (VA) – 6 January 1907

The Topeka State Journal – 17 October 1919

The Troy Budget – 5 September 1849

The Tucumcari News – 31 March 1906

Turner County Herald – 21 December 1911

Tyrone Constitution – 15 September 1848, 6 March 1908

Tyrone Courier – 26 July 1900, 12 December 1901

Ulster Echo – 30 November 1882

The Uncertainty of the Signs of Death by J.J. Bruhier d'Ablaincourt 1746

Union County Courier – 18 May 1887

University Missourian – 23 October 1908

Uxbridge & West Drayton Gazette – 20 January 1912

The Viet Cong Massacre at Hue by Alje Vennema

Vindicator – 25 May 1839, 23 August 1843

Waco Evening News – 27 August 1888

The Wadsworth Dispatch – 2 May 1896

Warwickshire Herald – 25 August 1892

The Washington Herald – 19 November 1922

Washington Star – 15 December 1897

Washington Times – 1 September 1918, 16 September 1924, 10 May 1928, 28 August
   1928, 5 September 1929, 19 May 1931

Waterbury Evening Democrat – 13 January 1904

Watertown Republican – 7 February 1877

Weekly Dispatch – 9 February 1896, 8 August 1909, 2 October 1921

Weekly Irish Times – 29 November 1890, 23 June 1900

Weekly News – 10 April 1891

Weekly North Carolina Standard – 29 October 1851

The Weekly Telegraph – 13 March 1852

The Weekly Times – 26 August 1832

Wells Journal – 25 January 1912

Wenatchee Daily World – 2 January 1906

Western Daily Press – 30 January 1923

Western Mail – 28 August 1902

Western Star – 15 April 1848

Westminster Gazette – 2 January 1919, 29 April 1926, 1 May 1926

Weston-Super-Mare Gazette – 13 March 1852

West Virginia Daily Oil Review – 15 January 1902

Wexford Conservative – 10 March 1841

White Bluff's News (Washington) – 27 August 1936

Wicklow People – 29 September 1900

Wicklow People – 20 June 1903, 28 January 1905

Wilmington Morning Star – 8 December 1941
Wimbledon News – 12 October 1895
Witney Gazette – 29 April 1899
Woman's Chronicle – 17 December 1892
Wood River Times – 18 June 1890
Worcester Democrat – 10 June 1922
The World of Chinese by Sun Jiahui
Yorkshire Evening Post – 4 May 1893, 10 March 1896
Yorkshire Telegraph – 25 May 1905

Index

Dear Reader,

We hope you have enjoyed this book, but why not share your views on social media? You can also follow our pages to see more about our other products: facebook.com/penandswordbooks or follow us on X @penswordbooks

You can also view our products at www.pen-and-sword.co.uk (UK and ROW) or www.penandswordbooks.com (North America).

To keep up to date with our latest releases and online catalogues, please sign up to our newsletter at: www.pen-and-sword.co.uk/newsletter

If you would like a printed catalogue with our latest books, then please email: enquiries@pen-and-sword.co.uk or telephone: 01226 734555 (UK and ROW) or email: uspen-and-sword@casematepublishers.com or telephone: (610) 853-9131 (North America).

We respect your privacy and we will only use personal information to send you information about our products.

Thank you!